Networking

FOR

DUMMIES

A Wiley Brand

10TH EDITION

by Doug Lowe

Networking For Dummies®, 10th Edition

Published by
John Wiley & Sons, Inc.
111 River Street
Hoboken, NJ 07030-5774

www.wiley.com

Copyright © 2013 by John Wiley & Sons, Inc., Hoboken, New Jersey

Published by John Wiley & Sons, Inc., Hoboken, New Jersey

Published simultaneously in Canada

For general information on our other products and services, please contact our Customer Care Department within the U.S. at 877-762-2974, outside the U.S. at 317-572-3993, or fax 317-572-4002.

For technical support, please visit www.wiley.com/techsupport.

Wiley publishes in a variety of print and electronic formats and by print-on-demand. Some material included with standard print versions of this book may not be included in e-books or in print-on-demand. If this book refers to media such as a CD or DVD that is not included in the version you purchased, you may download this material at http://booksupport.wiley.com. For more information about Wiley products, visit www.wiley.com.

Library of Congress Control Number: 2013933934

ISBN 978-1-118-47408-2 (pbk); ISBN 978-1-118-47412-9 (ebk); ISBN 978-1-118-47411-2 (ebk); ISBN 978-1-118-47414-3 (ebk)

Manufactured in the United States of America

10 9 8 7 6 5 4 3 2

About the Author

Doug Lowe has written enough computer books to line all the birdcages in California. His other books include *Networking All-in-One Desk Reference For Dummies* (now in its fourth edition), *PowerPoint 2013 For Dummies*, *Java All-in-One Desk Reference For Dummies*, and *Electronics All-in-One For Dummies*.

Although Doug has yet to win a Pulitzer Prize, he remains cautiously optimistic. He is hopeful that Claude-Michel Schönberg and Alain Boublil will turn this book into a musical, titled *Les Réseau Miserables*. (Hopefully the role of the vengeful network administrator will be played by someone who can sing.)

Doug lives in sunny Fresno, California, where the nearby Sierra Nevada mountains are visible through the smog at least three or four glorious days every year.

Dedication

This one is for mom. I will miss you so.

Author's Acknowledgments

I'd like to thank project editor Christopher Morris, who did a great job of managing all the editorial work that was required to put this book together, and Amy Fandrei, who made the whole project possible. I'd also like to thank Dan DiNicolo, who gave the entire manuscript a thorough technical review and offered many excellent suggestions, as well as copy editor Teresa Artman, who made sure the i's were crossed and the t's were dotted (oops, reverse that!). And, as always, thanks to all the behind-the-scenes people who chipped in with help I'm not even aware of.

Publisher's Acknowledgments

We're proud of this book; please send us your comments at http://dummies.custhelp.com. For other comments, please contact our Customer Care Department within the U.S. at 877-762-2974, outside the U.S. at 317-572-3993, or fax 317-572-4002.

Some of the people who helped bring this book to market include the following:

Acquisitions and Editorial

Sr. Project Editor: Christopher Morris

Acquisitions Editor: Amy Fandrei

Sr. Copy Editor: Teresa Artman

Technical Editor: Dan DiNicolo

Editorial Manager: Kevin Kirschner

Editorial Assistant: Annie Sullivan

Sr. Editorial Assistant: Cherie Case

Cover Photo: © Spectral-Design / iStockphoto

Composition Services

Project Coordinator: Katherine Crocker

Layout and Graphics: Jennifer Creasey, Joyce Haughey

Proofreaders: Jessica Kramer, Kathy Simpson

Indexer: Slivoskey Indexing Services

Publishing and Editorial for Technology Dummies

    Richard Swadley, Vice President and Executive Group Publisher

    Andy Cummings, Vice President and Publisher

    Mary Bednarek, Executive Acquisitions Director

    Mary C. Corder, Editorial Director

Publishing for Consumer Dummies

    Kathleen Nebenhaus, Vice President and Executive Publisher

Composition Services

    Debbie Stailey, Director of Composition Services

Contents at a Glance

Table of Contents

Introduction

Welcome to the tenth edition of *Networking For Dummies,* the book that's written especially for people who have this nagging feeling in the back of their minds that they should network their computers but haven't a clue about how to start or where to begin.

Do you often copy a spreadsheet to a flash drive just so you can give it to someone else in your office? Are you frustrated because you can't use the fancy color laser printer that's on the financial secretary's computer? Do you wait in line to use the computer that has the customer database? You need a network!

Or maybe you already have a network, but you have just one problem: Someone promised that a network would make your life easier, but it's instead turned your computing life upside down. Just when you had this computer thing figured out, someone popped into your office, hooked up a cable, and said, "Happy networking!" Makes you want to scream.

Regardless, you've found the right book. Help is here, within these humble pages.

This book talks about networks in everyday (and often irreverent) terms. The language is friendly; you don't need a graduate education to get through it. And the occasional potshot helps unseat the hallowed and sacred traditions of networkdom, bringing just a bit of fun to an otherwise dry subject. The goal is to bring the lofty precepts of networking down to earth, where you can touch them and squeeze them and say, "What's the big deal? I can do this!"

About This Book

This isn't the kind of book you pick up and read from start to finish, as if it were a cheap novel. If I ever see you reading it at the beach, I'll kick sand in your face. This book is more like a reference, the kind of book you can pick up, turn to just about any page, and start reading. Each chapter covers a specific aspect of networking, such as printing from the network, hooking up network cables, or setting up security so that bad guys can't break in. Just turn to the chapter you're interested in and start reading.

Each chapter is divided into self-contained chunks, all related to the major theme of the chapter. For example, the chapter on hooking up the network cable contains nuggets like these:

- ✔ What is Ethernet?
- ✔ All about cable
- ✔ To shield or not to shield
- ✔ Wall jacks and patch panels
- ✔ Switches

You don't have to memorize anything in this book. It's a need-to-know book: You pick it up when you need to know something. Need to know what 100BaseT is? Pick up the book. Need to know how to create good passwords? Pick up the book. Otherwise, put it down and get on with your life.

How to Use This Book

This book works like a reference. Start with the topic you want to find out about. Look for it in the Table of Contents or in the index to get going.

If you need to type something, you see the text you need to type like this: **Type this stuff**. In this example, you type **Type this stuff** at the keyboard and then press Enter. An explanation usually follows, just in case you're scratching your head and grunting, "Huh?"

Whenever I describe a message or information that you see on the screen, I present it this way:

```
A message from your friendly network
```

This book rarely directs you elsewhere for information; just about everything that you need to know about networks is right here. If you find the need for additional information, plenty of other *For Dummies* books can help. If you have a networking question that isn't covered in this book, allow me to suggest my own *Networking All-in-One For Dummies,* 5th Edition (Wiley), which is a much-expanded reference book that goes deeper into specific network operating systems and TCP/IP protocols. You can also find plenty of other *For Dummies* books that cover just about every operating system and application program known to humanity.

What You Don't Need to Read

Aside from the topics you can use right away, much of this book is skippable. I carefully placed extra-technical information in self-contained sidebars and clearly marked them so that you can steer clear of them. Don't read this stuff unless you're really into technical explanations and want to know a little of what's going on behind the scenes. Don't worry: My feelings won't be hurt if you don't read every word.

Foolish Assumptions

I'm making only two assumptions about who you are: You're someone who works with a PC, and you either have a network or you're thinking about getting one. I hope that you know (and are on speaking terms with) someone who knows more about computers than you do. My goal is to decrease your reliance on that person, but don't throw away his phone number yet.

Is this book useful for Macintosh users? Absolutely. Although the bulk of this book is devoted to showing you how to link Windows-based computers to form a network, you can find information about how to network Macintosh computers as well.

Windows 8? Gotcha covered. You'll find plenty of information about how to network with the latest and greatest Microsoft operating system.

How This Book Is Organized

Inside this book, you find chapters arranged in parts. Each chapter breaks down into sections that cover various aspects of the chapter's main subject. The chapters are in a logical sequence, so reading them in order (if you want to read the whole thing) makes sense, but the book is modular enough that you can pick it up and start reading at any point.

Here's the lowdown on what's in each part.

Part 1: Getting Started with Networking

The chapters in this part present a layperson's introduction to what networking is all about. This part is a good place to start if you're clueless about what a network is and why you're suddenly expected to use one. It's also a great place to start if you're a hapless network user who doesn't give a whit about "optimizing network performance" but wants to know what the network is and how to get the most out of it.

The best thing about this part is that it focuses on how to use a network without getting into the technical details of setting up a network or maintaining a network server. In other words, this part is aimed at ordinary network users who have to know how to get along with a network.

Part II: Setting Up a Network

Uh-oh. The boss just gave you an ultimatum: Get a network up and running by Friday or pack your things. The chapters in this section cover everything you need to know to build a network, from picking the network operating system to installing the cable.

Part III: Working with Servers

One of the most challenging aspects of setting up a network is installing and configuring server computers and the software that runs on them. The chapters in this part show you how to set up a basic server, create user accounts, and configure file, e-mail, and web servers.

Part IV: Cloudy with a Chance of Gigabytes

The chapters in this part introduce you to techniques for extending your network into the Internet using what has come to be known as *cloud computing*. Included in this part are chapters about integrating the new breed of mobile devices such as smartphones and tablet computers into your network, as well as extending your office network to your home computer.

Part V: Managing and Protecting Your Network

I hope that the job of managing the network doesn't fall on your shoulders, but in case it does, the chapters in this part can help you out. You find out all about backup, security, performance, dusting, mopping, changing the oil, and all the other stuff that network managers have to do.

You will also learn about network security: backing up your data, protecting your network from evil people who want to break your network's back, and hardening your network against threats such as viruses and spyware.

Part VI: More Ways to Network

The three chapters in this part cover some additional technologies you need to know to build and manage a successful network. First, you'll see how you can use *virtualization* in your network so that you can save money by buying fewer server computers. Then you'll discover about networking with the two most popular alternatives to Windows: Linux and Macintosh computers.

Part VII: The Part of Tens

This wouldn't be a *For Dummies* book without a collection of lists of interesting snippets: ten networking commandments, ten things you should keep in your closet, and more!

Icons Used in This Book

Those nifty little pictures in the margin aren't there just to pretty up the place. They also have practical functions.

Hold it — technical details lurk just around the corner. Read on only if you have a pocket protector.

Pay special attention to this icon; it lets you know that some particularly useful tidbit is at hand — perhaps a shortcut or a little-used command that pays off big.

Did I tell you about the memory course I took?

Danger, Will Robinson! This icon highlights information that may help you avoid disaster.

Where to Go from Here

Yes, you can get there from here. With this book in hand, you're ready to plow right through the rugged networking terrain. Browse through the Table of Contents and decide where you want to start. Be bold! Be courageous! Be adventurous! Above all, have fun!

Occasionally, we have updates to our technology books. If this book does have any technical updates, they'll be posted at

www.dummies.com/go/networkingonlinefd10eupdates

Part I

Getting Started with Networking

In this part...

- ✔ Learning what a network is and what you can do with one
- ✔ Comparing server and client computers
- ✔ Accessing network resources such as shared storage and network printers
- ✔ Using Microsoft Office and other software on a network

Chapter 1

Let's Network!

Computer networks get a bad rap in the movies. In the classic *Terminator* movies, Skynet (a computer network of the future) takes over the planet, builds deadly terminator robots, and sends them back through time to kill everyone unfortunate enough to have the name Sarah Connor. In the *Matrix* movies, a vast and powerful computer network enslaves humans and keeps them trapped in a simulation of the real world. And in *Eagle Eye,* Shia LaBeouf is chased around the country by a deranged supercomputer that has control of every imaginable networkable device, including traffic signals, mobile phones, and fast-food menus.

Fear not. These bad networks exist only in the dreams of science fiction writers. Real-world networks are much more calm and predictable. They don't think for themselves, they can't evolve into something you don't want them to be, and they won't hurt you, even if your name is Sarah Connor.

Now that you're over your fear of networks, you're ready to breeze through this chapter. It's a gentle, even superficial, introduction to computer networks, with a slant toward the concepts that can help you use a computer that's attached to a network. This chapter goes easy on the details; the detailed and boring stuff comes later.

Defining a Network

A *network* is nothing more than two or more computers connected by a cable or by a wireless radio connection so that they can exchange information.

Of course, computers can exchange information in ways other than networks. Most of us have used what computer nerds call the *sneakernet*. That's where you copy a file to a flash drive (or a CD or DVD) and then walk the data over to someone else's computer. (The term *sneakernet* is typical of computer nerds' feeble attempts at humor.)

The whole problem with the sneakernet is that it's slow, and it wears a trail in your carpet. One day, some penny-pinching computer geeks discovered that connecting computers with cables was cheaper than replacing the carpet every six months. Thus, the modern computer network was born.

You can create a simple computer network by hooking together all the computers in your office with cables and using the computer's *network interface* (an electronic circuit that resides inside your computer and has a special jack on the computer's backside). Then you tweak a few simple settings in the computer's operating system (OS) software, and *voilà!* You have a working network. That's all there is to it.

If you don't want to mess with cables, you can create a wireless network instead. In a wireless network, the computers use wireless network adapters that communicate via radio signals. All modern laptop computers have built-in wireless network adapters. To create a wireless network with a desktop computer, though, you'll need to purchase a separate wireless network adapter that plugs into one of the computer's USB ports.

Figure 1-1 shows a typical network with four computers. You can see that all four computers are connected by a network cable to a central network device: the *switch*. You can also see that Ward's computer has a fancy laser printer attached to it. Because of the network, June, Wally, and the Beaver can also use this laser printer. (Also, you can see that the Beaver stuck yesterday's bubble gum to the back of his computer. Although the bubble gum isn't recommended, it shouldn't adversely affect the network.)

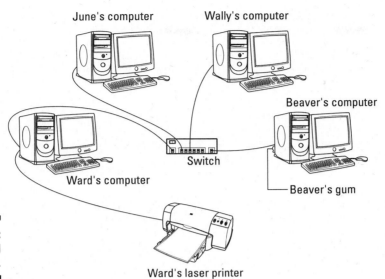

Figure 1-1:
A typical
network.

Computer networking has its own strange vocabulary. Although you don't have to know every esoteric networking term, it helps to be acquainted with a few of the basic buzzwords:

- **LAN:** Networks are often called LANs, short for *local area network.*

  LAN is the first *TLA* — or *three-letter acronym* — of this book. You don't really need to remember it or any of the many TLAs that follow. In fact, the only three-letter acronym you need to remember is TLA. You might guess that the acronym for *four-letter acronym* is *FLA.* Wrong! A four-letter acronym is an *ETLA,* which stands for *extended three-letter acronym.* After all, it just wouldn't be right if the acronym for *four-letter acronym* had only three letters.

- **On the network:** Every computer connected to the network is said to be "on the network." The technical term (which you can forget) for a computer that's on the network is a *node.*

- **Online, offline:** When a computer is turned on and can access the network, the computer is *online.* When a computer can't access the network, it's *offline.* A computer can be offline for several reasons. The computer can be turned off, the user may have disabled the network connection, the computer may be broken, the cable that connects it to the network can be unplugged, or a wad of gum can be jammed into the disk drive.

- **Up, down:** When a computer is turned on and working properly, it's *up.* When a computer is turned off, broken, or being serviced, it's *down.*

Turning off a computer is sometimes called *taking it down.* Turning it back on is sometimes called *bringing it up.*

✔ **Local, remote:** A resource such as a disk drive is *local* if it resides in your computer. It's *remote* if it resides in another computer somewhere else on your network.

✔ **Internet:** The *Internet* is a huge amalgamation of computer networks strewn about the entire planet. Networking the computers in your home or office so that they can share information with one another and connecting your computer to the worldwide Internet are two separate but related tasks.

Why Bother with a Network?

Frankly, computer networks are a bit of a pain to set up. So why bother? Because the benefits of having a network outweigh the difficulties of setting up one.

You don't have to be a PhD to understand the benefits of networking. In fact, you learned everything you need to know in kindergarten: Networks are all about sharing. Specifically, networks are about sharing three things: files, resources, and programs.

Sharing files

Networks enable you to share information with other computers on the network. Depending on how you set up your network, you can share files with your network friends in several different ways. You can send a file from your computer directly to a friend's computer by attaching the file to an e-mail message and then mailing it. Or you can let your friend access your computer over the network so that your friend can retrieve the file directly from your hard drive. Yet another method is to copy the file to a disk on another computer and then tell your friend where you put the file so that your friend can retrieve it later. One way or the other, the data travels to your friend's computer over the network cable and not on a CD or DVD or flash drive, as it would in a sneakernet.

Sharing resources

You can set up certain computer resources — such as hard drives or printers — so that all computers on the network can access them. For example, the laser printer attached to Ward's computer in Figure 1-1 is a *shared resource,* which means that anyone on the network can use it. Without the network, June, Wally, and the Beaver would have to buy their own laser printers.

Hard drives can be shared resources, too. In fact, you must set up a hard drive as a shared resource to share files with other users. Suppose that Wally wants to share a file with the Beaver, and a shared hard drive has been set up on June's computer. All Wally has to do is copy his file to the shared hard drive in June's computer and tell the Beaver where he put it. Then, when the Beaver gets around to it, he can copy the file from June's computer to his own (unless, of course, that hooligan Eddie Haskell deletes the file first).

You can share other resources, too, such as an Internet connection. In fact, sharing an Internet connection is one of the main reasons why many networks are created.

Sharing programs

Rather than keep separate copies of programs on each person's computer, putting programs on a drive that everyone shares is sometimes best. For example, if ten computer users all use a particular program, you can purchase and install ten copies of the program, one for each computer. Or you can purchase a ten-user license for the program and then install just one copy of the program on a shared drive. Each of the ten users can then access the program from the shared hard drive.

In most cases, however, running a shared copy of a program over the network is unacceptably slow. A more common way of using a network to share programs is to copy the program's installation disks or CDs to a shared network drive. Then you can use that copy to install a separate copy of the program on each user's local hard drive. For example, Microsoft Office enables you to do this if you purchase a license from Microsoft for each computer on which you install Office.

The advantage of installing Office from a shared network drive is that you don't have to lug around the installation disks or CDs to each user's computer. And the system administrator can customize the network installation so that the software is installed the same way on each user's computer. (However, these benefits are significant only for larger networks. If your network has fewer than about ten computers, you're probably better off installing the program separately on each computer directly from the installation disks or CDs.)

Remember that purchasing a single-user copy of a program and then putting it on a shared network drive — so that everyone on the network can access it — is illegal. If five people use the program, you need to either purchase five copies of the program or purchase a network license that specifically allows five or more users.

That being said, many software manufacturers sell their software with a concurrent usage license, which means that you can install the software on as many computers as you want, but only a certain number of people can use the software at any given time. Usually, special licensing software that runs on one of the network's server computers keeps track of how many people are currently using the software. This type of license is frequently used with more specialized (and expensive) software, such as accounting systems or computer drafting systems.

Another benefit of networking is that networks enable computer users to communicate with one another over the network. The most obvious way networks allow computer users to communicate is by passing messages back and forth, using e-mail or instant-messaging programs. Networks also offer other ways to communicate: For example, you can hold online meetings over the network. Network users who have inexpensive video cameras (webcams) attached to their computers can have videoconferences. You can even play a friendly game of Hearts over a network — during your lunch break, of course.

Servers and Clients

The network computer that contains the hard drives, printers, and other resources that are shared with other network computers is a *server*. This term comes up repeatedly, so you have to remember it. Write it on the back of your left hand.

Any computer that's not a server is a *client*. You have to remember this term, too. Write it on the back of your right hand.

Only two kinds of computers are on a network: servers and clients. Look at your left hand and then look at your right hand. Don't wash your hands until you memorize these terms.

The distinction between servers and clients in a network has parallels in sociology — in effect, a sort of class distinction between the "haves" and "have-nots" of computer resources:

✔ Usually, the most powerful and expensive computers in a network are the servers. There's a good technical reason: All users on the network share the server's resources.

✔ The cheaper and less-powerful computers in a network are the clients. *Clients* are the computers used by individual users for everyday work. Because clients' resources don't have to be shared, they don't have to be as fancy.

✔ Most networks have more clients than servers. For example, a network with ten clients can probably get by with one server.

✔ In many networks, a clean line of demarcation exists between servers and clients. In other words, a computer functions as either a server or a client, not both. For the sake of an efficient network, a server can't become a client, nor can a client become a server.

✔ Other (usually smaller) networks can be more evenhanded by allowing any computer in the network to be a server and allowing any computer to be both server and client at the same time.

Dedicated Servers and Peers

In some networks, a server computer is a server computer and nothing else. It's dedicated to the sole task of providing shared resources, such as hard drives and printers, to be accessed by the network client computers. This type of server is a *dedicated server* because it can perform no other task than network services.

Some smaller networks take an alternative approach by enabling any computer on the network to function as both a client and a server. Thus, any computer can share its printers and hard drives with other computers on the network. And while a computer is working as a server, you can still use that same computer for other functions, such as word processing. This type of network is a *peer-to-peer network* because all the computers are thought of as *peers,* or equals.

Here are some points to ponder concerning the differences between dedicated server networks and peer-to-peer networks while you're walking the dog tomorrow morning:

✔ Peer-to-peer networking features are built into Windows. Thus, if your computer runs Windows, you don't have to buy any additional software to turn your computer into a server. All you have to do is enable the Windows server features.

✔ The network server features that are built into desktop versions of Windows (such as Windows 7 and 8) aren't particularly efficient because these versions of Windows weren't designed primarily to be network servers.

If you dedicate a computer to the task of being a full-time server, use a special network operating system rather than the standard Windows operating system. A *network operating system* (NOS) is specially designed to handle networking functions efficiently.

- The most commonly used NOSes are the server versions of Windows.

  As of this writing, the current server version of Windows is Windows Server 20012. However, many companies still use the previous version (Windows Server 2008), and a few even use its predecessor, Windows 2003 Server.

- Another popular NOS is *Linux.* Linux is popular because it is free. However, it requires a more expertise to set up than Windows Server.

- ✔ Many networks are both peer-to-peer *and* dedicated-server networks at the same time. These networks have

    - At least one server computer that runs an NOS, such as Windows Server 2012

    - *Client* computers that use the server features of Windows to share their resources with the network

- ✔ Besides being dedicated, your servers should also be sincere.

What Makes a Network Tick?

To use a network, you don't really have to know much about how it works. Still, you may feel a little bit better about using the network if you realize that it doesn't work by voodoo. A network may seem like magic, but it isn't. The following list describes the inner workings of a typical network:

- ✔ **Network interface:** Inside any computer attached to a network is a special electronic circuit called the *network interface*. The network interface has either an external jack into which you can plug a network cable — or, in the case of a wireless network interface, an antenna.

- ✔ **Network cable:** The network cable physically connects the computers. It plugs into the network interface card (NIC) on the back of your computer.

    The type of network cable most commonly used is twisted-pair cable, so named because it consists of several pairs of wires twisted together in a certain way. Twisted-pair cable superficially resembles telephone cable. However, appearances can be deceiving. Most phone systems are wired using a lower grade of cable that doesn't work for networks.

    For the complete lowdown on networking cables, see Chapter 6.

    Network cable isn't necessary when wireless networking is used. For more information about wireless networking, see Chapter 9.

- ✔ **Network switch:** Networks built with twisted-pair cabling require one or more switches. A *switch* is a box with a bunch of cable connectors. Each computer on the network is connected by cable to the switch. The switch, in turn, connects all the computers to each other.

    In the early days of twisted-pair networking, devices known as *hubs* were used rather than switches. The term *hub* is sometimes used to refer to switches, but true hubs went out of style sometime around the turn of the century.

    In networks with just a few computers, the network switch is often combined with another networking device called a *router*. A router is used to connect two networks. Typically, a router is used to connect your network to the Internet. By combining a router and a switch in a single box, you can easily connect several computers to the Internet and to each other.

✔ **Network software:** Of course, the software makes the network work. To make any network work, a whole bunch of software has to be set up just right. For peer-to-peer networking with Windows, you have to play with the Control Panel to get networking to work. And an NOS such as Windows Server 2012 requires a substantial amount of tweaking to get it to work just right.

It's Not a Personal Computer Anymore!

If I had to choose one point that I want you to remember from this chapter more than anything else, it's this: After you hook up your personal computer (PC) to a network, it's not a "personal" computer anymore. You're now part of a network of computers, and in a way, you've given up one of the key concepts that made PCs so successful in the first place: independence.

I got my start in computers back in the days when mainframe computers ruled the roost. *Mainframe computers* are big, complex machines that used to fill entire rooms and had to be cooled with chilled water. My first computer was a water-cooled Binford Hex Core Model 2000. Argh, argh, argh. (I'm not making up the part about the water. A plumber was often required to install a mainframe computer. In fact, the really big ones were cooled by liquid nitrogen. I *am* making up the part about the Binford 2000.)

Mainframe computers required staffs of programmers and operators in white lab coats just to keep them going. The mainframes had to be carefully managed. A whole bureaucracy grew up around managing them.

Mainframe computers used to be the dominant computers in the workplace. Personal computers changed all that: They took the computing power out of the big computer room and put it on the user's desktop, where it belongs. PCs severed the tie to the centralized control of the mainframe computer. With a PC, a user could look at the computer and say, "This is mine — all mine!" Mainframes still exist, but they're not nearly as popular as they once were.

But networks have changed everything all over again. In a way, it's a change back to the mainframe-computer way of thinking: central location, distributed resources. True, the network isn't housed in the basement and doesn't have to be installed by a plumber. But you can no longer think of "your" PC as your own. You're part of a network — and like the mainframe, the network has to be carefully managed.

Here are several ways in which a network robs you of your independence:

✔ **You can't just indiscriminately delete files from the network.** They may not be yours.

✔ **You're forced to be concerned about network security.** For example, a server computer has to know who you are before it allows you to access its files. So you have to know your user ID and password to access the network. This precaution prevents some 15-year-old kid from hacking his way into your office network by using its Internet connection and stealing all your computer games.

✔ **You may have to wait for shared resources.** Just because Wally sends something to Ward's printer doesn't mean that it immediately starts to print. The Beav may have sent a two-hour print job before that. Wally just has to wait.

✔ **You may have to wait for access to documents.** You may try to retrieve an Excel spreadsheet file from a network drive, only to discover that someone else is using it. Like Wally, you just have to wait.

✔ **You don't have unlimited storage space.** If you copy a 100GB video file to a server's drive, you may get calls later from angry co-workers complaining that no room is left on the server's drive for their important files.

✔ **Your files can become infected from viruses given to you by someone over the network.** You may then accidentally infect other network users.

✔ **You have to be careful about saving sensitive files on the server.** If you write an angry note about your boss and save it on the server's hard drive, your boss may find the memo and read it.

✔ **The server computer must be up and running at all times.** For example, if you turn Ward's computer into a server computer, Ward can't turn his computer off when he's out of the office. If he does, you can't access the files stored on his computer.

✔ **If your computer is a server, you can't just turn it off when you're finished using it.** Someone else may be accessing a file on your hard drive or printing on your printer.

The Network Administrator

Because so much can go wrong — even with a simple network — designating one person as network administrator is important. This way, someone is responsible for making sure that the network doesn't fall apart or get out of control.

The network administrator doesn't have to be a technical genius. In fact, some of the best network administrators are complete idiots when it comes to technical stuff. What's important is that the administrator is organized. That person's job is to make sure that plenty of space is available on the file server, that the file server is backed up regularly, that new employees can access the network, among other tasks.

The network administrator's job also includes solving basic problems that the users themselves can't solve — and knowing when to call in an expert when something really bad happens. It's a tough job, but somebody's got to do it. Here are a few tips that might help:

- Part V of this book is devoted entirely to the hapless network administrator. So if you're nominated, read the chapters in that part. If you're lucky enough that someone *else* is nominated, celebrate by buying her a copy of this book.

- In small companies, picking the network administrator by drawing straws is common. The person who draws the shortest straw loses and becomes administrator.

- Of course, the network administrator can't be a *complete* technical idiot. I was lying about that. (For those of you in Congress, the word is *testifying*.) I exaggerated to make the point that organizational skills are more important than technical skills. The network administrator needs to know how to do various maintenance tasks. Although this knowledge requires at least a little technical know-how, the organizational skills are more important.

What Have They Got That You Don't Got?

With all this technical stuff to worry about, you may begin to wonder whether you're smart enough to use your computer after it's attached to the network. Let me assure you that you are. If you're smart enough to buy this book because you know that you need a network, you're more than smart enough to use the network after it's put in. You're also smart enough to install and manage a network yourself. It isn't rocket science.

I know people who use networks all the time. They're no smarter than you are, but they do have one thing that you don't have: a certificate. And so, by the powers vested in me by the International Society for the Computer Impaired, I present you with the certificate in Figure 1-2, confirming that you've earned the coveted title Certified Network Dummy, better known as CND. This title is considered much more prestigious in certain circles than the more stodgy CNE or MCSE badges worn by real network experts.

Congratulations, and go in peace.

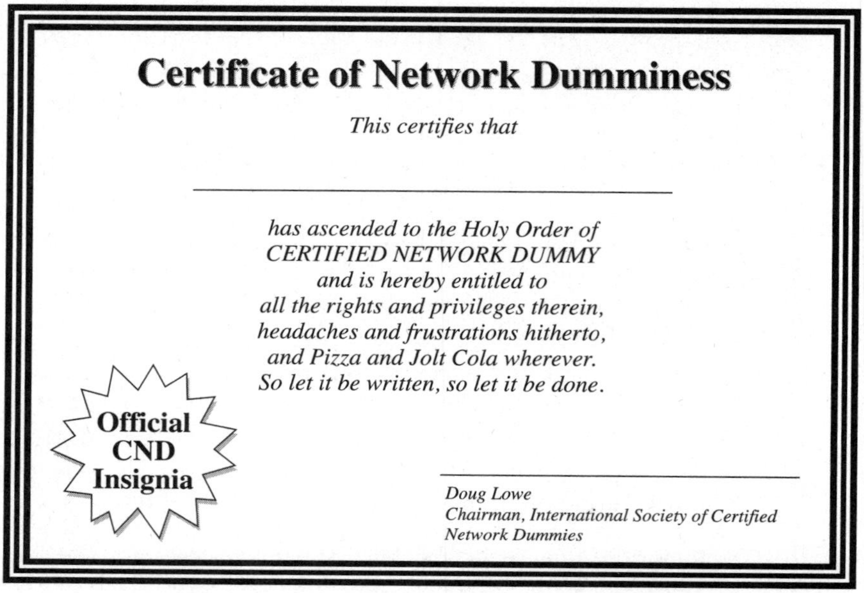
Certificate of Network Dumminess
This certifies that
has ascended to the Holy Order of
CERTIFIED NETWORK DUMMY
and is hereby entitled to
all the rights and privileges therein,
headaches and frustrations hitherto,
and Pizza and Jolt Cola wherever.
So let it be written, so let it be done.
Official CND Insignia
Doug Lowe
Chairman, International Society of Certified Network Dummies

Figure 1-2: Your official CND certificate.

Chapter 2

Life on the Network

After you hook up your PC to a network, it's not an island anymore, separated from the rest of the world like some kind of isolationist fanatic waving a "Don't tread on me" flag. The network connection changes your PC forever. Now your computer is part of a system, connected to other computers on the network. You have to worry about annoying network details, such as using local and shared resources, logging on and accessing network drives, using network printers, logging off, and who knows what else.

Oh, bother.

This chapter brings you up to speed on what living with a computer network is like. Unfortunately, this chapter gets a little technical at times, so you may need your pocket protector.

Distinguishing between Local Resources and Network Resources

In case you don't catch this statement in Chapter 1, one of the most important differences between using an isolated computer and using a network computer lies in the distinction between local resources and network resources. *Local resources* are items — such as hard drives, printers, and CD or DVD drives — that are connected directly to your computer. You can use local resources whether you're connected to the network or not. *Network resources,* on the other hand, are the hard drives, printers, optical drives, and other devices that are connected to the network's server computers. You can use network resources only after your computer is connected to the network.

Whenever you use a computer network, you need to know which resources are local resources (belong to you) and which are network resources (belong to the network). In most networks, your C: drive is a local drive, as is your My Documents folder. If a printer is sitting next to your PC, it's probably a local printer. You can do anything you want with these resources without affecting the network or other users on the network (as long as the local resources aren't shared on the network). Keep these points in mind:

✔ You can't tell just by looking at a resource whether it's a local resource or a network resource. The printer that sits right next to your computer is probably your local printer, but then again, it may be a network printer. The same statement is true for hard drives: The hard drive in your PC is probably your own, but it (or part of it) may be shared on the network, thus enabling other users to access it.

✔ Because dedicated network servers are full of resources, you may say that they're not only dedicated (and sincere), but also resourceful. (Groan. Sorry. This is yet another in a tireless series of bad computer-nerd puns.)

What's in a Name?

Just about everything on a computer network has a name: The computers themselves have names, the people who use the computers have names, the hard drives and printers that can be shared on the network have names, and the network itself has a name. Knowing all the names used on your network isn't essential, but you do need to know some of them.

Here are some additional details about network names:

✔ **Every person who can use the network has a username (sometimes called a *user ID*).** You need to know your username to log on to the network. You also need to know the usernames of your buddies, especially if you want to steal their files or send them nasty notes.

You can find more information about usernames and logging on in the section "Logging On to the Network," later in this chapter.

✔ **Letting folks on the network use their first names as their usernames is tempting but not a good idea.** Even in a small office, you eventually run into a conflict. (And what about Mrs. McCave — made famous by Dr. Seuss — who had 23 children and named them all Dave?)

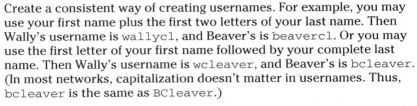

Create a consistent way of creating usernames. For example, you may use your first name plus the first two letters of your last name. Then Wally's username is `wallycl`, and Beaver's is `beavercl`. Or you may use the first letter of your first name followed by your complete last name. Then Wally's username is `wcleaver`, and Beaver's is `bcleaver`. (In most networks, capitalization doesn't matter in usernames. Thus, `bcleaver` is the same as `BCleaver`.)

✔ **Every computer on the network must have a unique computer name.**

You don't have to know the names of all the computers on the network, but it helps if you know your own computer's name and the names of any server computers you need to access.

The computer's name is sometimes the same as the username of the person who uses the computer, but that's usually a bad idea because in many companies, people come and go more often than computers. Sometimes the names indicate the physical location of the computer, such as `office-12` or `back-room`. Server computers often have names that reflect the group that uses the server most, like `acctng-server` or `cad-server`.

Some network nerds like to assign techie-sounding names, like `BL3K5-87a`. And some like to use names from science fiction movies; `HAL`, `Colossus`, `M5`, and `Data` come to mind. Cute names like `Herbie` aren't allowed. (However, `Tigger` and `Pooh` are entirely acceptable — recommended, in fact. Networks are what Tiggers like the best.)

Usually, the sensible approach to computer naming is to use names that have numbers, such as `computer001` or `computer002`.

✔ **Network resources, such as shared disk folders and printers, have names.** For example, a network server may have two printers, named `laser` and `inkjet` (to indicate the type of printer), and two shared disk folders, named `AccountingData` and `MarketingData`.

✔ **Server-based networks have a username for the network administrator.**

If you log on using the administrator's username, you can do anything you want: add new users, define new network resources, change Wally's password, anything. The administrator's username is usually something clever such as `Administrator`.

✔ **The network itself has a name.**

The Windows world has two basic types of networks:

- *Domain networks* are the norm for large corporate environments that have dedicated servers with IT staff to maintain them.

- *Workgroup networks* are more common in homes or in small offices that don't have dedicated servers or IT staff.

A domain network is known by — you guessed it — a *domain name*. And a workgroup network is identified by — drum roll, please — a *workgroup name*. Regardless of which type of network you use, you need to know this name to gain access to the network.

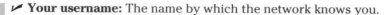

Logging On to the Network

To use network resources, you must connect your computer to the network, and you must go through the supersecret process of logging on, which is how you let the network know who you are so that it can decide whether you're one of the good guys.

Logging on is a little bit like cashing a check. You must have two forms of identification:

- ✔ **Your username:** The name by which the network knows you.

    Your username is usually some variation of your real name, like *Beav* for the Beaver.

    Everyone who uses the network must have a username.

- ✔ **Your password:** A secret word that only you and the network know. If you type the correct password, the network believes that you are who you say you are.

    Every user has a different password, and the password should be a secret.

In the early days of computer networking, you had to type a logon command at a stark MS-DOS prompt and then supply your user ID and password. Nowadays, the glory of Windows is that you get to log on to the network through a special network logon screen. Figure 2-1 shows the Windows 8 version of this dialog box.

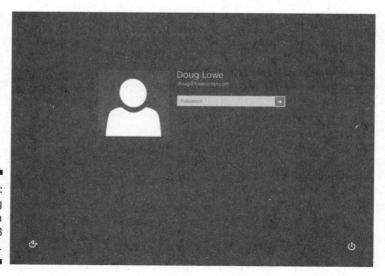

Figure 2-1:
Logging
in to a
Windows 8
system.

Here are some more logon points to ponder:

✔ The terms *user ID* and *logon name* are sometimes used instead of *username*. They all mean the same thing.

✔ As long as we're talking about words that mean the same thing, *log in* and *log on* mean the same thing, as do (respectively) *log out* and *log off* as ways of saying, "I'm outta here." Although you see both out there in the world, this book uses *log on* and *log off* throughout — and if there's any exception, the book says why and grouses about it a bit.

✔ As far as the network's concerned, you and your computer aren't the same thing. Your username refers to you, not to your computer. That's why you have a username and your computer has a computer name. You can log on to the network by using your username from any computer that's attached to the network. Other users can log on at your computer by using their own usernames.

When others log on at your computer by using their own usernames, they can't access any of your network files that are protected by your password. However, they *can* access any local files that you haven't protected. Be careful which people you allow to use your computer.

✔ If you're logging on to a domain network on a Windows Vista, Windows 7, or Windows 8 computer, you must type the domain name before your username, separated from it by a backslash. For example:

```
lowewriter\dlowe
```

Here, the domain name is `lowewriter`, and the username is `dlowe`.

Note that Windows remembers the domain and username from your last login, so ordinarily all you have to enter is your password. To log on to a different domain or as a different user, you must click Switch User. Then you can click the Other User icon and enter a different domain name and username, along with the password for the user you want to log on as.

✔ On an older Windows XP system, the logon dialog box has a field in which you can enter the domain name you want to log on to.

✔ Your computer may be set up so that it logs you on automatically whenever you turn it on. In that case, you don't have to type your username and password. This setup makes the task of logging on more convenient but takes the sport out of it. And it's a terrible idea if you're the least bit worried about bad guys getting into your network or personal files.

✔ Guard your password with your life. I'd tell you mine, but then I'd have to shoot you.

Understanding Shared Folders

Long ago, in the days Before Network (B.N.), your computer probably had just one hard drive, known as the C: drive. Maybe it had two — C: and D:. The second drive might be another hard disk, or possibly a CD-ROM or DVD-ROM drive. Even to this day, the descendants of those drives are physically located inside your PC. They're your *local drives*.

Now that you're on a network, however, you may have access to drives that aren't located inside your PC but are located instead in one of the other computers on the network. These network drives can be located on a dedicated server computer or, in the case of a peer-to-peer network, on another client computer.

In some cases, you can access an entire network drive over the network. But in most cases, you can't access the entire drive. Instead, you can access only certain folders on the network drives. Either way, the shared drives or folders are known in Windows terminology as *shared folders*.

Here's where it gets confusing: The most common way to access a shared folder is to assign a drive letter to it. Suppose that a server has a shared folder named Marketing. You can assign drive letter M to this shared folder. Then you access the Marketing folder as drive M:. The M: drive is then called a *network drive* because it uses the network to access data in a shared folder. Assigning a drive letter to a shared folder is *mapping a drive*.

Shared folders can be set up with restrictions on how you can use them. For example, you may be granted full access to some shared folders so that you can copy files to or from them, delete files on them, or create or remove folders on them. On other shared folders, your access may be limited in certain ways. For example, you may be able to copy files to or from the shared folder but not delete files, edit files, or create new folders. You may also be asked to enter a password before you can access a protected folder. The amount of disk space you're allowed to use on a shared folder may also be limited. For more information about file-sharing restrictions, see Chapter 12.

 In addition to accessing shared folders that reside on other people's computers, you can designate your computer as a server to enable other network users to access folders that you share. To find out how to share folders on your computer with other network users, see Chapter 3.

Four Good Uses for a Shared Folder

After you know which shared network folders are available, you may wonder what you're supposed to do with them. This section describes four good uses for a network folder.

Store files that everybody needs

A shared network folder is a good place to store files that more than one user needs to access. Without a network, you have to store a copy of the file on everyone's computer, and you have to worry about keeping the copies synchronized (which you can't do, no matter how hard you try). Or you can keep the file on a disk and pass it around. Or you can keep the file on one computer and play Musical Chairs; whenever someone needs to use the file, he goes to the computer that contains the file.

On a network, you can keep one copy of the file in a shared folder on the network, and everyone can access it.

Store your own files

You can also use a shared network folder as an extension of your own hard drive storage. For example, if you filled up all the free space on your hard drive with pictures, sounds, and movies that you downloaded from the Internet, but the network server has billions and billions of gigabytes of free space, you have all the drive space you need. Just store your files on the network drive!

Here are a few guidelines for storing files on network drives:

- ✔ **Using the network drive for your own files works best if the network drive is set up for private storage that other users can't access.** That way, you don't have to worry about the nosy guy down in Accounting who likes to poke around in other people's files.

- ✔ **Don't overuse the network drive.** Remember that other users have probably filled up their own hard drives, so they want to use the space on the network drive too.

- ✔ **Before you store personal files on a network drive, make sure that you have permission.** A note from your mom will do.

- ✔ **On domain networks, a drive (typically, drive H:) is commonly mapped to a user's home folder.** The *home folder* is a network folder that's unique for each user. You can think of it as a network version of My Documents. If your network is set up with a home folder, use it rather than My Documents for any important work-related files. That's because the home folder is usually included in the network's daily backup schedule. By contrast, most networks do *not* back up data you store in My Documents.

Make a temporary resting place for files on their way to other users

"Hey, Wally, could you send me a copy of last month's baseball stats?"

"Sure, Beav." But how? If the baseball stats file resides on Wally's local drive, how does Wally send a copy of the file to Beaver's computer? Wally can do it by copying the file to a network drive. Then Beaver can copy the file to his local hard drive.

Here are some tips to keep in mind when you use a network drive to exchange files with other network users:

- ✔ **Remember to delete files that you saved to the network drive after they're picked up!** Otherwise, the network drive quickly fills up with unnecessary files.

- ✔ **Create a folder on the network drive specifically intended for holding files en route to other users.** I like to name this folder PITSTOP.

In many cases, it's easier to send files to other network users by e-mail than by using a network folder. Just send a message to the other network user and attach the file you want to share. The advantage of sending a file by e-mail is that you don't have to worry about details like where to leave the file on the server and who's responsible for deleting the file.

Back up your local hard drive

If enough drive space is available on the file server, you can use it to store backup copies of the files on your hard drive. Just copy the files that you want to back up to a shared network folder.

Obviously, if you copy *all* your data files to the network drive — and everybody else follows suit — it can fill up quickly. Check with the network manager before you start storing backup copies of your files on the server. The manager may have already set up a special network drive that's designed just for backups. And if you're lucky, your network manager may be able to set up an automatic backup schedule for your important data so that you don't have to remember to back it up manually.

I hope that your network administrator also routinely backs up the contents of the network server's disk to tape. (Yes, *tape* — see Chapter 20 for details.) That way, if something happens to the network server, the data can be recovered from the backup tapes.

Oh, the Network Places You'll Go

Windows enables you to access network resources, such as shared folders, by browsing the network. In Windows XP, you do this by double-clicking the My Network Places icon that resides on your desktop. In Windows Vista and Windows 7, choose Network from the Start menu. In Windows 8, open Windows Explorer (click File Explorer on the taskbar) and then click Network. Figure 2-2 shows the Windows 8 version of the network browser.

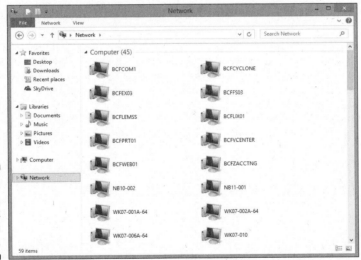

Figure 2-2: Browsing the network in Windows 8.

The network shown in Figure 2-2 consists of 45 computers, with names such as BCFCOM1, BCFFS03, and so on. You can open one of the computers by double-clicking its icon to reveal a list of shared resources available on the computer. For example, Figure 2-3 shows the resources shared by the BCFFS03 computer.

Figure 2-3:
The
resources
available
on a server
computer.

You can also browse the network from any Windows application program. For example, you may be working with Microsoft Word 2010 and want to open a document file that's stored in a shared folder on your network. All you have to do is use the Open command to bring up the dialog box. (In Office 2003 and 2010, this command is on the File menu. In Office 2007, you'll find it by clicking the Office button.) Choose Network in the list that appears in the pane on the left of the Open dialog box to browse the network, as shown in Figure 2-4.

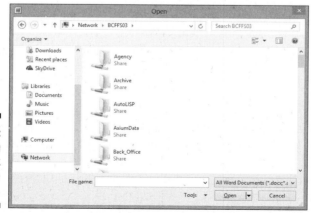

Figure 2-4:
Browsing
the network
in Office
2010.

Mapping Network Drives

If you often access a particular shared folder, you may want to use the special trick known as mapping to access the shared folder more efficiently. *Mapping* assigns a drive letter to a shared folder. Then you can use the drive letter to access the shared folder as though it were a local drive. In this way, you can access the shared folder from any Windows program without having to browse the network.

For example, you can map a shared folder named Data on the server named SERVER01 Files to drive K: on your computer. Then, to access files stored in the shared Data folder, you look on drive K.

To map a shared folder to a drive letter, follow these steps:

1. **Open File Explorer.**

   - *Windows Vista or 7:* Choose Start⇨Computer.

   - *Windows 8:* Open the desktop and click the File Explorer icon on the taskbar, and then click Computer in the Location list on the left side of the screen.

2. **Open the Map Network Drive dialog box.**

   - *Windows Vista and 7:* Access this dialog by clicking the Map Network Drive button located on the toolbar.

   - *Windows 8:* Click Map Network Drive on the ribbon.

   Figure 2-5 shows the Map Network Drive dialog box for Windows 8. The dialog box for earlier versions of Windows is similar.

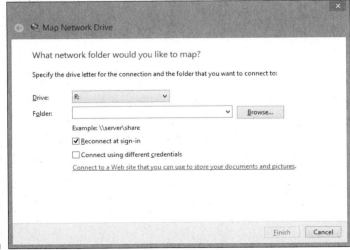

Figure 2-5: The Map Network Drive dialog box.

3. **(Optional) Change the drive letter in the Drive drop-down list.**

You probably don't have to change the drive letter that Windows selects (in Figure 2-5, drive R). If you're picky, though, you can select the drive letter from the Drive drop-down list.

4. **Click the Browse button.**

This step summons the dialog box shown in Figure 2-6.

Figure 2-6:
Browsing
for the
folder to
map.

5. **Use the Browse for Folder dialog box to find and select the shared folder you want to use.**

You can navigate to any shared folder on any computer in the network.

6. **Click OK.**

The Browse for Folder dialog box is dismissed, and you return to the Map Network Drive dialog box (refer to Figure 2-5).

7. **(Optional) If you want this network drive to be automatically mapped each time you log on to the network, select the Reconnect at Sign-in check box.**

If you leave the Reconnect at Logon check box deselected, the drive letter is available only until you shut down Windows or log out of the network. If you select this option, the network drive reconnects automatically each time you log on to the network.

Be sure to select the Reconnect at Logon check box if you use the network drive often.

8. **Click OK.**

You return to the Computer window, as shown in Figure 2-7. Here, you can see the newly mapped network drive.

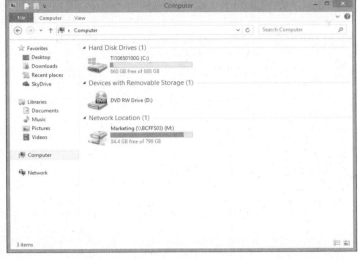

Figure 2-7:
The
Computer
folder
shows a
mapped net-
work drive.

Your network administrator may have already set up your computer with one or more mapped network drives. If so, you can ask her to tell you which network drives have been mapped. Or you can just open the Computer folder (My Computer on Windows XP) and have a look.

Here are a few additional tips:

- ✓ **If you're using Windows XP, the procedure for mapping a network drive is similar to the one for Windows Vista.** Start by opening My Computer and choosing Tools⇨Map Network Drive. Then follow the preceding set of steps, starting at Step 3.

- ✓ **Assigning a drive letter to a network drive is called *mapping the drive,* or *linking the drive,* by network nerds.** "Drive Q: is mapped to a network drive," they say.

- ✓ **Network drive letters don't have to be assigned the same way for every computer on the network.** For example, a network drive that's assigned drive letter M on your computer may be assigned drive letter Z on someone else's computer. In that case, your drive M: and the other computer's drive Z: refer to the same data. This arrangement can be confusing. If your network is set up this way, put pepper in your network administrator's coffee.

- ✓ **Accessing a shared network folder through a mapped network drive is much faster than accessing the same folder by browsing the network.** Windows has to browse the entire network to list all available computers whenever you browse the network. By contrast, Windows doesn't have to browse the network to access a mapped network drive.

✓ **If you select the Reconnect at Logon option for a mapped drive (refer to Figure 2-5), you receive a warning message if the drive isn't available when you log on.** In most cases, the problem is that the server computer isn't turned on. Sometimes, however, this message is caused by a broken network connection. For more information about fixing network problems such as this one, see Chapter 19.

Using a Network Printer

Using a network printer is much like using a network hard drive: You can print to a network printer from any Windows program by choosing the Print command to call up a Print dialog box from any program and choosing a network printer from the list of available printers. In Office 2003 and 2010, this command is on the File menu. In Office 2007, you can reach it by clicking the Office button.

Keep in mind, however, that printing on a network printer isn't exactly the same as printing on a local printer; you have to take turns. When you print on a local printer, you're the only one using it. When you print to a network printer, however, you are (in effect) standing in line behind other network users, waiting to share the printer. This line complicates the situation in several ways:

✓ **If several users print to the network printer at the same time, the network has to keep the print jobs separate from one another.** If it didn't, the result would be a jumbled mess, with your 268-page report getting mixed in with the payroll checks. That would be bad. Fortunately, the network takes care of this situation by using the fancy *print spooling* feature.

✓ **Network printing works on a first-come, first-served basis (unless you know some of the tricks that I discuss in Chapter 3).** Invariably, when I get in line at the hardware store, the person in front of me is trying to buy something that doesn't have a product code on it. I end up standing there for hours waiting for someone in Plumbing to pick up the phone for a price check. Network printing can be like that. If someone sends a two-hour print job to the printer before you send your half-page memo, you have to wait.

✓ **You may have access to a local printer and several network printers.** Before you were forced to use the network, your computer probably had just one printer attached to it. You may want to print some documents on your cheap (oops, I mean *local)* inkjet printer but use the network laser printer for important stuff. To do that, you have to find out how to use your programs' functions for switching printers.

Adding a network printer

Before you can print to a network printer, you have to configure your computer to access the network printer that you want to use. From the Start menu, open the Control Panel and then double-click the Printers icon. If your computer is already configured to work with a network printer, an icon for the network printer appears in the Printers folder. You can tell a network printer from a local printer by the shape of the printer icon. Network printer icons have a pipe attached to the bottom of the printer.

If you don't have a network printer configured for your computer, you can add one by using the Add Printer Wizard. Just follow these steps:

1. **Open the Control Panel.**

   - *Windows 7 or earlier:* Choose Start➪Control Panel.

   - *Windows 8:* Press the Windows key, type **Control**, and then click the Control Panel icon.

2. **Click Devices and Printers.**

3. **Click the Add a Printer button on the toolbar.**

   This step starts the Add Printer Wizard, as shown in Figure 2-8.

4. **Click the printer you want to use.**

   If you can't find the printer you want to use, ask your network administrator for the printer's *UNC path,* which is the name used to identify the printer on the network, or its IP address. Then click The Printer That I Want Isn't Listed and enter the UNC or IP address for the printer when prompted.

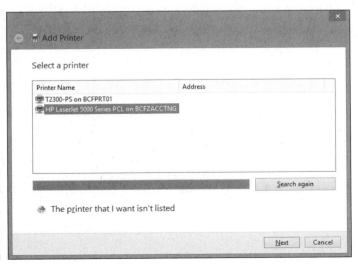

Figure 2-8:
The Add Printer Wizard asks you to pick a printer.

5. **Click Next to add the printer.**

   The wizard copies to your computer the correct printer driver for the network printer. (You may be prompted to confirm that you want to add the driver. If so, click Install Driver to proceed.)

   The Add Printer Wizard displays a screen that shows the printer's name and asks whether you want to designate the printer as your default printer.

6. **(Optional) Designate the printer as your default printer.**

7. **Click Next to continue.**

   A final confirmation dialog box is displayed.

8. **Click Finish.**

   You're done!

Many network printers, especially newer ones, are connected directly to the network by using a built-in Ethernet card. Setting up these printers can be tricky. You may need to ask the network administrator for help in setting up this type of printer. (Some printers that are connected directly to the network have their own web addresses, such as `Printer.CleaverFamily.com`. If that's the case, you can often set up the printer in a click or two: Use your browser to go to the printer's web page and then click a link that enables you to install the printer.)

Printing to a network printer

After you install the network printer in Windows, printing to the network printer is a snap. You can print to the network printer from any Windows program by using the Print command to summon the Print dialog box, which is usually found on the File menu. For example, Figure 2-9 shows the Print dialog box for WordPad (the free text-editing program that comes with Windows). The available printers are listed near the top of this dialog box. Choose the network printer from this list and then click OK to print your document. That's all there is to it!

Playing with the print queue

After you send your document to a network printer, you usually don't have to worry about it. You just go to the network printer, and voilà! Your printed document is waiting for you.

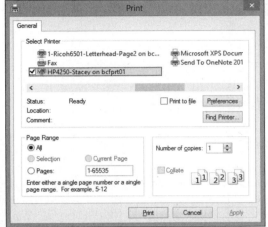

Figure 2-9:
A typical
Print
dialog box.

That's what happens in the ideal world. In the real world, where you and I live, all sorts of things can happen to your print job between the time you send it to the network printer and the time it prints:

- ✔ You discover that someone else already sent a 50 trillion–page report ahead of you that isn't expected to finish printing until the national debt is paid off.

- ✔ The price of a framis valve suddenly goes up by $2, rendering foolish the recommendations you made in your report.

- ✔ Your boss calls and tells you that his brother-in-law will be attending the meeting, so won't you please print an extra copy of the proposal for him? Oh, and a photocopy won't do. Originals only, please.

- ✔ You decide to take lunch, so you don't want the output to print until you get back.

Fortunately, your print job isn't totally beyond your control just because you already sent it to the network printer. You can easily change the status of jobs that you already sent. You can change the order in which jobs print, hold a job so that it doesn't print until you say so, or cancel a job.

You can probably make your network print jobs do other tricks, too: shake hands, roll over, and play dead. But the basic tricks — hold, cancel, and change the print order — are enough to get you started.

To play with the printer queue, open the Control Panel by choosing Start↪ Control Panel in Windows 7 or earlier; or press the Windows key, type **Control**, and the click the Control Panel icon. Then click Devices and Printers and double-click the icon for the printer that you want to manage. A window similar to the one shown in Figure 2-10 appears. You can see that just one document has been sent to the printer.

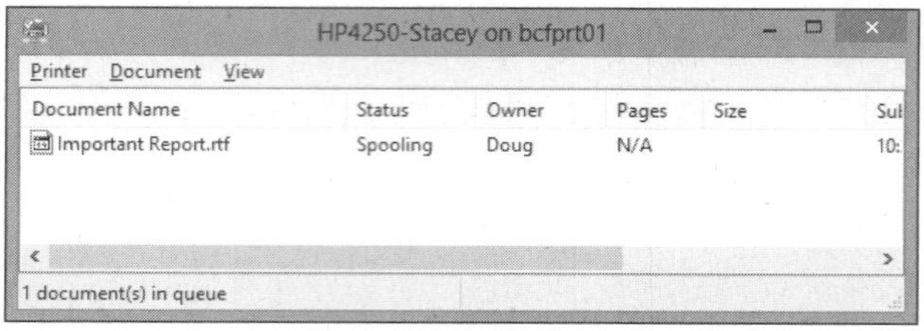

HP4250-Stacey on bcfprt01					
Printer Document View					
Document Name	Status	Owner	Pages	Size	Sul
Important Report.rtf	Spooling	Doug	N/A		10:

1 document(s) in queue

Figure 2-10:
Managing a
print queue.

To manipulate the print jobs that appear in the print queue or in the printer itself, use these tricks:

- **To temporarily stop a job from printing:** Select the job and choose Document⇨Pause Printing. Choose the same command again to release the job from its state of frustration and print it out, already.

- **To delete a print job:** Select the job and choose Document⇨Cancel Printing.

- **To stop the printer:** Choose Printer⇨Pause Printing. To resume, choose the command again.

- **To delete all print jobs:** Choose Printer⇨Purge Print Documents.

- **To cut to the front of the line:** Drag to the top of the list the print job that you want to print.

All these tips apply to your print jobs only. Unfortunately, you can't capriciously delete other people's print jobs.

The best thing about Windows printer management is that it shelters you from the details of working with different network operating systems. Whether you print on a NetWare printer, a Windows 2003 network printer, or a shared Windows printer, the Printer window icon manages all print jobs in the same way.

Logging Off the Network

After you finish using the network, log off. Logging off the network makes the network drives and printers unavailable. Your computer is still physically connected to the network (unless you cut the network cable with pruning shears; it's a bad idea — don't do it!), but the network and its resources are unavailable to you.

Here are a few other tips to keep in mind when you log off:

- After you turn off your computer, you're automatically logged off the network. After you start your computer, you have to log on again.

  Logging off the network is a good idea if you're going to leave your computer unattended for a while. As long as your computer is logged in to the network, anyone can use it to access the network. And because unauthorized users can access it under your user ID, you get the blame for any damage they do.

- In Windows, you can log off the network by clicking the Start button and choosing the Log Off command. This process logs you off the network without restarting Windows:

  - *In Windows XP:* You can reach this command directly from the Start menu.

  - *In Windows Vista or 7:* Click Start and then click the right-facing arrow that appears next to the little padlock icon.

  - *In Windows 8:* Press Ctrl+Alt+Del and then choose Sign Out.

Chapter 3

More Ways to Use Your Network

Chapter 2 introduces you to the basics of using a network: logging on, accessing data on shared network folders, printing, and logging off. In this chapter, I go beyond these basics. You find out how to turn your computer into a server that shares its own files and printers, how to use one of the most popular network computer applications — e-mail — and how to work with Office on a network.

Sharing Your Stuff

As you probably know, networks consist of two types of computers: client computers and server computers. In the economy of computer networks, *client computers* are the consumers — the ones that use network resources, such as shared printers and disk drives. *Servers* are the providers — the ones that offer their own printers and hard drives to the network so that the client computers can use them.

This chapter shows you how to turn your humble Windows client computer into a server computer so that other computers on your network can use your printer and any folders that you decide you want to share. In effect, your computer functions as both a client and a server at the same time. A couple of examples show how:

✔ It's a **client** when you send a print job to a network printer or when you access a file stored on another server's hard drive.

✔ It's a **server** when someone else sends a print job to your printer or accesses a file stored on your computer's hard drive.

Enabling File and Printer Sharing (Windows XP)

Before you can share your files or your printer with other network users, you must set up a Windows File and Printer Sharing feature. Without this feature installed, your computer can be a network client but not a server. This section shows you how to enable this feature for Windows XP. For Windows Vista, see the next section, "Enabling File and Printer Sharing (Windows Vista)."

If you're lucky, the File and Printer Sharing feature is already set up on your computer. To find out, double-click the My Computer icon on your desktop. Select the icon for your C: drive and then click File on the menu bar to reveal the File menu. If the menu includes a Sharing command, File and Printer Sharing is already set up, so you can skip the rest of this section. If you can't find a Sharing command on the File menu, you have to install File and Printer Sharing before you can share a file or printer with other network users.

To enable File and Printer Sharing on a Windows XP system, follow these steps:

1. **From the Start menu, choose Settings⇨Control Panel.**

   The Control Panel comes to life.

2. **Double-click the Network Connections icon.**

   The Network Connections window appears.

3. **Right-click Local Area Connection and choose Properties.**

   The Local Area Connection properties dialog box appears, as shown in Figure 3-1.

4. **Make sure the File and Print Sharing for Microsoft Networks option is checked.**

5. **Click OK.**

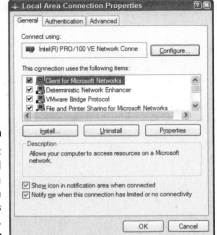

Figure 3-1:
The Local
Area
Connection
Properties
dialog box.

While you're working in the Network dialog box, don't mess around with any of the other network settings. You can safely change the File and Print Sharing options, but leave the rest of the settings in the Network dialog box alone.

Enabling File and Printer Sharing (Windows Vista)

To enable file and printer sharing in Windows Vista, follow these steps:

1. **Choose Start➪Network.**

   This step opens the Network folder.

2. **Click the Network and Sharing Center button on the toolbar.**

   This step opens the Network and Sharing Center, as shown in Figure 3-2.

3. **Click the down arrow to the right of File Sharing in the Sharing and Discovery section.**

   This step reveals the controls that enable you to activate file sharing, as shown in Figure 3-3.

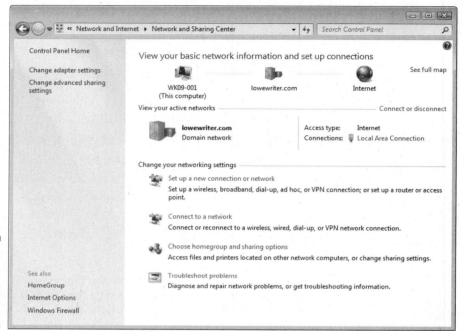

Figure 3-2:
The
Network
and Sharing
Center.

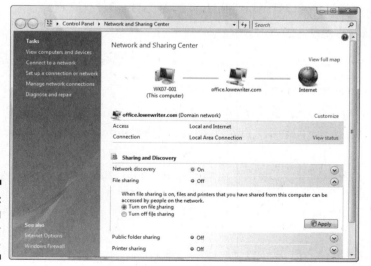

Figure 3-3:
Activating
the file shar-
ing feature.

4. **Select the Turn on File Sharing option and then click Apply.**

   This file sharing feature is activated.

5. **Select the Printer Sharing option.**

   This step reveals the controls that enable you to activate printer sharing.

6. **Select the Turn on Printer Sharing option and then click Apply.**

   This file sharing feature is activated.

7. **Close the Network and Sharing Center folder.**

   You're done; you can now share your files and printers.

Enabling File and Printer Sharing (Windows 7 and 8)

Here are the steps to enable file and printer sharing in Windows 7:

1. **Click the Start button, type** Control Panel, **and press Enter.**

   This step opens the Control Panel.

2. **Double-click the Network and Sharing Center icon and then click Change Advanced Sharing Settings.**

   This step opens the Advanced Sharing Settings page, which lists network settings for each network you're connected to.

   - *For a home computer running Windows 7:* Two networks are listed: Home or Work, and Public.

   - *In Windows 8:* The Home or Work network is called Private.

   - *For a computer connected to a domain network:* A third network named Domain is listed.

3. **Click the down arrow next to the network you want to enable file and printer sharing for.**

   - *For a home computer:* Click the down arrow next to Home or Work (Windows 7) or Private (Windows 8).

   - *For a computer connected to a domain network:* Click the down arrow next to Domain.

   Figure 3-4 shows the settings for a Domain network. The settings for a Home or Work network are the same.

Do *not* enable file or printer sharing for the Public network. Enabling file or printer sharing on a public network exposes your computer's data to other users on the same public network.

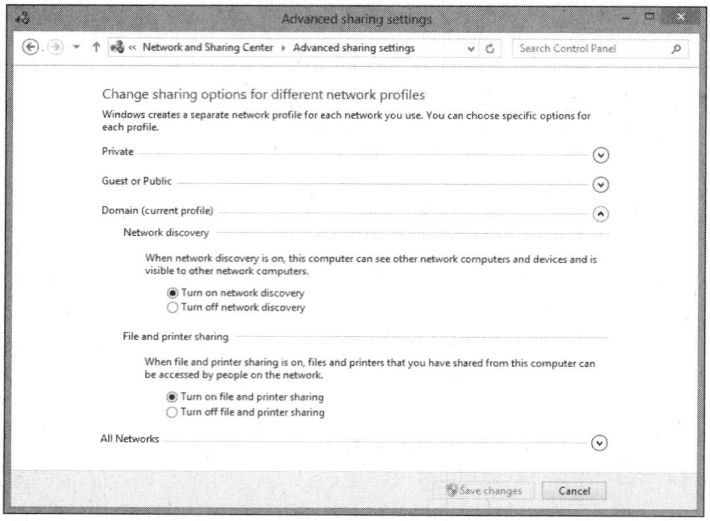

Figure 3-4:
Enabling file
and printer
sharing in
Windows 8.

4. **Select the Turn on File and Printer Sharing option.**

5. **Click the Save Changes button.**

   This action saves your changes and closes the Advanced Sharing
   Settings page.

Sharing a Folder

To enable other network users to access files that reside on your hard drive,
you must designate a folder on the drive as a *shared* folder. Note that you can
also share an entire drive, if you so desire. If you share an entire drive, other
network users can access all the files and folders on the drive. If you share
a folder, network users can access only those files that reside in the folder
you share. (If the folder you share contains other folders, network users can
access files in those folders, too.)

Don't share an entire hard drive unless you want to grant *everyone on the network* the freedom to sneak a peek at every file on your hard drive. Instead, you
should share just the folder or folders containing the specific documents that
you want others to be able to access. For example, if you store all your Word
documents in the My Documents folder, you can share your My Documents
folder so that other network users can access your Word documents.

Sharing a folder in Windows XP

To share a folder on a Windows XP computer, follow these steps:

1. Double-click the My Computer icon on your desktop.

The My Computer window comes to center stage.

2. Select the folder that you want to share.

Click the icon for the drive that contains the folder you want to share, and then find the folder itself and click it.

3. Choose File⇨Sharing and Security.

The Properties dialog box for the folder that you want to share appears. Notice that the sharing options are grayed out.

4. Select the Share This Folder on the Network option.

After you select this option, the rest of the sharing options come alive, as shown in Figure 3-5.

If you prefer, you can skip Steps 2–4. Instead, just right-click the folder you want to share and then choose Sharing and Security from the menu that appears.

Figure 3-5:
The Sharing options come to life when you select the Share This Folder on the Network check box (in Windows XP).

5. (Optional) Change the share name if you don't like the name that Windows proposes.

The *share name* is the name that other network users use to access the shared folder. You can give it any name you want, but the name can be no more than 12 characters long. Uppercase and lowercase letters are treated the same in a share name, so the name My Documents is the same as MY DOCUMENTS.

Windows proposes a share name for you, based on the actual folder name. If the folder name has 12 or fewer characters, the proposed share name is the same as the folder name. If the folder name is longer than 12 characters, however, Windows abbreviates it. For example, the name Multimedia Files becomes MULTIMEDIA F.

If the name that Windows chooses doesn't make sense or seems cryptic, you can change the share name to something better. For example, I would probably use MEDIA FILES rather than MULTIMEDIA F.

6. **(Optional) If you want to allow other network users to change the files in this folder, select the Allow Network Users to Change My Files check box.**

   If you leave this option deselected, other network users can open your files, but they can't save any changes they make.

7. **Click OK.**

   The Properties dialog box vanishes, and a hand is added to the icon for the folder to show that the folder is shared.

If you change your mind and decide that you want to stop sharing a folder, double-click the My Computer icon, select the folder or drive that you want to stop sharing, and choose File⇨Sharing to summon the Properties dialog box. Deselect the Share This Folder on the Network check box and then click OK.

Sharing a folder in Windows Vista, 7, or 8

To share a folder in Windows Vista, Windows 7, or Windows 8, follow these steps:

1. **Open File Explorer.**

   • *Windows Vista or 7:* Choose Start⇨Computer.

   • *Windows 8:* Open the desktop and click the File Explorer icon on the taskbar; then click Computer in the Location list on the left side of the screen.

2. **Navigate to the folder you want to share.**

3. **Right-click the folder you want to share and choose Properties.**

   The Properties dialog box appears.

4. **Click the Sharing tab and then click the Share button.**

   The File Sharing dialog box appears, as shown in Figure 3-6.

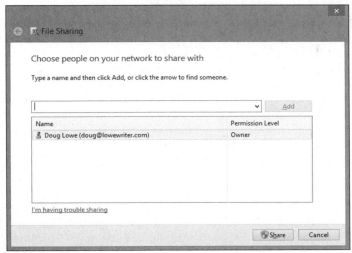

Figure 3-6:
The File
Sharing
dialog box
(Windows 8).

5. **Click the arrow in the drop-down list, choose Everyone, and then click Add.**

   This action designates that anyone on your network can access the shared folder.

   If you prefer, you can limit access to just certain users. To do so, select each person you want to grant access to and then click Add.

6. **Select the level of access you want to grant each user.**

   You can use the drop-down list in the Permission Level column to choose from three levels of access:

   - *Reader:* A reader can open files but can't modify or create new files or folders.

   - *Contributor:* A contributor can add files to the share but can change or delete only her own files.

   - *Owner:* An owner has full access to the shared folder. He or she can create, change, or delete any file in the folder.

7. **Click Share.**

   A confirmation dialog box appears to confirm that the folder has been shared.

Using the Public Folder in Windows Vista or Windows 7 or 8

Windows Vista, Windows 7, and Windows 8 include an alternative method of sharing files on the network: the Public folder. The *Public folder* is simply a folder that's designated for public access. Files you save in this folder can be accessed by other users on the network and by any user who logs on to your computer.

Before you can use the Public folder, you must enable it. In Windows 7 or 8, just follow the steps listed in the section "Enabling File and Printer Sharing (Windows 7 and 8)" earlier in this chapter, but choose the Turn on Sharing option in the Public Sharing Settings section. For Windows Vista, follow the steps in the earlier section "Enabling File and Printer Sharing (Windows Vista)," but choose the Public Sharing option instead of the File Sharing and Printer Sharing options.

After you enable Public folder sharing, you can access the Public folder on your own computer in Windows Vista by choosing Start⇨Computer and then clicking the Public icon in the pane on the left side of the window. To open the Public folder in Windows 7, choose Start⇨Computer, expand the Libraries item in the left pane, and then expand the Documents, Music, Pictures, or Videos items. In Windows 8, open the desktop, click the File Explorer icon on the taskbar, expand the Libraries item in the left pane, and then expand the Documents, Music, Pictures or Videos items.

Figure 3-7 shows an example of a Public folder in Windows 8.

As you can see, the Public folder includes several predefined subfolders designed for sharing documents, downloaded files, music, pictures, and videos. You can use these subfolders if you want, or you can create your own subfolders to help organize the data in your Public folder.

To access the Public folder of another computer, use the techniques that I describe in Chapter 2 to either browse to the Public folder or map it to a network drive.

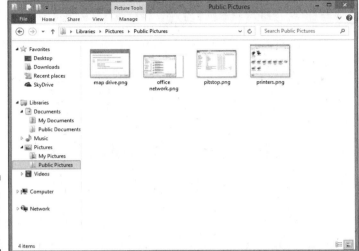

Figure 3-7:
A Public
folder in
Windows 8.

Sharing a Printer

Sharing a printer is much more traumatic than sharing a hard drive. When you share a hard drive, other network users access your files from time to time. When they do, you hear your drive click a few times, and your computer may hesitate for a half-second or so. The interruptions caused by other users accessing your drive are sometimes noticeable but rarely annoying.

When you share a printer, you get to see Murphy's Law in action: Your co-worker down the hall is liable to send a 140-page report to your printer just moments before you try to print a 1-page memo that has to be on the boss's desk in two minutes. The printer may run out of paper — or worse, jam — during someone else's print job — and you're expected to attend to the problem.

Although these interruptions can be annoying, sharing your printer makes a lot of sense in some situations. If you have the only decent printer in your office or workgroup, everyone will bug you to let them use it anyway. You may as well share the printer on the network. At least this way, they won't line up at your door to ask you to print their documents for them.

Sharing a printer in Windows XP

The following procedure shows you how to share a printer in Windows XP:

1. From the Start menu, choose Printers and Faxes.

The Printers and Faxes folder appears, as shown in Figure 3-8. In this example, the Printers folder lists a single printer, named HP PSC 750.

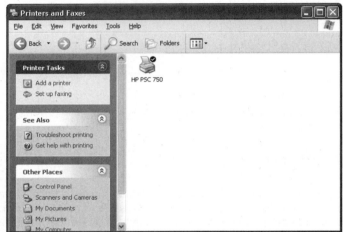

Figure 3-8:
The Printers
and Faxes
folder.

2. Select the printer that you want to share.

Click the icon for the printer to select the printer.

3. Choose File➪Sharing.

You're right: This command doesn't make sense. You're sharing a *printer,* not a file, but the Sharing command is on the File menu. Go figure.

When you choose File➪Sharing, the Properties dialog box for the printer appears.

4. Select the Share This Printer option.

5. (Optional) Change the share name if you don't like the name suggested by Windows.

Other computers use the share name to identify the shared printer, so choose a meaningful or descriptive name.

6. Click OK.

You return to the Printers folder, where a hand is added to the printer icon to show that the printer is now a shared network printer.

To take your shared printer off the network so that other network users can't access it, follow Steps 1–3 in the preceding set of steps to open the Printer Properties dialog box. Select the Do Not Share This Printer option and then click OK. The hand disappears from the printer icon to indicate that the printer is no longer shared.

Sharing a printer in Windows Vista, Windows 7, or Windows 8

To share a printer in Windows Vista, Windows 7, or Windows 8, follow these steps:

1. **Open the Control Panel.**

    - *Windows 7 or earlier:* Choose Start⇨Control Panel.

    - *Windows 8:* Press the Windows key, type **Control**, and then click the Control Panel icon.

2. **Click Devices and Printers.**

3. **Right-click the printer that you want to share and choose Printer Properties.**

    The Properties dialog box for the printer appears.

4. **Click the Sharing tab.**

    The Sharing tab appears, as shown in Figure 3-9. Notice that the options for sharing the printer are disabled.

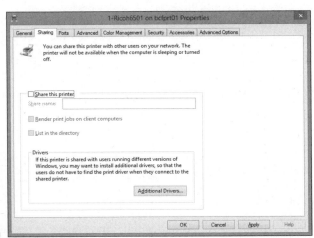

Figure 3-9:
Sharing a printer in Windows 8.

5. **Select the Share This Printer option.**

6. **(Optional) Change the share name if you don't like the name suggested by Windows.**

   Because other computers will use the share name to identify the shared printer, pick a descriptive name.

7. **Click OK.**

   You return to the Printers folder. The icon for the printer is modified to indicate that it has been shared.

To take your shared printer off the network so that other network users can't access it, follow Steps 1–4 in the preceding set of steps. Deselect the Share This Printer check box and then click OK.

Using Microsoft Office on a Network

Microsoft Office is far and away the most popular suite of application programs used on personal computers, and it includes the most common types of application programs used in an office: a word processing program (Word), a spreadsheet program (Excel), a presentation program (PowerPoint), and an excellent e-mail program (Outlook). Depending on the version of Office you purchase, you may also get a database program (Access), a desktop publishing program (Publisher), a set of Ginsu knives (KnifePoint), and a slicer and dicer (ActiveSalsa).

This section describes the networking features of Microsoft Office System 2010, the latest and greatest version of Office. Most of these features also work with previous versions of Office.

To get the most from using Office on a network, you should purchase the Microsoft Office Resource Kit. The Office Resource Kit, also known as *ORK,* contains information about installing and using Office on a network and comes with a CD that has valuable tools. If you don't want to purchase the ORK, you can view it online and download the ORK tools from the Microsoft TechNet website (`http://technet.microsoft.com/en-US/`). Nanoo-nanoo, Earthling.

Installing Office on a network — some options

You need to make some basic decisions when you prepare to install Microsoft Office on a network. In particular, here are some possible approaches to installing Microsoft Office on your network clients:

✔ You can simply ignore the fact that you have a network and purchase a separate copy of Office for each user on the network. Then you can install Office from the CD on each computer. This option works well if

- • Your network is small.

- • Each computer has ample disk space to hold the necessary Office files.

- • Each computer has its own CD-ROM drive. (If the computer doesn't have a CD-ROM drive, you can share a CD-ROM drive on another computer and install the software from the shared drive.)

✔ On a larger network, you can use the Office Setup program in Administrative Setup mode. This option lets you create a special type of setup on a network server disk from which you can install Office on network computers. Administrative Setup enables you to control the custom features selected for each network computer and reduce the amount of user interaction required to install Office on each computer.

If you choose to use Administrative Setup, you can use the Network Installation Wizard, which comes with the Office Resource Kit. The Network Installation Wizard lets you customize settings for installing Office on client computers. For example, you can choose which Office components to install, provide default answers to yes/no questions that Setup asks the user while installing Office, and select the amount of interaction you want the Setup program to have with the user while installing Office.

No matter which option you choose for installing Office on your network, you must purchase either a copy of Office or a license to install Office for every computer that uses Office. Purchasing a single copy of Office and installing it on more than one computer is illegal.

Accessing network files

Opening a file that resides on a network drive is almost as easy as opening a file on a local drive. All Office programs use File➪Open to summon the Open dialog box, as shown in its Excel incarnation in Figure 3-10. (The Open dialog box is nearly identical in other Office programs.)

To access a file that resides on a network volume that's mapped to a drive letter, all you have to do is use the drop-down list at the top of the dialog box to select the network drive.

You can map a network drive directly from the Open dialog box by navigating to the folder you want to map, right-clicking the folder, and choosing Map Network Drive.

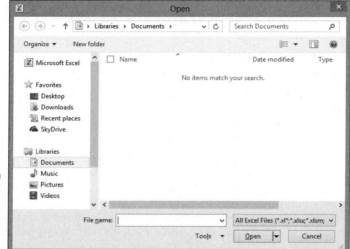

Figure 3-10:
The Open
dialog box in
Excel 2010.

 If you try to open a file that another network user has opened already, Office tells you that the file is already in use and offers to let you open a read-only version of the file. You can read and edit the read-only version, but Office doesn't let you overwrite the existing version of the file. Instead, you have to use the Save As command to save your changes to a new file.

Using workgroup templates

Although an occasional sacrifice to the Office gods may make your computing life a bit easier, a template isn't a place of worship. Rather, a *template* is a special type of document file that holds formatting information, boilerplate text, and other customized settings that you can use as the basis for new documents.

Three Office programs — Word, Excel, and PowerPoint — enable you to specify a template whenever you create a new document. When you create a new document in Word, Excel, or PowerPoint by choosing File⇨New, you see a dialog box that lets you choose a template for the new document.

Office comes with a set of templates for the most common types of documents. These templates are grouped under the various tabs that appear across the top of the New dialog box.

In addition to the templates that come with Office, you can create your own templates in Word, Excel, and PowerPoint. Creating your own templates is especially useful if you want to establish a consistent look for documents prepared by your network users. For example, you can create a Letter template that includes your company's letterhead or a Proposal template that includes a company logo.

Office enables you to store templates in two locations. Where you put them depends on what you want to do with them:

✔ **The User Templates folder on each user's local disk drive:** If a particular user needs a specialized template, put it here.

✔ **The Workgroup Templates folder on a shared network drive:** If you have templates that you want to make available to all network users on the network server, put them here. This arrangement still allows each user to create templates that aren't available to other network users.

When you use both a User Templates folder and a Workgroup Templates folder, Office combines the templates from both folders and lists them in alphabetical order in the New dialog box. For example, the User Templates folder may contain templates named Blank Document and Web Page, and the Workgroup Templates folder may contain a template named Company Letterhead. In this case, three templates appear in the New dialog box, in this order: Blank Document, Company Letterhead, and Web Page.

To set the location of the User Templates and Workgroup Templates folders, follow these steps in Microsoft Word:

1. **Click the Office button and then click Word Options.**

   The Word Options dialog box opens.

2. **Click the Advanced tab.**

   The Advanced options appear.

3. **Scroll down to the General section and then click the File Locations button.**

   The File Locations dialog box appears, as shown in Figure 3-11.

4. **Double-click the Workgroup Templates item.**

   This step opens a dialog box that lets you browse to the location of your template files.

5. **Browse to the template files and then click OK.**

   You return to the File Locations dialog box.

6. **Click OK to dismiss the File Locations dialog box.**

   You return to the Word Options dialog box.

7. **Click OK again.**

   The Word Options dialog box is dismissed.

Figure 3-11:
Setting the
file loca-
tions in
Word 2010.

Although the User Templates and Workgroup Templates settings affect Word, Excel, and PowerPoint, you can change these settings only from Word. The Options dialog boxes in Excel and PowerPoint don't show the User Templates or Workgroup Templates options.

When you install Office, the standard templates that come with Office are copied into a folder on the computer's local disk drive, and the User Templates option is set to this folder. The Workgroup Templates option is left blank. You can set the Workgroup Templates folder to a shared network folder by clicking Network Templates, clicking the Modify button, and specifying a shared network folder that contains your workgroup templates.

Networking an Access database

If you want to share a Microsoft Access database among several network users, be aware of a few special considerations. Here are the most important ones:

✔ When you share a database, more than one user may try to access the same record at the same time. This situation can lead to problems if two or more users try to update the record. To handle this potential traffic snarl, Access locks the record so that only one user at a time can update it. Access uses one of three methods to lock records:

  • *Edited Record:* This method locks a record whenever a user begins to edit a record. For example, if a user retrieves a record in a form that allows the record to be updated, Access locks the record while the user edits it so that other users can't edit the record until the first record is finished.

- *No Locks:* This method doesn't really mean that the record isn't locked. Instead, No Locks means that the record isn't locked until a user writes a change to the database. This method can be confusing to users because it enables one user to overwrite changes made by another user.

- *All Records:* All Records locks an entire table whenever a user edits any record in the table.

✔ Access lets you split a database so that the forms, queries, and reports are stored on each user's local disk drive, but the data itself is stored on a network drive. This feature can make the database run more efficiently on a network, but it's a little more difficult to set up. (To split a database, choose Tools➪Database Utilities➪Database Splitter.)

✔ Access includes built-in security features that you should use if you share an Access database from a Windows client computer. If you store the database on a domain server, you can use the server's security features to protect the database.

✔ Access automatically refreshes forms and datasheets every 60 seconds. That way, if one user opens a form or datasheet and another user changes the data a few seconds later, the first user sees the changes within one minute. If 60 seconds is too long (or too short) an interval, you can change the refresh rate by using the Advanced tab in the Options dialog box.

Working with Offline Files

Desktop computers are by nature stationary beasts. As a result, they're almost always connected to their networks. Notebook computers, however, are more transitory. If you have a notebook computer, you're likely to tote it around from place to place. If you have a network at work, you probably connect to the network when you're at work. But then you take the notebook computer home for the weekend, and you aren't connected to your network.

Of course, your boss wants you to spend your weekends working, so you need a way to access your important network files while you're away from the office and disconnected from the network. That's where the offline files feature comes in. It lets you access your network files even while you're disconnected from the network.

It sounds like magic, but it isn't really. Imagine how you'd work away from the network without this feature. You simply copy the files you need to work on to your notebook computer's local hard disk. Then, when you take the computer home, you work on the local copies. When you get back to the office, you connect to the network and copy the modified files back to the network server.

That's essentially how the offline files feature works, except that Windows does all the copying automatically. Windows also uses smoke and mirrors to make it look like the copies are actually on the network even though you're not connected to the network. For example, if you map a drive (drive M:, for example) and make it available offline, you can still access the offline copies of the file on the M: drive. That's because Windows knows that when you aren't connected to the network, it should redirect drive M: to its local copy of the drive M: files.

The main complication of working with offline files, of course, is what happens when two or more users want to access the same offline files. Windows can attempt to straighten that mess out for you, but it doesn't do a great job of it. Your best bet is to not use the offline files feature with network resources that other users may want available offline, too. In other words, it's okay to make your home drive available offline because that drive is accessible only to you. I don't recommend making shared network resources available offline, though, unless they're read-only resources that don't contain files you intend to modify.

Using the offline files feature is easy:

- **Windows Vista, Windows 7, or Windows 8:** Open the Computer folder, right-click the mapped network drive you want to make available offline, and choose Always Available Offline.

- **Windows XP:** Open My Computer, right-click the mapped drive, and choose Make Available Offline.

If you don't want to designate an entire mapped drive for offline access, you can designate individual folders within a mapped drive by using the same technique: Right-click the folder and then choose Always Available Offline (Make Available Offline in Windows XP).

When you first designate a drive or folder as available offline, Windows copies all the files on the drive or folder to local storage. Depending on how many files are involved, this process can take a while, so plan accordingly.

After you designate a drive as available offline, Windows takes care of the rest. Each time you log on to or out of the network, Windows synchronizes your offline files. Windows compares the time stamp on each file on both the server and the local copy and then copies any files that have changed.

Here are a few other thoughts to consider about offline files:

- If you want, you can force Windows to synchronize your offline files by right-clicking the drive or folder and choosing Sync.

- Make sure that no files in the folder are currently open at the time you set the Make Available Offline option. If any files are open, you'll receive

an error message. You have to close the open files before you can designate the folder for offline access.

✔ The Properties dialog box for mapped drives includes an Offline Files
tab, as shown in Figure 3-12.

✔ Employers love the offline files feature because it encourages their
employees to work at home during evenings and weekends. In fact,
every time you use the offline files feature to work at home, your boss
sends Bill Gates a nickel. That's how he got so rich.

Figure 3-12:
Offline file
properties.

Part II
Setting Up a Network

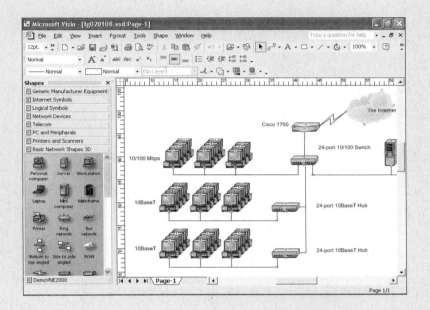

Find out a great way to test the network you set up at www.dummies.com/
extras/networking

In this part...

- ✔ Creating a network plan
- ✔ Understanding and using TCP/IP
- ✔ Working with cables, network adapters, switches, and other important networking components
- ✔ Configuring Windows computers for networking
- ✔ Getting connected to the Internet
- ✔ Using wireless devices in your network

Chapter 4

Planning a Network

· ·

In This Chapter

▶ Making a network plan

▶ Taking stock of your computer stock

▶ Making sure that you know why you need a network

▶ Making the three basic network decisions that you can't avoid

▶ Using a starter kit

▶ Looking at a sample network

· ·

*O*kay, so you're convinced that you need to network your computers. What now? Do you stop by Computers-R-Us on the way to work, install the network before drinking your morning coffee, and expect the network to be fully operational by noon?

I don't think so.

Networking your computers is just like any other worthwhile endeavor: Doing it right requires a bit of planning. This chapter helps you to think through your network before you start spending money. It shows you how to come up with a networking plan that's every bit as good as the plan that a network consultant would charge thousands of dollars for. See? This book is already saving you money!

Making a Network Plan

Before you begin any networking project, whether a new network installation or an upgrade of an existing network, start with a detailed plan. If you make technical decisions too quickly before studying all the issues that affect the project, you'll regret it. You'll discover too late that a key application won't run over the network, the network has unacceptably slow performance, or key components of the network don't work together.

Here are some general thoughts to keep in mind while you create your network plan:

- **Don't rush the plan.** The most costly networking mistakes are the ones that you make before you install the network. Think things through and consider alternatives.

- **Write down the network plan.** The plan doesn't have to be a fancy, 500-page document. If you want to make it look good, pick up a small three-ring binder. This binder will be big enough to hold your network plan with room to spare.

- **Ask someone else to read your network plan before you buy anything.** Preferably, ask someone who knows more about computers than you do.

- **Keep the plan up to date.** If you add to the network, dig up the plan, dust it off, and update it.

"The best laid schemes of mice and men gang aft agley, and leave us naught but grief and pain for promised joy." Robert Burns lived a few hundred years before computer networks, but his famous words ring true. A network plan isn't chiseled in stone. If you discover that something doesn't work how you thought it would, that's okay. Just change your plan.

Being Purposeful

One of the first steps in planning your network is making sure that you understand why you want the network in the first place. Here are some of the more common reasons for needing a network, all of them quite valid:

- My co-worker and I exchange files using CDs or flash drives just about every day. With a network, it would be easier to trade files.

- I don't want to buy everyone a color laser printer when I know the one we have now just sits there taking up space most of the day. So wouldn't investing in a network be better than buying a color laser printer for every computer?

- I want everyone to be able to access the Internet. (Many networks, especially smaller ones, exist solely for sharing an Internet connection.)

- Business is so good that one person typing in orders eight hours each day can't keep up. With a network, I can have two people entering orders, and I won't have to pay overtime to either person.

- My brother-in-law just put in a network at his office, and I don't want him to think that I'm behind the times.

- I already have a network, but it's so old it may as well be made of kite string and tin cans. An improved network will speed up access to shared files, provide better security, and be easier to manage.

Make sure that you identify all the reasons why you think you need a network and then write them down. Don't worry about winning the Pulitzer Prize for your stunning prose. Just make sure that you write down what you expect a network to do for you.

If you were making a 500-page networking proposal, you'd place the description of why a network is needed in a tabbed section labeled "Justification." In your network binder, file the description under "Purpose."

As you consider the reasons why you need a network, you may conclude that you don't need a network after all. That's okay. You can always use the binder for your stamp collection.

Taking Stock

One of the most challenging parts of planning a network is figuring out how to work with the computers that you already have. In other words, how do you get from here to there? Before you can plan how to get "there," you have to know where "here" is. In other words, you have to take a thorough inventory of your current computers.

What you need to know

You need to know the following information about each of your computers. Don't sweat it right now if some of these terms don't make sense. They're all just pieces of the puzzle.

✔ **The processor type and, if possible, its clock speed:** It would be nice if each of your computers had a shiny new Core i7 six-core processor. In most cases, though, you find a mixture of computers: some new, some old, some borrowed, some blue. You may even find a few archaic Pentium computers.

You can't usually tell what kind of processor that a computer has just by looking at the computer's case. Most computers, however, display the processor type when you turn them on or reboot them. If the information on the startup screen scrolls too quickly for you to read it, try pressing the Pause key to freeze the information. After you finish reading it, press the Pause key again so that your computer can continue booting.

✔ **The size of the hard drive and the arrangement of its partitions:** To find out the size of your computer's hard drive in Windows 8, 7, or Vista, open the Computer window (click Start, then click Computer), right-click the drive icon, and choose the Properties command from the shortcut menu that appears. Figure 4-1 shows the Properties dialog box for a 922GB hard drive that has about 867GB of free space.

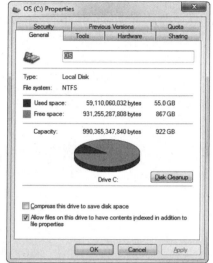

Figure 4-1:
The
Properties
dialog box
for a disk
drive.

If your computer has more than one hard drive, Windows lists an icon for each drive in the Computer window. Jot down the size and amount of free space available on each drive.

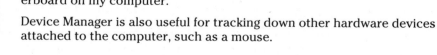 **The amount of memory:** To find this information in Windows, right-click Computer from the Start menu and choose the Properties command. The amount of memory on your computer is shown in the dialog box that appears. For example, Figure 4-2 shows the System Properties dialog box for a computer with 8GB of RAM.

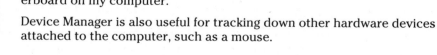 **The operating system version:** This you can also deduce from the System Properties dialog box. For example, the Properties page shown in Figure 4-2 indicates that the computer is running Windows 7 Ultimate.

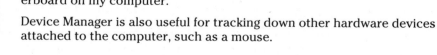 **What type of network card, if any, is installed in the computer:** The easiest way to get this information is to right-click Computer on the Start menu, choose Manage, click Device Manager, right-click the network adapter, and choose Properties. For example, Figure 4-3 shows the Properties dialog box for the network adapter that's built into the motherboard on my computer.

Device Manager is also useful for tracking down other hardware devices attached to the computer, such as a mouse.

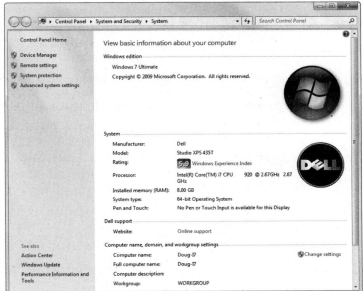

Figure 4-2:
The
Properties
page for a
computer
with 8GB of
RAM.

Figure 4-3:
The
Properties
page for
a network
adapter.

✔ **What network protocols are in use:**

- *Windows Vista:* Choose Start➪Open Control Panel➪Network and Sharing Center. Click Manage Network Connections, right-click the Local Area connection, and choose Properties.

- *Windows 7 or 8:* Choose Start➪Control Panel, click Network and Sharing Center, click Change Adapter Settings, right-click the Local Area Connection, and choose Properties. The dialog box shown in Figure 4-4 appears.

Figure 4-4: The Properties page for a local area network connection.

✔ **What kind of printer, if any, is attached to the computer:** Usually, you can tell just by looking at the printer. You can also tell by double-clicking the Printers icon in Control Panel.

✔ **Any other devices connected to the computer:** A DVD or Blu-ray drive? Scanner? External disk or tape drive? Video camera? Battle droid? Hot tub?

✔ **Which driver and installation disks are available:** Hopefully, you'll be able to locate the disks or CDs required by hardware devices such as the network card, printers, scanners, and so on. If not, you may be able to locate the drivers on the Internet.

✔ **What software is used on the computer: Microsoft Office?** AutoCAD? QuickBooks? Make a complete list and include version numbers.

✔ **Does the computer have wireless capability?** Nearly all laptops do. Most desktops do not, but you can always add an inexpensive USB wireless adapter if you want your network to be entirely wireless.

Programs that gather information for you

Gathering information about your computers is a lot of work if you have more than a few computers to network. Fortunately, several software programs are available that can automatically gather the information for you. These programs inspect various aspects of a computer, such as the CPU type and speed, amount of RAM, and the size of the computer's hard drives. Then they show the information on the screen and give you the option of saving the information to a hard drive file or printing it.

Windows comes with just such a program, called Microsoft System Information. Microsoft System Information gathers and prints information about your computer. You can start Microsoft System Information by choosing Start⇨All Programs⇨Accessories⇨System Tools⇨System Information.

When you fire up Microsoft System Information, you see a window similar to the one shown in Figure 4-5. Initially, Microsoft System Information displays basic information about your computer, such as your version of Microsoft Windows, the processor type, the amount of memory on the computer, and so on. You can obtain more detailed information by clicking Hardware Resources, Components, or other categories in the left side of the window.

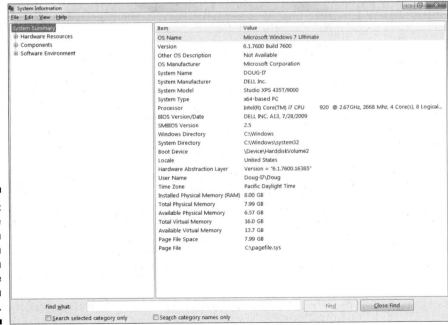

Figure 4-5:
Let the System Information program gather the data you need.

To Dedicate or Not to Dedicate: That Is the Question

One of the most basic questions that a network plan must answer is whether the network will have one or more dedicated servers or rely completely on peer-to-peer networking. If the only reason for purchasing your network is to share a printer and exchange an occasional file, you may not need a dedicated server computer. In that case, you can create a peer-to-peer network by using the computers that you already have. However, all but the smallest networks will benefit from having a separate, dedicated server computer.

- ✔ **Using a dedicated server computer makes the network faster, easier to work with, and more reliable.** Consider what happens, though, when the user of a server computer that doubles as a workstation decides to turn off the computer, not realizing that someone else is accessing files on his hard drive.

- ✔ **You don't necessarily have to use your biggest and fastest computer as your server computer.** I've seen networks where the slowest computer on the network is the server. This advice is especially true when the server is mostly used to share a printer or to store a small number of shared files. So if you need to buy a computer for your network, consider promoting one of your older computers to be the server and using the new computer as a client.

Assuming that your network will require one or more dedicated servers, you should next consider what types of servers the network will need. In some cases, a single server computer can fill one or more of these roles. Whenever possible, limit each server computer to a single server function.

File servers

File servers provide centralized disk storage that can be conveniently shared by client computers on the network. The most common task of a file server is to store shared files and programs. For example, members of a small workgroup can use disk space on a file server to store their Microsoft Office documents.

File servers must ensure that two users don't try to update the same file at the same time. The file servers do this by *locking* a file while a user updates the file so that other users can't access the file until the first user finishes. For document files (for example, word processing or spreadsheet files), the whole file is locked. For database files, the lock can be applied just to the portion of the file that contains the record or records being updated.

Print servers

Sharing printers is one of the main reasons that many small networks exist. Although it isn't necessary, a server computer can be dedicated for use as a *print server,* whose sole purpose is to collect information being sent to a shared printer by client computers and print it in an orderly fashion.

- ✔ A single computer may double as both a file server and a print server, but performance is better if you use separate print and file server computers.

- ✔ With inexpensive inkjet printers running about $100 each, just giving each user his or her own printer is tempting. However, you get what you pay for. Instead of buying $100 printers for 15 users, you may be better off buying one $1,500 laser printer and sharing it. The $1,500 laser printer will be much faster, will probably produce better-looking output and will be less expensive to operate.

Web servers

A *web server* is a server computer that runs software that enables the computer to host an Internet website. The two most popular web server programs are Microsoft's IIS (Internet Information Services) and Apache, an open source web server managed by the Apache Software Foundation.

Mail servers

A *mail server* is a server that handles the network's e-mail needs. It is configured with e-mail server software, such as Microsoft Exchange Server. Exchange Server is designed to work with Microsoft Outlook, the e-mail client software that comes with Microsoft Office.

Most mail servers actually do much more than just send and receive electronic mail. For example, here are some of the features that Exchange Server offers beyond simple e-mail:

- ✔ Collaboration features that simplify the management of collaborative projects.

- ✔ Audio and video conferencing.

- ✔ Chat rooms and instant messaging (IM) services.

- ✔ Microsoft Exchange Forms Designer, which lets you develop customized forms for applications, such as vacation requests or purchase orders.

Database servers

A *database server* is a server computer that runs database software, such as Microsoft's SQL Server 2012. Database servers are usually used along with customized business applications, such as accounting or marketing systems.

Choosing a Server Operating System

If you determine that your network will require one or more dedicated servers, the next step is to determine what network operating system those servers should use. If possible, all the servers should use the same network operating system (NOS) so that you don't find yourself supporting different operating systems.

Although you can choose from many network operating systems, from a practical point of view, your choices are limited to the following:

✔ Windows Server 2012 or 2008

✔ Linux or another version of Unix

For more information, see Chapter 10.

Planning the Infrastructure

You also need to plan the details of how you will connect the computers in the network. This task includes determining which network topology the network will use, what type of cable will be used, where the cable will be routed, and what other devices (such as repeaters, bridges, hubs, switches, and routers) will be needed.

Although you have many cabling options to choose from, you'll probably use Cat 5e or better UTP (unshielded twisted pair) for most — if not all — of the desktop client computers on the network. However, you have many decisions to make beyond this basic choice:

✔ Will you use hubs (less expensive) or switches (faster but more expensive)?

✔ Where will you place workgroup hubs or switches — on a desktop somewhere within the group or in a central wiring closet?

✔ How many client computers will you place on each hub or switch, and how many hubs or switches will you need?

✔ If you need more than one hub or switch, what type of cabling will you use to connect the hubs and switches to one another?

For more information about network cabling, see Chapter 6.

If you're installing new network cable, don't scrimp on the cable itself. Because installing network cable is a labor-intensive task, the cost of the cable itself is a small part of the total cable installation cost. And if you spend a little extra to install higher-grade cable now, you won't have to replace the cable in a few years when it's time to upgrade the network.

Drawing Diagrams

One of the most helpful techniques for creating a network plan is to draw a picture of it. The diagram can be a detailed floor plan, showing the actual location of each network component. This type of diagram is sometimes called a "physical map." If you prefer, the diagram can be a *logical map,* which is more abstract and Picasso-like. Any time you change the network layout, update the diagram. Also include a detailed description of the change, the date that the change was made, and the reason for the change.

You can diagram very small networks on the back of a napkin, but if the network has more than a few computers, you'll want to use a drawing program to help you create the diagram. One of the best programs for this purpose is Microsoft Visio, shown in Figure 4-6.

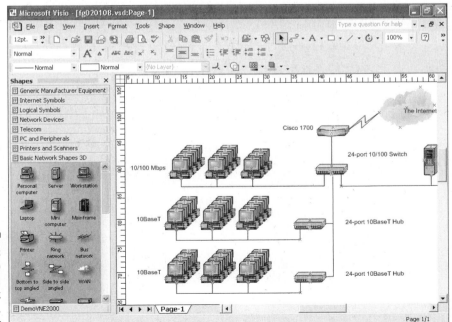

Figure 4-6: Using Visio to draw a network diagram.

Here's a rundown of some of the features that make Visio so useful:

- ✔ Smart shapes and connectors maintain the connections you've drawn between network components, even if you rearrange the layout of the components on the page.

- ✔ Stencils provide dozens of useful shapes for common network components — not just for client and server computers, but for routers, hubs, switches, and just about anything else you can imagine. If you're really picky about the diagrams, you can even purchase stencil sets that have accurate drawings of specific devices, such as Cisco routers or IBM mainframe computers.

- ✔ You can add information to each computer or device in the diagram, such as the serial number or physical location. Then, you can quickly print an inventory that lists this information for each device in the diagram.

- ✔ You can easily create large diagrams that span multiple pages.

Sample Network Plans

In what's left of this chapter, I present some network plans that are drawn from real-life situations. These examples illustrate many of the network design issues I've covered so far in this chapter. The stories you're about to read are true. The names have been changed to protect the innocent.

Building a small network: California Sport Surface, Inc.

California Sport Surface, Inc. (CSS) is a small company specializing in the installation of outdoor sports surfaces, such as tennis courts, running tracks, and football fields. CSS has an administrative staff of just four employees who work out of a home office. The company currently has three computers:

- ✔ A brand-new Dell desktop computer running Windows 8, shared by the president (Mark) and vice president (Julie) to prepare proposals and marketing brochures, to handle correspondence, and to do other miscellaneous chores. This computer has a built-in gigabit Ethernet network port.

- ✔ An older Gateway computer running Windows XP Home Edition, used by the bookkeeper (Erin), who uses QuickBooks to handle the company's accounting needs. This computer has a built-in 10/100 Mbps Ethernet port.

- ✔ A notebook that runs Windows 7 Ultimate, used by the company's chief engineer (Daniel), who often takes it to job sites to help with engineering needs. This computer has a built-in wireless networking and a gigabit Ethernet port.

The company owns just one printer, a moderately priced inkjet printer that's connected to Erin's computer. The computers aren't networked, so whenever Mark, Julie, or Daniel needs to print something, the file must be copied to a flash drive and given to Erin, who then prints the document. The computer shared by Mark and Julie is connected to the Internet via a residential DSL connection.

The company wants to install a network to support these three computers. Here are the primary goals of the network:

- ✔ Provide shared access to the printer so that users don't have to exchange data on flash drives to print their documents.

- ✔ Provide shared access to the Internet connection so that users can access the Internet from any of the computers.

- ✔ Allow for the addition of another desktop computer, which the company expects to purchase within the next six months, and potentially another notebook computer. (If business is good, the company hopes to hire another engineer.)

- ✔ The network should be intuitive to the users and shouldn't require extensive upkeep.

CSS's networking needs can be met with the simple peer-to-peer network diagrammed in Figure 4-7.

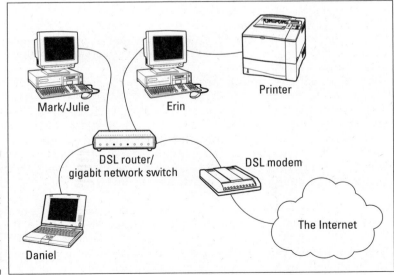

Figure 4-7: California Sport Surface's new peer-to-peer network.

Here's what the network requires:

- ✔ The network needs a combination DSL router and four-port gigabit network switch. The company may outgrow this device when it adds a laptop, but if and when that happens, another 4- or 8-port switch can be added at that time.

- ✔ The firewall features of the DSL router will need to be enabled to protect the network from Internet hackers.

- ✔ File and printer sharing will need to be activated on Erin's computer, and the printer will need to be shared.

Connecting two networks: Creative Course Development, Inc.

Creative Course Development, Inc. (CCD) is a small educational publisher located in central California that specializes in integrated math and science curriculum for primary and secondary grades. It publishes a variety of course materials, including textbooks, puzzle books, and CD-ROM software.

CCD leases two office buildings that are adjacent to each other, separated only by a small courtyard. The creative staff, which consists of a dozen writers and educators, works in Building A. The sales, marketing, and administrative staff, which consists of six employees, works in Building B.

The creative staff (Building A) has a dozen relatively new personal computers, all running Windows Vista Business Edition, and a server computer running Windows 2003 Server. These computers are networked via a single 24-port gigabit network switch. A fractional T1 line that's connected to the network through a small Cisco router provides Internet access.

The sales, marketing, and administrative staff (Building B) has a hodgepodge of computers, some running Windows 8 but most running Windows 7. They have a small Windows 2008 server that meets their needs. The older computers have 10/100BaseT network interfaces; the newer ones have gigabit interfaces. However, the computers are all connected to a 10/100 Mbps Ethernet switch with 12 ports. Internet access is provided by an ISDN connection.

Both groups are happy with their computers and networks. The problem is that the networks can't communicate with each other. For example, the creative team in Building A prepares weekly product-development status reports to share with the Administrative staff in Building B, and they frequently go to the other building to look into important sales trends.

Although several solutions to this problem exist, the easiest is to bridge the networks with a pair of wireless switches. To do this, CCD will purchase two wireless access points. One will be plugged into the gigabit switch in Building A, and the other will be plugged into the switch in Building B. After the access points are configured, the two networks will function as a single network. Figure 4-8 shows a logical diagram for the completed network.

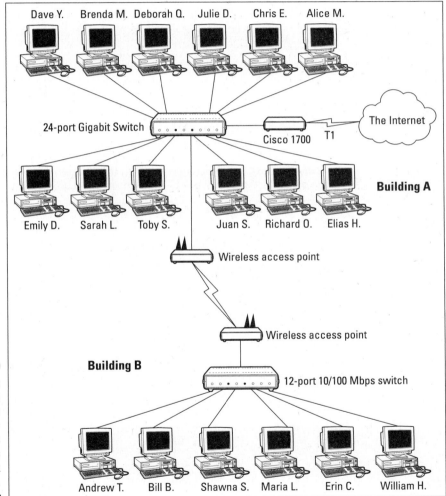

Figure 4-8:
Creative Course Development's wireless network solution.

Although the wireless solution to this problem sounds simple, a number of complications still need to be dealt with. Specifically:

- ✔ Depending on the environment, the wireless access points may have trouble establishing a link between the buildings. It may be necessary to locate the devices on the roof. In that case, CCD will have to spend a little extra money for weatherproof enclosures.

- ✔ Before the networks were connected, each network had its own DHCP server to assign IP addresses to users as needed. Unfortunately, both DHCP servers have the same local IP address (`192.168.0.1`). When the networks are combined, one of these DHCP servers will have to be disabled.

- ✔ In addition, both networks had their own Internet connections. With the networks bridged, CCD can eliminate the ISDN connection altogether. Users in both buildings can get their Internet access via the shared T1 connection.

- ✔ The network administrator will also have to determine how to handle directory services for the network. Previously, each network had its own domain. With the networks bridged, CCD may opt to keep these domains separate, or it may decide to merge them into a single domain. (Doing so will require considerable work, so the company will probably leave the domains separate.)

Improving network performance: DCH Accounting

DCH Accounting is an accounting firm that has grown in two years from 15 employees to 35, all located in one building. Here's the lowdown on the existing network:

- ✔ The network consists of 35 client computers and three servers running Windows 2008 Server.

- ✔ The 35 client computers run a variety of Windows operating systems. About a third (a total of 11) run Windows Vista Professional. The rest run Windows XP Professional. None of the computers run Windows 7 or 8.

- ✔ The Windows Vista computers all have gigabit Ethernet cards. The older computers have 10/100 Mbps cards.

- ✔ The server computers are somewhat older computers that have 10/100 Mbps network interfaces.

- ✔ All the offices in the building are wired with Cat 5e wiring to a central wiring closet, where a small equipment rack holds two 24-port 10/100 switches.

- ✔ Internet access is provided through a T1 connection with a Cisco 1700 router.

Lately, network performance has been noticeably slow, particularly Internet access and large file transfers between client computers and the servers. Users have started to complain that sometimes the network seems to crawl.

The problem is most likely that the network has outgrown the old 10/100BaseT switches. All network traffic must flow through them, and they're limited to the speed of 100 Mbps. As a result, the new computers with the gigabit Ethernet cards are connecting to the network at 100 Mbps.

The performance of this network can be dramatically improved in two steps. The first step is to replace the 10/100 Mbps network interface cards in the three servers with gigabit cards (or, better yet, replace the servers with newer models). Second, add a 24-port gigabit switch to the equipment rack. The equipment rack can be rewired, as shown in Figure 4-9.

1. **Connect the servers, the Cisco router, and the gigabit clients to the new gigabit switch. This will use 15 of the 24 ports.**

2. **Connect the two 10/100 switches to the new gigabit switch. This will use two more ports, leaving 7 ports for future growth.**

3. **Divide the remaining clients between the two 10/100 switches. Each switch will have 12 computers connected.**

This arrangement connects all the gigabit clients to gigabit switch ports and 100 Mbps clients to 100 Mbps switch ports.

For even better performance, DCH can simply replace both switches with 24-port gigabit switches.

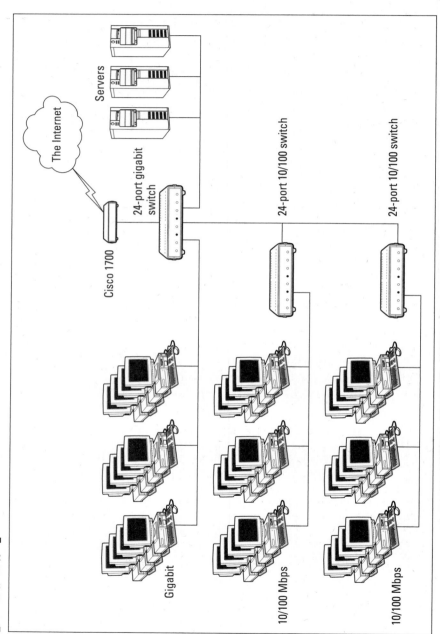

Figure 4-9:
DCH
Accounting's
switched
network.

Chapter 5

Dealing with TCP/IP

- -

In This Chapter

▶ Getting a handle (or two) on the binary system

▶ Digging into IP addresses

▶ Finding out how subnetting works

▶ Understanding private and public IP addresses

▶ Looking at network address translation

▶ Finding out how DHCP works

▶ Understanding how DNS works

- -

*T*ransfer Control Protocol/Internet Protocol — TCP/IP — is the basic protocol by which computers on a network talk to each other. Without TCP/IP, networks wouldn't work. In this chapter, I introduce you to the most important concepts of TCP/IP.

This chapter is far and away the most technical chapter in this book. It helps you examine the binary system, the details of how IP addresses are constructed, how subnetting works, and how two of the most important TCP/IP services — Dynamic Host Configuration Protocol (DHCP) and Domain Name System (DNS) — work. You don't need to understand every detail in this chapter to set up a simple TCP/IP network. However, the more you understand the information in this chapter, the more TCP/IP will start to make sense. Be brave.

Understanding Binary

Before you can understand the details of how TCP/IP — in particular, IP — addressing works, you need to understand how the binary numbering system works because binary is the basis of IP addressing. If you already understand binary, please skip right over this section to the next main section, "Introducing IP Addresses." I don't want to bore you with stuff that's too basic.

Counting by ones

The *binary* counting system uses only two numerals: 0 and 1. In the decimal system to which most people are accustomed, you use ten numerals: 0 through 9. In an ordinary decimal number, such as 3,482, the rightmost digit represents ones; the next digit to the left, tens; the next, hundreds; the next, thousands; and so on. These digits represent powers of ten: first 10^0 (which is 1); next, 10^1 (10); then 10^2 (100); then 10^3 (1,000); and so on.

In binary, you have only two numerals rather than ten, which is why binary numbers look somewhat monotonous, as in 110011, 101111, and 100001.

The positions in a binary number (called *bits* rather than *digits*) represent powers of two rather than powers of ten: 1, 2, 4, 8, 16, 32, and so on. To figure the decimal value of a binary number, you multiply each bit by its corresponding power of two and then add the results. The decimal value of binary 10101, for example, is calculated as follows:

```
    1 × 2⁰ = 1 ×  1  =    1
  + 0 × 2¹ = 0 ×  2  =    0
  + 1 × 2² = 1 ×  4  =    4
  + 0 × 2³ = 0 ×  8  =    0
  + 1 × 2⁴ = 1 × 16  =   16
                          21
```

Fortunately, a computer is good at converting a number between binary and decimal — so good, in fact, that you're unlikely ever to need to do any conversions yourself. The point of knowing binary isn't to be able to look at a number, such as 1110110110110, and say instantly, "Ah! Decimal 7,606!" (If you could do that, you would probably be interviewed on the *Today* show, and they would even make a movie about you.)

Instead, the point is to have a basic understanding of how computers store information and — most important — to understand how the hexadecimal counting system works (which I describe in the following section).

Here are some of the more interesting characteristics of binary and how the system is similar to and differs from the decimal system:

✔ The number of bits allotted for a binary number determines how large that number can be. If you allot eight bits, the largest value that number can store is 11111111, which happens to be 255 in decimal.

✔ To quickly determine how many different values you can store in a binary number of a given length, use the number of bits as an exponent of two. An eight-bit binary number, for example, can hold 2^8 values. Because 2^8 is 256, an 8-bit number can have any of 256 different values, which is why a byte, which is eight bits, can have 256 different values.

✔ This powers-of-two concept is why computers don't use nice, even, round numbers in measuring such values as memory or disk space. A value of 1K, for example, isn't an even 1,000 bytes — it's 1,024 bytes because 1,024 is 2^{10}. Similarly, 1MB isn't an even 1,000,000 bytes but rather is 1,048,576 bytes, which happens to be 2^{20}.

Doing the logic thing

One of the great things about binary is that it's very efficient at handling special operations called *logical operations*. Four basic logical operations exist, although additional operations are derived from the basic four operations. Three of the operations — AND, OR, and XOR — compare two binary digits (bits). The fourth (NOT) works on just a single bit.

The following list summarizes the basic logical operations:

✔ **AND:** An AND operation compares two binary values. If both values are 1, the result of the AND operation is 1. If one value is 0 or both of the values are 0, the result is 0.

✔ **OR:** An OR operation compares two binary values. If at least one of the values is 1, the result of the OR operation is 1. If both values are 0, the result is 0.

✔ **XOR:** An XOR operation compares two binary values. If exactly one of them is 1, the result is 1. If both values are 0 or if both values are 1, the result is 0.

✔ **NOT:** The NOT operation doesn't compare two values. Instead, it simply changes the value of a single binary value. If the original value is 1, NOT returns 0. If the original value is 0, NOT returns 1.

Logical operations are applied to binary numbers that have more than one binary digit by applying the operation one bit at a time. The easiest way to do this manually is to

   1. Line one of the two binary numbers on top of the other.

   2. Write the result of the operation beneath each binary digit.

The following example shows how you calculate 10010100 AND 11001101:

```
      10010100
AND   11001101
      10000100
```

As you can see, the result is 10000100.

Introducing IP Addresses

An *IP address* is a number that uniquely identifies every host on an IP network. IP addresses operate at the Network layer of the TCP/IP protocol stack, so they're independent of lower-level addresses, such as MAC addresses. (MAC stands for *Media Access Control.*)

IP addresses are 32-bit binary numbers, which means that theoretically, a maximum of something in the neighborhood of 4 billion unique host addresses can exist throughout the Internet. You'd think that'd be enough, but TCP/IP places certain restrictions on how IP addresses are allocated. These restrictions severely limit the total number of usable IP addresses, and about half of the total available IP addresses have already been assigned. However, new techniques for working with IP addresses have helped to alleviate this problem, and a new standard for 128-bit IP addresses (known as *IPv6)* is on the verge of winning acceptance.

Networks and hosts

The primary purpose of Internet Protocol (IP) is to enable communications between networks. As a result, a 32-bit IP address consists of two parts:

  ✔ **The network ID (or network address):** Identifies the network on which a host computer can be found

  ✔ **The host ID (or host address):** Identifies a specific device on the network indicated by the network ID

Most of the complexity of working with IP addresses has to do with figuring out which part of the complete 32-bit IP address is the network ID and which part is the host ID. The original IP specification uses the *address classes* system to determine which part of the IP address is the network ID and which part is the host ID. A newer system — classless IP addresses — is rapidly taking over the address classes system. You come to grips with both systems later in this chapter.

The dotted-decimal dance

IP addresses are usually represented in a format known as *dotted-decimal notation.* In dotted-decimal notation, each group of eight bits — an *octet* — is represented by its decimal equivalent. For example, consider the following binary IP address:

```
11000000101010001000100000011100
```

The dotted-decimal equivalent to this address is

```
192.168.136.28
```

Here, 192 represents the first eight bits (11000000); 168, the second set of eight bits (10101000); 136, the third set of eight bits (10001000); and 28, the last set of eight bits (00011100). This is the format in which you usually see IP addresses represented.

Classifying IP Addresses

When the original designers of the IP protocol created the IP addressing scheme, they could have assigned an arbitrary number of IP address bits for the network ID. The remaining bits would then be used for the host ID. For example, the designers may have decided that half of the address (16 bits) would be used for the network and the remaining 16 bits would be used for the host ID. The result of that scheme would be that the Internet could have a total of 65,536 networks, and each of those networks could have 65,536 hosts.

In the early days of the Internet, this scheme probably seemed like several orders of magnitude more than would ever be needed. However, the IP designers realized from the start that few networks would actually have tens of thousands of hosts. Suppose that a network of 1,000 computers joins the Internet and is assigned one of these hypothetical network IDs. Because that network uses only 1,000 of its 65,536 host addresses, more than 64,000 IP addresses would be wasted.

As a solution to this problem, the idea of IP address classes was introduced. The IP protocol defines five different address classes: A, B, C, D, and E. Each of the first three classes, A–C, uses a different size for the network ID and host ID portion of the address. Class D is for a special type of address called a *multicast address*. Class E is an experimental address class that isn't used.

The first four bits of the IP address are used to determine into which class a particular address fits:

- ✔ If the first bit is 0, the address is a Class A address.
- ✔ If the first bit is 1 and the second bit is 0, the address is a Class B address.
- ✔ If the first two bits are both 1 and the third bit is 0, the address is a Class C address.
- ✔ If the first three bits are all 1 and the fourth bit is 0, the address is a Class D address.
- ✔ If the first four bits are all 1, the address is a Class E address.

Because Class D and E addresses are reserved for special purposes, I focus the rest of this discussion on Class A, B, and C addresses. Table 5-1 summarizes the details of each address class.

Table 5-1			IP Address Classes		
Class	**Address Range**	**Starting Bits**	**Length of Network ID**	**Number of Networks**	**Number of Hosts**
A	1-126. x.y.z	0	8	126	16,777,214
B	128-191. x.y.z	10	16	16,384	65,534
C	192-223. x.y.z	110	24	2,097,152	254

Class A addresses

Class A addresses are designed for very large networks. In a Class A address, the first octet of the address is the network ID, and the remaining three octets are the host ID. Because only eight bits are allocated to the network ID and the first of these bits is used to indicate that the address is a Class A address, only 126 Class A networks can exist in the entire Internet. However, each Class A network can accommodate more than 16 million hosts.

Only about 40 Class A addresses are assigned to companies or organizations. The rest are either reserved for use by the Internet Assigned Numbers Authority (IANA) or are assigned to organizations that manage IP assignments for geographic regions, such as Europe, Asia, and Latin America.

Just for fun, Table 5-2 lists some of the better-known Class A networks. You probably recognize many of them. In case you're interested, you can find a complete list of all the Class A address assignments at www.iana.org/ assignments/ipv4-address-space.

Table 5-2	Some Well-Known Class A Networks		
Net	*Description*	*Net*	*Description*
3	General Electric Company	19	Ford Motor Company
6	Army Information Systems Center	20	Computer Sciences Corporation
9	IBM	25	UK Ministry of Defense
11	DoD Intel Information Systems	26	Defense Information Systems Agency
12	AT&T Bell Laboratories	28	Decision Sciences Institute (North)
13	Xerox Corporation	29–30	Defense Information Systems Agency
15	Hewlett-Packard Company	45	Interop Show Network
16	Digital Equipment Corporation	48	Prudential Securities Inc.
17	Apple Computer, Inc.	51	Department of Social Security of UK
18	MIT	54	Merck and Co., Inc.
22	Defense Information Systems Agency	56	U.S. Postal Service

Class B addresses

In a Class B address, the first two octets of the IP address are used as the network ID, and the second two octets are used as the host ID. Thus, a Class B address comes close to my hypothetical scheme of splitting the address down the middle, using half for the network ID and half for the host ID. It isn't identical to this scheme, however, because the first two bits of the first octet are required to be 10, to indicate that the address is a Class B address. Thus, a total of 16,384 Class B networks can exist. All Class B addresses fall within the range $128.x.y.z$ to $191.x.y.z$. Each Class B address can accommodate more than 65,000 hosts.

The problem with Class B networks is that even though they're much smaller than Class A networks, they still allocate far too many host IDs. Very few networks have tens of thousands of hosts. Thus, the careless assignment of Class B addresses can lead to a large percentage of the available host addresses being wasted on organizations that don't need them.

What about IPv6?

Most of the current Internet is based on version 4 of the Internet Protocol, also known as IPv4. IPv4 has served the Internet well for more than 20 years. However, the growth of the Internet has put a lot of pressure on IPv4's limited 32-bit address space. This chapter describes how IPv4 has evolved to make the best possible use of 32-bit addresses, but eventually all the addresses will be assigned; the IPv4 address space will be filled to capacity. When that happens, the Internet will have to migrate to the next version of IP, known as IPv6.

IPv6 is also called *IP next generation,* or *IPng,* in honor of the favorite television show of most Internet gurus, *Star Trek: The Next Generation.*

IPv6 offers several advantages over IPv4, but the most important is that it uses 128 bits for Internet addresses rather than 32 bits. The number of host addresses possible with 128 bits is a number so large that it would make Carl Sagan proud. It doesn't just double or triple the number of available addresses. Just for the fun of it, here's the number of unique Internet addresses provided by IPv6:

340,282,366,920,938,463,463,374,607,431,768,211,456

This number is so large that it defies understanding. If the IANA had been around at the creation of the universe and started handing out IPv6 addresses at a rate of one per millisecond, it would now, 15 billion years later, have not yet allocated even 1 percent of the available addresses.

Unfortunately, the transition from IPv4 to IPv6 has been a slow one. Thus, the Internet will continue to be driven by IPv4 for at least a few more years.

Class C addresses

In a Class C address, the first three octets are used for the network ID, and the fourth octet is used for the host ID. With only eight bits for the host ID, each Class C network can accommodate only 254 hosts. However, with 24 network ID bits, Class C addresses allow for more than 2 million networks.

The problem with Class C networks is that they're too small. Although few organizations need the tens of thousands of host addresses provided by a Class B address, many organizations need more than a few hundred. The large discrepancy between Class B networks and Class C networks led to the development of subnetting, which I describe in the next section.

Subnetting

Subnetting is a technique that lets network administrators use the 32 bits available in an IP address more efficiently by creating networks that aren't limited to the scales provided by Class A, B, and C IP addresses. With subnetting, you can create networks with more realistic host limits.

Subnetting provides a more flexible way to designate which portion of an IP address represents the network ID and which portion represents the host ID. With standard IP address classes, only three possible network ID sizes exist: 8 bits for Class A, 16 bits for Class B, and 24 bits for Class C. Subnetting lets you select an arbitrary number of bits to use for the network ID.

Two reasons compel me to use subnetting. The first is to allocate the limited IP address space more efficiently. If the Internet were limited to Class A, B, or C addresses, every network would be allocated 254, 65,000, or 16 million IP addresses for host devices. Although many networks with more than 254 devices exist, few (if any) exist with 65,000, let alone 16 million. Unfortunately, any network with more than 254 devices would need a Class B allocation and probably waste tens of thousands of IP addresses.

The second reason for subnetting is that even if a single organization has thousands of network devices, operating all those devices with the same network ID would slow the network to a crawl. The way TCP/IP works dictates that all the computers with the same network ID must be on the same physical network. The physical network comprises a single *broadcast domain,* which means that a single network medium must carry all the traffic for the network. For performance reasons, networks are usually segmented into broadcast domains that are smaller than even Class C addresses provide.

Subnets

A *subnet* is a network that falls within another (Class A, B, or C) network. Subnets are created by using one or more of the Class A, B, or C host bits to extend the network ID. Thus, rather than the standard 8-, 15-, or 24-bit network ID, subnets can have network IDs of any length.

Figure 5-1 shows an example of a network before and after subnetting has been applied. In the unsubnetted network, the network has been assigned the Class B address 144.28.0.0. All the devices on this network must share the same broadcast domain.

In the second network, the first four bits of the host ID are used to divide the network into two small networks, identified as subnets 16 and 32. To the outside world (that is, on the other side of the router), these two networks still appear to be a single network identified as 144.28.0.0. For example, the outside world considers the device at 144.28.16.22 to belong to the 144.28.0.0 network. As a result, a packet sent to this device is delivered to the router at 144.28.0.0. The router then considers the subnet portion of the host ID to decide whether to route the packet to subnet 16 or subnet 32.

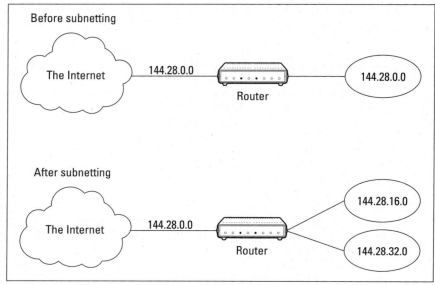

Figure 5-1:
A network
before and
after
subnetting.

Subnet masks

For subnetting to work, the router must be told which portion of the host ID to use for the subnet's network ID. This little sleight of hand is accomplished by using another 32-bit number, known as a *subnet mask*. Those IP address bits that represent the network ID are represented by a 1 in the mask, and those bits that represent the host ID appear as a 0 in the mask. As a result, a subnet mask always has a consecutive string of ones on the left, followed by a string of zeros.

For example, the subnet mask for the subnet, as shown in Figure 5-1, in which the network ID consists of the 15-bit network ID plus an additional 4-bit subnet ID, would look like this:

```
11111111 11111111 11110000 00000000
```

In other words, the first 20 bits are ones; the remaining 12 bits are zeros. Thus, the complete network ID is 20 bits in length, and the actual host ID portion of the subnetted address is 12 bits in length.

To determine the network ID of an IP address, the router must have both the IP address and the subnet mask. The router then performs a bitwise operation called a *logical AND* on the IP address to extract the network ID. To perform a logical AND, each bit in the IP address is compared to the corresponding bit in the subnet mask. If both bits are 1, the resulting bit in the network ID is set to 1. If either of the bits is 0, the resulting bit is set to 0.

For example, here's how the network address is extracted from an IP address using the 20-bit subnet mask from the previous example:

```
                 144  .   28  .   16  .   17
IP address:   10010000 00011100 00100000 00001001
Subnet mask:  11111111 11111111 11110000 00000000
Network ID:   10010000 00011100 00100000 00000000
                 144  .   28  .   16  .    0
```

Thus, the network ID for this subnet is 144.28.16.0.

The subnet mask itself is usually represented in dotted-decimal notation. As a result, the 20-bit subnet mask used in the previous example would be represented as 255.255.240.0:

```
Subnet mask:  11111111 11111111 11110000 00000000
                 255  .   255  .   240  .    0
```

 Don't confuse a subnet mask with an IP address. A subnet mask doesn't represent any device or network on the Internet. It's just a way of indicating which portion of an IP address should be used to determine the network ID. (You can spot a subnet mask right away because the first octet is always 255, and 255 isn't a valid first octet for any class of IP address.)

The great subnet roundup

You should know about a few additional restrictions that are placed on subnet masks — in particular:

- The minimum number of network ID bits is eight. As a result, the first octet of a subnet mask is always 255.

- The maximum number of network ID bits is 30. You have to leave at least two bits for the host ID portion of the address, to allow for at least two hosts. If you used all 32 bits for the network ID, that would leave no bits for the host ID. Obviously, that doesn't work. Leaving just one bit for the host ID doesn't work, either. That's because a host ID of all ones is reserved for a broadcast address — and all zeros refers to the network itself. Thus, if you used 31 bits for the network ID and left only one for the host ID, host ID 1 would be used for the broadcast address and host ID 0 would be the network itself, leaving no room for actual hosts. That's why the maximum network ID size is 30 bits.

- Because the network ID is always composed of consecutive bits set to 1, only nine values are possible for each octet of a subnet mask (including counting 0). For your reference, these values are listed in Table 5-3.

Table 5-3	The Eight Subnet Octet Values		
Binary Octet	**Decimal**	**Binary Octet**	**Decimal**
00000000	0	11111000	248
10000000	128	11111100	252
11000000	192	11111110	254
11100000	224	11111111	255
11110000	240		

Private and public addresses

Any host with a direct connection to the Internet must have a globally unique IP address. However, not all hosts are connected directly to the Internet. Some are on networks that aren't connected to the Internet. Some hosts are hidden behind firewalls, so their Internet connection is indirect.

Several blocks of IP addresses are set aside just for this purpose — for use on private networks that aren't connected to the Internet or to use on networks hidden behind a firewall. Three such ranges of addresses exist, as summarized in Table 5-4. Whenever you create a private TCP/IP network, use IP addresses from one of these ranges.

Table 5-4	Private Address Spaces
Subnet Mask	**Address Range**
255.0.0.0	10.0.0.1–10.255.255.254
255.255.240.0	172.16.1.1–172.31.255.254
255.255.0.0	192.168.0.1–192.168.255.254

Understanding Network Address Translation

Many firewalls use a technique called *network address translation* (NAT) to hide the actual IP address of a host from the outside world. When that's the case, the NAT device must use a globally unique IP to represent the host to the Internet; behind the firewall, however, the host can use any IP address it wants. As packets cross the firewall, the NAT device translates the private IP address to the public IP address, and vice versa.

One of the benefits of NAT is that it helps slow down the rate at which the IP address space is assigned because a NAT device can use a single public IP address for more than one host. It does this by keeping track of outgoing packets so that it can match up incoming packets with the correct host. To understand how this process works, consider this sequence of steps:

1. A host whose private address is 192.168.1.100 sends a request to 74.125.226.1, which happens to be www.google.com. The NAT device changes the source IP address of the packet to 208.23.110.22, the IP address of the firewall. That way, Google will send its reply back to the firewall router. The NAT records that 192.168.1.100 sent a request to 74.125.226.1.

2. Now another host, at address 192.168.1.107, sends a request to 64.4.11.37, which happens to be www.microsoft.com. The NAT device changes the source of this request to 208.23.110.22 so that Microsoft will reply to the firewall router. The NAT records that 192.168.1.107 sent a request to 64.4.11.37.

3. A few seconds later, the firewall receives a reply from 74.125.226.1. The destination address in the reply is 208.23.110.22, the address of the firewall. To determine to whom to forward the reply, the firewall checks its records to see who's waiting for a reply from 74.125.226.1. It discovers that 192.168.1.100 is waiting for that reply, so it changes the destination address to 192.168.1.100 and sends the packet on.

Actually, the process is a little more complicated than that because it's very likely that two or more users may have pending requests from the same public IP. In that case, the NAT device uses other techniques to figure out to which user each incoming packet should be delivered.

Configuring Your Network for DHCP

Every host on a TCP/IP network must have a unique IP address. Each host must be properly configured so that it knows its IP address. When a new host comes online, it must be assigned an IP address within the correct range of addresses for the subnet — one that's not already in use. Although you can manually assign IP addresses to each computer on your network, that task quickly becomes overwhelming if the network has more than a few computers.

That's where Dynamic Host Configuration Protocol (DHCP) comes into play. DHCP automatically configures the IP address for every host on a network, thus ensuring that each host has a valid, unique IP address. DHCP even automatically reconfigures IP addresses as hosts come and go. As you can imagine, DHCP can save a network administrator many hours of tedious configuration work.

In this section, you discover the ins and outs of DHCP: what it is, how it works, and how to set it up.

Understanding DHCP

DHCP allows individual computers on a TCP/IP network to obtain their configuration information — in particular, their IP addresses — from a server. The DHCP server keeps track of which IP addresses have already been assigned so that when a computer requests an IP address, the DHCP servers offer it an IP address that isn't already in use.

The alternative to DHCP is to assign each computer on your network a static IP address, which can be good or problematic:

- ✔ Static IP addresses are okay for networks with a handful of computers.
- ✔ For networks with more than a few computers, using static IP addresses is a huge mistake. Eventually, some poor, harried administrator (guess who?) will make the mistake of assigning two computers the same IP address. Then you have to manually check each computer's IP address to find the conflict. DHCP is a must for any but the smallest networks.

Although the primary job of DHCP is to assign IP addresses, DHCP provides more configuration information than just the IP address to its clients. The additional configuration information is referred to as *DHCP options.* The following list describes some common DHCP options that can be configured by the server:

- ✔ Router address, also known as the default gateway address
- ✔ Expiration time for the configuration information
- ✔ Domain name
- ✔ DNS server address
- ✔ Windows Internet Name Service (WINS) server address

DHCP servers

A DHCP server can be a server computer located on the TCP/IP network. Fortunately, all modern server operating systems have a built-in DHCP server capability. To set up DHCP on a network server, all you have to do is enable the server's DHCP function and configure its settings. In the section "Managing a Windows Server 2012 DHCP Server," later in this chapter, I show you how to configure a DHCP server for Windows 2012.

A server computer running DHCP doesn't have to be devoted entirely to DHCP unless the network is very large. For most networks, a file server can share duty as a DHCP server, especially if you provide long leases for your IP addresses. (I explain the idea of leases later in this chapter.)

Most multifunction routers also have built-in DHCP servers. So if you don't want to burden one of your network servers with the DHCP function, you can enable the router's built-in DHCP server. An advantage of allowing the router to be your network's DHCP server is that you rarely need to power down a router. By contrast, you occasionally need to restart or power down a file server to perform system maintenance, to apply upgrades, or to do some needed troubleshooting.

Most networks require only one DHCP server. Setting up two or more servers on the same network requires that you carefully coordinate the IP address ranges (known as *scopes)* for which each server is responsible. If you accidentally set up two DHCP servers for the same scope, you may end up with duplicate address assignments if the servers attempt to assign the same IP address to two different hosts. To prevent this situation from happening, set up just one DHCP server unless your network is so large that one server can't handle the workload.

Understanding scopes

A *scope* is simply a range of IP addresses that a DHCP server is configured to distribute. In the simplest case, in which a single DHCP server oversees IP configuration for an entire subnet, the scope corresponds to the subnet. However, if you set up two DHCP servers for a subnet, you can configure each one with a scope that allocates only one part of the complete subnet range. In addition, a single DHCP server can serve more than one scope.

You must create a scope before you can enable a DHCP server. When you create a scope, you can provide it these properties:

- A **scope name,** which helps you identify the scope and its purpose.
- A **scope description,** which lets you provide additional details about the scope and its purpose.
- A **starting IP address** for the scope.
- An **ending IP address** for the scope.
- A **subnet mask** for the scope. You can specify the subnet mask with dotted decimal notation or with Classless Inter Domain Routing (CIDR) notation.
- **One or more ranges of excluded addresses.** These addresses aren't assigned to clients. (For more information, see the section "Feeling excluded?," later in this chapter.)
- **One or more reserved addresses.** These addresses are always assigned to particular host devices. (For more information, see the section "Reservations suggested," later in this chapter.)

✔ The **lease duration,** which indicates how long the host is allowed to use
     the IP address. The client attempts to renew the lease when half of the
     lease duration has elapsed. For example, if you specify a lease duration
     of eight days, the client attempts to renew the lease after four days have
     passed. The host then has plenty of time to renew the lease before the
     address is reassigned to some other host.

   ✔ The **router address** for the subnet.

     This value is also known as the *default gateway address.*

   ✔ The **domain name and the IP address** of the network's DNS servers and
     WINS servers.

Feeling excluded?

Everyone feels excluded once in a while. With a wife and three daughters, I
know how that feels. Sometimes, however, being excluded is a good thing. In
the case of DHCP scopes, exclusions can help you prevent IP address conflicts
and can enable you to divide the DHCP workload for a single subnet among
two or more DHCP servers.

An *exclusion* is a range of addresses not included in a scope but falling within
the range of the scope's starting and ending addresses. In effect, an exclusion
range lets you punch a hole in a scope: The IP addresses that fall within the
hole aren't assigned.

Here are a couple of reasons to exclude IP addresses from a scope:

   ✔ **The computer that runs the DHCP service itself must usually have
     a static IP address assignment.** As a result, the address of the DHCP
     server should be listed as an exclusion.

   ✔ **You may want to assign static IP addresses to your other servers.** In
     that case, each server IP address should be listed as an exclusion.

     Reservations are often better solutions to this problem, as I describe in
     the next section.

Reservations suggested

In some cases, you may want to assign a specific IP address to a particular
host. One way to do this is to configure the host with a static IP address so
that the host doesn't use DHCP to obtain its IP configuration. However, two
major disadvantages to that approach exist:

✔ **TCP/IP configuration supplies more than just the IP address.** If you use static configuration, you must manually specify the subnet mask, default gateway address, DNS server address, and other configuration information required by the host. If this information changes, you have to change it not only at the DHCP server, but also at each host that you configured statically.

✔ **You must remember to exclude the static IP address from the DHCP server's scope.** Otherwise, the DHCP server doesn't know about the static address and may assign it to another host. Then comes the problem: You have two hosts with the same address on your network.

A better way to assign a fixed IP address to a particular host is to create a DHCP reservation. A *reservation* simply indicates that whenever a particular host requests an IP address from the DHCP server, the server should provide it the address that you specify in the reservation. The host doesn't receive the IP address until the host requests it from the DHCP server, but whenever the host does request IP configuration, it always receives the same address.

To create a reservation, you associate the IP address that you want assigned to the host with the host's MAC address. Accordingly, you need to get the MAC address from the host before you create the reservation:

✔ Usually, you can get the MAC address by running the command `ipconfig /all` from a command prompt.

✔ If TCP/IP has not yet been configured on the computer, you can get the MAC address by choosing the System Information command:

Choose Start➪All Programs➪Accessories➪System Tools➪System Information.

If you set up more than one DHCP server, be sure to specify the same reservations on each server. If you forget to repeat a reservation on one of the servers, that server may assign the address to another host.

How long to lease?

One of the most important decisions that you make when you configure a DHCP server is the length of time to specify for the lease duration. The default value is eight days, which is appropriate in many cases. However, you may encounter situations in which a longer or shorter interval may be appropriate:

✔ The more stable your network, the longer the lease duration can safely exist. If you only periodically add new computers to your network (or replace existing computers), you can safely increase the lease duration past eight days.

✔ The more volatile the network, the shorter the lease duration should be. For example, you may have a wireless network in a university library, used by students who bring their laptop computers into the library to work for a few hours at a time. For this network, a duration as short as one hour may be appropriate.

Don't configure your network to allow leases of infinite duration. Although some administrators feel that this duration cuts down the workload for the DHCP server on stable networks, no network is permanently stable. Whenever you find a DHCP server that's configured with infinite leases, look at the active leases. I guarantee that you'll find IP leases assigned to computers that no longer exist.

Managing a Windows Server 2012 DHCP Server

The exact steps to follow when you configure and manage a DHCP server depend on the network operating system or router you're using. The following paragraphs describe how to work with a DHCP server in Windows Server 2012. The procedures for other operating systems are similar.

If you haven't already installed the DHCP server on the server, install it using the Server Manager (click Server Manager on the taskbar). Once the DHCP server role is installed, you can manage it by opening the DHCP management console, as shown in Figure 5-2. To open this console, open System Manager and choose Tools⇨DHCP.

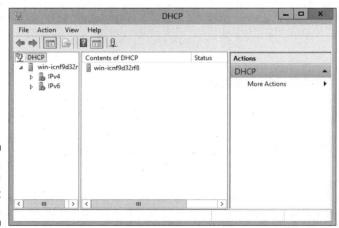

Figure 5-2:
The DHCP management console.

To get started with a DHCP server, you must create at least one scope. You can create a scope by using the New Scope Wizard, which you start by selecting the server you want to create the scope on and then clicking New Scope. The wizard asks for the essential information required to define the scope, including the scope's name, its starting and ending IP addresses, and the subnet mask. You can also specify any IP addresses you want to exclude from the scope, the lease duration (the default is eight days), the IP address of your gateway router, the domain name for your network, and the IP addresses for the DNS servers you want the client computers to use. Figure 5-3 shows the New Scope Wizard in action.

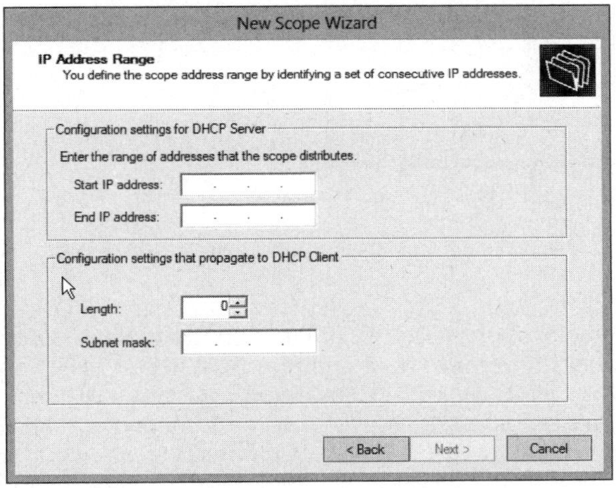

Figure 5-3:
The New
Scope
Wizard.

Configuring a Windows DHCP Client

Configuring a Windows client for DHCP is easy. The DHCP client is included automatically when you install the TCP/IP protocol, so all you have to do is configure TCP/IP to use DHCP. To do this, open the Network Properties dialog box by choosing Network or Network Connections in the Control Panel (depending on which version of Windows the client is running). Then select the TCP/IP protocol and click the Properties button. This action opens the TCP/IP Properties dialog box, as shown in Figure 5-4. To configure the computer to use DHCP, select the Obtain an IP Address Automatically and Obtain DNS Server Address Automatically options. Click OK, and you're done.

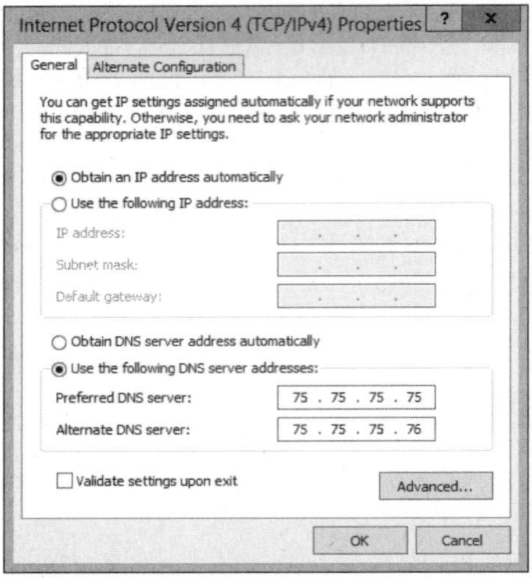

Figure 5-4:
Configuring
a Windows
client to use
DHCP.

Using DNS

DNS (Domain Name System) is the TCP/IP facility that lets you use names rather than numbers to refer to host computers. Without DNS, you'd buy books from 72.21.194.212 rather than from www.amazon.com, you'd sell your used furniture at 66.135.200.161 rather than on www.ebay.com, and you'd search the web at 74.125.224.147 rather than at www.google.com.

Understanding how DNS works and how to set up a DNS server is crucial to setting up and administering a TCP/IP network. The rest of this chapter introduces you to the basics of DNS, including how the DNS naming system works and how to set up a DNS server.

Domains and domain names

To provide a unique DNS name for every host computer on the Internet, DNS uses a time-tested technique: divide and conquer. DNS uses a hierarchical naming system that's similar to the way folders are organized hierarchically on a Windows computer. Instead of folders, however, DNS organizes its names into *domains.* Each domain includes all the names that appear directly beneath it in the DNS hierarchy.

For example, Figure 5-5 shows a small portion of the DNS domain tree. At the top of the tree is the *root domain,* which is the anchor point for all domains. Directly beneath the root domain are four *top-level domains,* named edu, com, org, and gov.

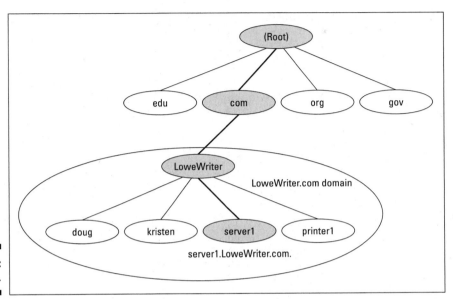

Figure 5-5:
DNS names.

In reality, many more top-level domains than this exist in the Internet's root domain. In fact, at the time I wrote this, there were more than 87 million of them.

Beneath the com domain in Figure 5-5 is another domain named LoweWriter, which happens to be my own personal domain. (Pretty clever, eh?) To completely identify this domain, you have to combine it with the name of its *parent domain* (in this case, com) to create the complete domain name: LoweWriter.com. Notice that the parts of the domain name are separated from each other by periods, which are pronounced "dot." As a result, when you read this domain name, you should pronounce it "LoweWriter dot com."

Beneath the LoweWriter node are four host nodes, named doug, kristen, server1, and printer1. These nodes correspond to three computers and a printer on my home network. You can combine the host name with the domain name to get the complete DNS name for each of my network's hosts. For example, the complete DNS name for my server is server1. LoweWriter.com. Likewise, my printer is printer1.LoweWriter.com.

Here are a few additional details that you need to remember about DNS names:

✔ DNS names aren't case-sensitive. As a result, LoweWriter and Lowewriter are treated as the same name, as are LOWEWRITER, LOWEwriter, and LoWeWrItEr. When you use a domain name, you can use capitalization to make the name easier to read, but DNS ignores the difference between capital and lowercase letters.

✔ The name of each DNS node can be up to 63 characters long (not including the dot) and can include letters, numbers, and hyphens. No other special characters are allowed.

✔ A *subdomain* is a domain that's beneath an existing domain. For example, the `com` domain is a subdomain of the `root` domain. Likewise, `LoweWriter` is a subdomain of the `com` domain.

✔ DNS is a hierarchical naming system that's similar to the hierarchical folder system used by Windows. However, one crucial difference exists between DNS and the Windows naming convention. When you construct a complete DNS name, you start at the bottom of the tree and work your way up to the root. Thus, `doug` is the lowest node in the name `doug.LoweWriter.com`. By contrast, Windows paths are the opposite: They start at the root and work their way down. For example, in the path `\Windows\System32\dns`, `dns` is the lowest node.

✔ The DNS tree can be up to 127 levels deep. However, in practice, the DNS tree is pretty shallow. Most DNS names have just three levels (not counting the root), and although you sometimes see names with four or five levels, you rarely see more levels than that.

✔ Although the DNS tree is shallow, it's very broad. In other words, each of the top-level domains has a huge number of second-level domains immediately beneath it. For example, at the time I wrote this book, the `com` domain had more than two million second-level domains beneath it.

Fully qualified domain names

If a domain name ends with a trailing dot, that trailing dot represents the root domain, and the domain name is said to be a *fully qualified domain name* (FQDN). A fully qualified domain name — also called an *absolute name* — is unambiguous because it identifies itself all the way back to the root domain. In contrast, if a domain name doesn't end with a trailing dot, the name may be interpreted in the context of some other domain. Thus, DNS names that don't end with a trailing dot are *relative names*.

This concept is similar to the way relative and absolute paths work in Windows. For example, if a path begins with a backslash, such as `\Windows\System32\dns`, the path is absolute. However, a path that doesn't begin with a backslash, such as `System32\dns`, uses the current folder as its starting point. If the current folder happens to be `\Windows`, `\Windows\System32\dns` and `System32\dns` refer to the same location.

In many cases, relative and fully qualified domain names are interchangeable because the software that interprets them always interprets relative names in the context of the root domain. That's why, for example, you can type `www.wiley.com` — without the trailing dot — rather than `www.wiley.com.` to go to the Wiley home page in a web browser. Some applications, such as DNS servers, may interpret relative names in the context of a domain other than the root.

Working with the Windows DNS Server

The procedure for installing and managing a DNS server depends on the network operating system you're using. This section is specific to working with a DNS server in Windows 2008. Working with a DNS server in a Linux or Unix environment is similar but without the help of a graphical user interface.

You can install the DNS server on Windows Server 2012 from the Server Manager (choose Server Manager on the taskbar). After you install the DNS server, you can manage it from the DNS management console. Here, you can perform common administrative tasks, such as adding additional zones, changing zone settings, or adding new records an existing zone. The DNS management console hides the details of the resource records from you, thus allowing you to work with a friendly graphical user interface instead.

To add a new host (which is defined by a DNS record called an A record) to a zone, right-click the zone in the DNS management console and choose the Add New Host command. This action opens the New Host dialog box, as shown in Figure 5-6.

Figure 5-6:
The New Host dialog box.

Here, you specify the following information:

- ✔ **Name:** The host name for the new host.
- ✔ **IP Address:** The host's IP address.
- ✔ **Create Associated Pointer (PTR) Record:** Automatically creates a PTR record in the reverse lookup zone file. Select this option if you want to

allow reverse lookups for the host. (A *reverse lookup* determines the domain name for a given IP address. It's called that because the normal type of DNS lookup determines the IP address for a given domain name.)

✓ **Allow Any Authenticated User to Update:** Select this option if you want to allow other users to update this record or other records with the same host name. You should usually leave this option deselected.

✓ **Time to Live:** The TTL value for this record, which indicates how long (in seconds) the data should be cached.

You can add other records, such as MX records, in the same way.

Configuring a Windows DNS Client

Client computers don't need much configuration to work properly with DNS. The client must have the address of at least one DNS server. Usually, this address is supplied by DHCP, so if the client is configured to obtain its IP address from a DHCP server, it also obtains the DNS server address from DHCP.

To configure a client computer to obtain the DNS server location from DHCP, open the Network Properties dialog box by choosing Network or Network Connections in the Control Panel (depending on which version of Windows the client is running). Then select the TCP/IP protocol and click the Properties button. This action summons the TCP/IP Properties dialog box, which is shown back in Figure 5-4. To configure the computer to use DHCP, select the Obtain an IP Address Automatically and the Obtain DNS Server Address Automatically options. Click OK, and you're done.

Chapter 6

Oh, What a Tangled Web We Weave: Cables, Switches, and Routers

Cable is the plumbing of your network. In fact, working with network cable is a lot like working with pipe: You have to use the right pipe (cable), the right valves and connectors (switches and routers), and the right fixtures (network interface cards).

And network cables have an advantage over pipes: You don't get wet when they leak.

This chapter tells you far more about network cables than you probably need to know. I introduce you to *Ethernet,* the most common system of network cabling for small networks. Then you find out how to work with the cables used to wire an Ethernet network. You also find out how to install a network interface card (NIC), which enables you to connect the cables to your computer.

What Is Ethernet?

Ethernet is a standardized way of connecting computers to create a network.

Obligatory filler about network topology

A networking book wouldn't be complete without the usual textbook description of the three basic network topologies. One type of network topology is a *bus,* in which network nodes (that is, computers) are strung together in a line, like this:

A *bus* is the simplest type of topology, but it has some drawbacks. If the cable breaks somewhere in the middle, the whole network breaks.

A second type of topology is the ring:

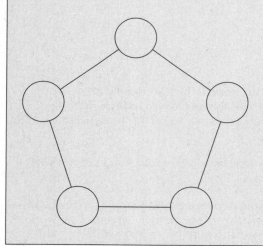

A ring is very much like a bus except with no end to the line: The last node on the line is connected to the first node, forming an endless loop.

A third type of topology is a star:

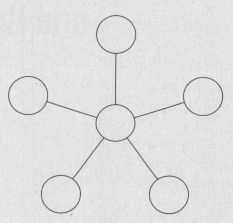

In a star network, all the nodes are connected to a central hub. In effect, each node has an independent connection to the network, so a break in one cable doesn't affect the others.

Ethernet networks are based on a bus design. However, fancy cabling tricks make an Ethernet network appear to be wired like a star when twisted-pair cable is used.

You can think of Ethernet as a kind of municipal building code for networks: It specifies what kind of cables to use, how to connect the cables, how long the cables can be, how computers transmit data to one another by using the cables, and more.

Although Ethernet is now the overwhelming choice for networking, that wasn't always the case. In ye olde days, Ethernet had two significant competitors:

✔ **Token Ring:** This IBM standard for networking is still in some organizations (especially where IBM mainframe or midrange systems are in use).

✔ **ARCnet:** This standard is still commonly used for industrial network applications, such as building automation and factory robot control.

But these older networks are now pretty much obsolete, so you don't need to worry about them. Ethernet is now the only real choice for new networks — small or large.

Here are a few tidbits you're likely to run into at parties where the conversation is about Ethernet standards:

✔ Ethernet is a set of standards for the infrastructure on which a network is built. All the operating systems that I discuss in this book can operate on an Ethernet network. If you build your network on a solid Ethernet base, you can change network operating systems later.

✔ Ethernet is often referred to by network gurus as 802.3 (pronounced "eight-oh-two-dot-three"), which is the official designation used by the *IEEE* (pronounced "eye-triple-ee," not *"aieeee!"*), a group of electrical engineers who wear bow ties and have nothing better to do than argue all day long about things like inductance and cross-talk — and it's a good thing they do. If not for them, you couldn't mix and match Ethernet components made by different companies.

✔ The original vintage Ethernet transmits data at a rate of 10 million bits per second, or 10 Mbps. (*Mbps* is usually pronounced "megabits per second.") Because 8 bits are in a byte, that translates into roughly 1.2 million bytes per second. In practice, Ethernet can't move information that fast because data must be transmitted in packages of no more than 1,500 bytes, called *packets*. So 150KB of information has to be split into 100 packets.

Ethernet's transmission speed has nothing to do with how fast electrical signals move on the cable. The electrical signals travel at about 70 percent of the speed of light, or as Captain Kirk would say, "Warp factor point-seven-oh."

✔ A faster version of Ethernet, called *100 Mbps Ethernet* or *Fast Ethernet,* moves data ten times as fast as normal Ethernet.

✔ The most common version of Ethernet today is *gigabit Ethernet,* which moves data at 1,000 Mbps.

✔ Most networking components that you can buy these days support 10, 100 Mbps and 1,000 Mbps. These components are called *10/100/1000 Mbps components.*

All about Cable

Although you can use wireless technology to create networks without cables, most networks still use cables to physically connect each computer to the network. Over the years, various types of cables have been used with Ethernet networks. Almost all networks are now built with twisted-pair cable. In this type of cable, pairs of wires are twisted around each other to reduce electrical interference. (You almost need a PhD in physics to understand why twisting the wires helps to reduce interference, so don't feel bad if this concept doesn't make sense.)

You may encounter other types of cable in an existing network; for example, on older networks, you may encounter two types of *coaxial* cable (also known as *coax,* pronounced "COE-ax"). The first type, which resembles television cable, is RG-58 cable. The second type is a thick, yellow cable that used to be the only type of cable used for Ethernet. You may also encounter fiber optic cables that span long distances at high speeds or thick twisted-pair bundles that carry multiple sets of twisted-pair cable between wiring closets in a large building. Most networks, however, use simple twisted-pair cable.

Twisted-pair cable is sometimes called *UTP.* (The *U* stands for *u*nshielded, but "twisted-pair" is the standard name.) Figure 6-1 shows a twisted-pair cable.

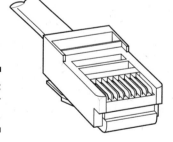

Figure 6-1:
Twisted-pair
cable.

When you use UTP cable to construct an Ethernet network, you connect the computers in a star arrangement, as Figure 6-2 illustrates. In the center of this star is a *switch.* Depending on the model, Ethernet switches enable you to connect 4 to 48 computers (or more) by using twisted-pair cable.

In the UTP star arrangement, if one cable goes bad, only the computer attached to that cable is affected. The rest of the network continues to chug along.

Cable categories

Twisted-pair cable comes in various grades: categories. These categories are specified by the ANSI/EIA Standard 568. (*ANSI* stands for American National

Standards Institute; *EIA* stands for Electronic Industries Association). The standards indicate the data capacity — bandwidth — of the cable. Table 6-1 lists the various categories of twisted-pair cable.

Although higher-category cables are more expensive, the real cost of installing Ethernet cabling is the labor required to pull the cables through the walls. You should never install anything less than Category (Cat) 5e cable. And if at all possible, invest in Cat 6 cable to allow for upgrades to your network.

To sound like the cool kids, say "Cat 6" rather than "Category 6."

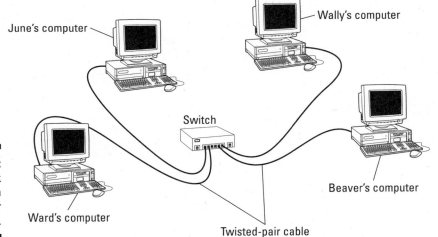

Figure 6-2:
A network cabled with twisted-pair cable.

Table 6-1	Twisted-Pair Cable Categories	
Category	*Maximum Data Rate*	*Intended Use*
1	1 Mbps	Voice only
2	4 Mbps	4 Mbps Token Ring
3	16 Mbps	10BaseT Ethernet
4	20 Mbps	16 Mbps Token Ring
5	100 Mbps (2-pair)	100BaseT Ethernet
	1000 Mbps (4-pair)	1000BaseTX
5e	1000 Mbps (2-pair)	1000BaseT
6	1000 Mbps (2-pair)	1000BaseT and faster broadband applications
6a	10000 Mbps (2-pair)	Future standard that will provide for 10 Gbps Ethernet

What's with the pairs?

Most twisted-pair cable has four pairs of wires, for a total of eight wires. Standard Ethernet uses only two of the pairs, so the other two pairs are unused. You may be tempted to save money by purchasing cable with just two pairs of wires, but that's a bad idea. If a network cable develops a problem, you can sometimes fix it by switching over to one of the extra pairs. If you use two-pair cable, though, you don't have any spare pairs to use.

Don't use the extra pairs for some other purpose, such as a voice line or a second data line. The electrical "noise" in the extra wires can interfere with your network.

To shield or not to shield

Unshielded twisted-pair cable (UTP) is designed for normal office environments. When you use UTP cable, you must be careful not to route cable close to fluorescent light fixtures, air conditioners, or electric motors (such as automatic door motors or elevator motors). UTP is the least expensive type of cable.

In environments that have a lot of electrical interference (such as factories), you may want to use shielded twisted-pair cable (STP). Because STP can be as much as three times more expensive than regular UTP, you don't want to use STP unless you have to. With a little care, UTP can withstand the amount of electrical interference found in a normal office environment.

Most STP cable is shielded by a layer of aluminum foil. For buildings with unusually high amounts of electrical interference, the more expensive braided-copper shielding offers even more protection.

When to use plenum cable

The outer sheath of shielded and unshielded twisted-pair cable comes in two kinds:

- **PVC:** The most common and least expensive type.
- **Plenum:** A special type of fire-retardant cable designed for use in the plenum space (definition coming right up) of a building. Plenum cable has a special Teflon coating that not only resists heat, but also gives off fewer toxic fumes if it does burn. Unfortunately, plenum cable costs more than twice as much as ordinary PVC cable.

Most local building codes require plenum cable when the wiring is installed in the building's *plenum space* (a compartment that's part of the building's air-distribution system, usually the space above a suspended ceiling or under a raised floor).

The area above a suspended ceiling is *not* a plenum space if both the delivery and return lines of the air-conditioning and heating systems are ducted. Plenum cable is required only if the air-conditioning and heating systems aren't ducted. When in doubt, have the local inspector look at your facility before you install cable.

Sometimes solid, sometimes stranded

The actual copper wire that makes up the cable comes in two varieties: solid and stranded. Your network will have some of each:

✔ **Stranded:** Each conductor is made from a bunch of very small wires that are twisted together. Stranded cable is more flexible than solid cable, so it doesn't break as easily. However, stranded cable is more expensive than solid cable and isn't very good at transmitting signals over long distances. Stranded cable is best used for *patch cables* (such as patch panels to hubs and switches).

Strictly speaking, the cable that connects your computer to the wall jack is a station cable — not a patch cable — but it's an appropriate use for stranded cable. (Although not technically correct, most people refer to the cable that connects a computer to a wall jack as a "patch cable.")

✔ **Solid:** Each conductor is a single, solid strand of wire. Solid cable is less expensive than stranded cable and carries signals farther, but it isn't very flexible. If you bend it too many times, it breaks. Typically, you find solid cable in use as permanent wiring within the walls and ceilings of a building.

Installation guidelines

The hardest part of installing network cable is the physical task of pulling the cable through ceilings, walls, and floors. This job is just tricky enough that I recommend you don't attempt it yourself, except for small offices. For large jobs, hire a professional cable installer. You may even want to hire a professional for small jobs if the ceiling and wall spaces are difficult to access.

Keep these pointers in mind if you install cable yourself:

✔ You can purchase twisted-pair cable in prefabricated lengths, such as 10, 15, or 20 feet. Longer lengths, such as 50 feet or 100 feet, are also available.

✔ Alternatively, you can purchase cable in bulk rolls, cut them to length, and attach the connectors yourself.

✔ Always use a bit more cable than you need, especially if you're running cable through walls. For example, when you run a cable up a wall, leave a few feet of slack in the ceiling above the wall. That way, you have plenty of cable if you need to make a repair.

✔ When running cable, avoid sources of interference, such as fluorescent lights, big motors, X-ray machines, nuclear reactors, cyclotrons, or other gadgets you may have hidden in behind closed doors in your office.

Fluorescent lights are the most common sources of interference for cables behind ceiling panels. Give light fixtures a wide berth. Three feet should do it.

✔ The maximum allowable cable length between the hub and the computer is 100 meters (about 328 feet).

✔ If you must run cable across the floor where people walk, cover the cable so no one trips over it. Cable protectors are available at most hardware stores.

✔ When running cables through walls, label each cable at both ends. Most electrical supply stores carry pads of cable labels that are perfect for the job. These pads contain 50 sheets or so of precut labels with letters and numbers. They look much more professional than wrapping a loop of masking tape around the cable and writing on the tape with a marker.

Alternatively, you can just write directly on the label with a permanent marker.

✔ If you're installing cable in new construction, label each end of the cable at least three times, leaving about a foot of space between the labels. The drywallers or painters will probably spray mud or paint all over your cables, making the labels difficult to find.

✔ When several cables come together, tie them with plastic cable ties. Avoid masking tape if you can; the tape doesn't last, but the sticky glue stuff does. It's a mess a year later. Cable ties are available at electrical supply stores.

✔ Cable ties have all sorts of useful purposes. Once, on a backpacking trip, I used a pair of cable ties to attach an unsuspecting buddy's hat to a high tree limb. He wasn't impressed with my innovative use of the cable ties, but my other hiking companions were.

✔ When you run cable above suspended ceiling panels, use cable ties, hooks, or clamps to secure the cable to the ceiling or to the metal frame that supports the ceiling tiles. Don't just lay the cable on top of the panels.

The tools you need

Of course, to do a job right, you must have the right tools:

✔ Start with a basic set of computer tools, which you can get for about $15 from any computer store and most office-supply stores. These kits include socket wrenches and screwdrivers to open your computers and insert adapter cards.

The computer tool kit probably contains everything you need if

- All your computers are in the same room.
- You're running the cables along the floor.
- You're using prefabricated cables.

If you don't have a computer tool kit, make sure that you have several flat-head and Phillips screwdrivers of various sizes.

✔ If you're using bulk cable and plan on attaching your own connectors, you also need the following tools in addition to the basic computer tool kit:

- *Wire cutters:* You need big ones for coax; smaller ones work for twisted-pair cable. For yellow cable, you need the Jaws of Life.

- *A crimp tool:* You need the crimp tool to attach the connectors to the cable. Don't use a cheap $25 crimp tool. A good crimp tool costs $100 and will save you many headaches in the long run.

  When you crimp, you mustn't scrimp.

- *Wire stripper:* You need this tool only if the crimp tool doesn't include a wire stripper.

✔ If you plan on running cables through walls, you need these additional tools:

- *A hammer*
- *A keyhole saw:* This one is useful if you plan on cutting holes through walls to route your cable.
- *A flashlight*
- *A ladder*
- *Someone to hold the ladder*
- *Fish tape:* Possibly. A *fish tape* is a coiled-up length of stiff metal tape. To use it, you feed the tape into one wall opening and fish it toward the other opening, where a partner is ready to grab it when the tape arrives. Next, your partner attaches the cable to the fish tape and yells something like "Let 'er rip!" or "Bombs away!" Then you reel in the fish tape and the cable along with it. (You can find fish tape in the electrical section of most well-stocked hardware stores.)

If you plan on routing cable through a concrete subfloor, you need to rent a jackhammer and a backhoe and then hire someone to hold a yellow flag while you work. Better yet, find some other route for the cable.

Pinouts for twisted-pair cables

Each pair of wires in a twisted-pair cable is one of four colors: orange, green, blue, or brown. The two wires that make up each pair are complementary: one is white with a colored stripe; the other is colored with a white stripe. For example, the orange pair has an orange wire with a white stripe (the *orange wire*) and a white wire with an orange stripe (the *white/orange wire*). Likewise, the blue pair has a blue wire with a white stripe (the *blue wire*) and a white wire with a blue stripe (the *white/blue wire*).

When you attach a twisted-pair cable to a modular connector or jack, you must match up the right wires to the right pins. It's harder than it sounds; you can use any of several different standards to wire the connectors. To confuse matters further, you can use one of the two popular standard ways of hooking up the wires: EIA/TIA 568A or EIA/TIA 568B, also known as AT&T 258A. Both of these wiring schemes are shown in Table 6-2.

It doesn't matter which of these wiring schemes you use, but pick one and stick with it. If you use one wiring standard on one end of a cable and the other standard on the other end, the cable doesn't work.

Table 6-2		Pin Connections for Twisted-Pair Cable	
Pin	*Function*	*EIA/TIA 568A*	*EIA/TIA568B AT&T 258A*
1	Transmit +	White/Green	White/orange wire
2	Transmit −	Green	Orange wire
3	Receive +	White/Orange	White/green wire
4	Unused	Blue	Blue wire
5	Unused	White/Blue	White/blue wire
6	Receive −	Orange	Green wire
7	Unused	White/Brown	White/brown wire
8	Unused	Brown	Brown wire

Ethernet only uses two of the four pairs, connected to Pins 1, 2, 3, and 6. One pair transmits data; the other receives data. The only difference between the two wiring standards is which pair transmits and which receives. In the EIA/TIA 568A standard, the green pair is used for transmit, and the orange pair is used for receive. In the EIA/TIA 568B and AT&T 258A standards, the orange pair is used for transmit and the green pair for receive.

If you want, you can get away with connecting only Pins 1, 2, 3, and 6. However, I suggest that you connect all four pairs, as indicated in Table 6-2.

RJ-45 connectors

RJ-45 connectors for twisted-pair cables aren't too difficult to attach if you have the right crimping tool. The only trick is making sure that you attach each wire to the correct pin and then press the tool hard enough to ensure a good connection.

Here's the procedure for attaching an RJ-45 connector:

1. **Cut the end of the cable to the desired length.**

   Make sure that you make a square cut — not a diagonal cut.

2. **Insert the cable into the stripper portion of the crimp tool so that the end of the cable is against the stop.**

   Squeeze the handles and slowly pull out the cable, keeping it square. This strips off the correct length of outer insulation without puncturing the insulation on the inner wires.

3. **Arrange the wires so that they lie flat and line up according to Table 6-2.**

   You have to play with the wires a little bit to get them to lay out in the right sequence.

4. **Slide the wires into the pinholes on the connector.**

   Double-check to make sure all the wires are slipped into the correct pinholes.

5. **Insert the plug and wire into the crimping portion of the tool and then squeeze the handles to crimp the plug.**

   Squeeze it tight!

6. **Remove the plug from the tool and double-check the connection.**

   You're done!

Here are a few other points to remember when dealing with RJ-45 connectors and twisted-pair cable:

✔ The pins on the RJ-45 connectors aren't numbered.

  You can tell which is Pin 1 by holding the connector so that the metal conductors are facing up, as shown in Figure 6-3. Pin 1 is on the left.

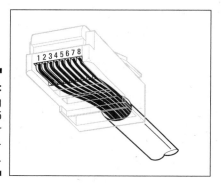

Figure 6-3:
Attaching
an RJ-45
connector
to twisted-
pair cable.

✔ Some people wire the cable differently — using the green-and-white pair for Pins 1 and 2, and the orange-and-white pair for Pins 3 and 6. Doing it this way doesn't affect the operation of the network (the network is color blind) *as long as the connectors on both ends of the cable are wired the same way!*

✔ When you attach the connectors, don't untwist more than half an inch of cable. And, don't try to stretch the cable runs beyond the 100-meter maximum. When in doubt, have the cable professionally installed.

Crossover cables

A *crossover cable* can directly connect two devices without a hub or switch. You can use a crossover cable to connect two computers directly to each other, but crossover cables are more often used to daisy-chain hubs and switches to each other.

If you want to create your own crossover cable, you must reverse the wires on one end of the cable, as shown in Table 6-3. This table shows how you should wire both ends of the cable to create a crossover cable. Connect one of the ends according to the Connector A column and the other according to the Connector B column.

Note that you don't need to use a crossover cable if one of the switches or hubs that you want to connect has a crossover port, usually labeled Uplink or Daisy-chain. If the hub or switch has an Uplink port, you can daisy-chain it by using a normal network cable. For more information about daisy-chaining hubs and switches, see the section "Daisy-Chaining Switches," later in this chapter.

If you study Table 6-3 long enough and then compare it with Table 6-2, you may notice that a crossover cable is a cable that's wired according to the 568A standard on one end and the 568B standard on the other end.

Table 6-3	Creating a Crossover Cable	
Pin	*Connector A*	*Connector B*
1	White/green	White/orange
2	Green	Orange
3	White/orange	White/green
4	Blue	Blue
5	White/blue	White/blue
6	Orange	Green
7	White/brown	White/brown
8	Brown	Brown

Wall jacks and patch panels

If you want, you can run a single length of cable from a network hub or switch in a wiring closet through a hole in the wall, up the wall to the space above the ceiling, through the ceiling space to the wall in an office, down the wall, through a hole, and all the way to a desktop computer. That's not a good idea. For example, every time someone moves the computer or even cleans behind it, the cable will get moved a little bit. Eventually, the connection will fail, and the RJ-45 plug will have to be replaced. Then the cables in the wiring closet will quickly become a tangled mess.

The alternative is to put a wall jack in the wall at the user's end of the cable and connect the other end of the cable to a patch panel. Then the cable itself is completely contained within the walls and ceiling spaces. To connect a computer to the network, you plug one end of a patch cable (properly called a *station cable*) into the wall jack and plug the other end into the computer's network interface. In the wiring closet, you use a patch cable to connect the wall jack to the network hubs or switches. Figure 6-4 shows how this arrangement works.

Connecting a twisted-pair cable to a wall jack or a patch panel is similar to connecting it to an RJ-45 plug. However, you don't usually need any special tools. Instead, the back of the jack has a set of slots that you lay each wire across. You then snap a removable cap over the top of the slots and press it down. This action forces the wires into the slots, where little metal blades pierce the insulation and establish the electrical contact.

When you connect the wire to a jack or a patch panel, be sure to untwist as little of the wire as possible. If you untwist too much of the wire, the signals that pass through the wire may become unreliable.

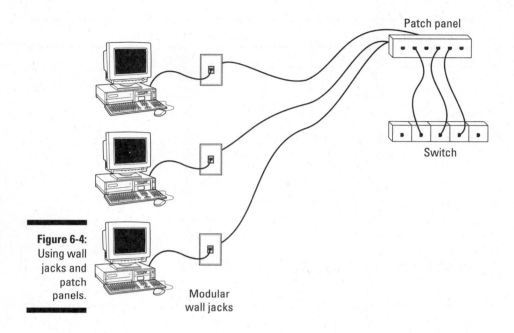

Figure 6-4:
Using wall
jacks and
patch
panels.

Patch panel

Switch

Modular
wall jacks

Working with Switches

When you use twisted-pair cable to wire a network, you don't plug the computers into each other. Instead, each computer plugs into a separate device called a *switch*.

You need to know only a few details when working with switches. Here they are:

- ✔ Installing a switch is usually very simple. Just plug in the power cord and then plug in patch cables to connect the network.

- ✔ Each port on the switch has an RJ-45 jack and a single LED indicator, labeled *Link,* that lights up when a connection is made on the port.

If you plug one end of a cable into the port and the other end into a computer or other network device, the Link light should come on. If it doesn't, something is wrong with the cable, the hub or switch port, or the device on the other end of the cable.

✔ Each port may have an LED indicator that flashes to indicate network activity.

If you stare at a switch for a while, you can find out who uses the network most by noting which activity indicators flash the most.

✔ The ports may also have a collision indicator that flashes whenever a packet collision occurs on the port.

It's perfectly acceptable for the collision indicator to flash now and then, but if it flashes a lot, you may have a problem with the network:

- Usually, the flashing means that the network is overloaded and should be segmented with a switch to improve performance.

- In some cases, the flashing may be caused by a faulty network node that clogs the network with bad packets.

Daisy-Chaining Switches

If a single switch doesn't have enough ports for your entire network, you can connect switches by *daisy-chaining* them, as shown in Figure 6-5.

You can often increase the overall performance of your network by using two (or more) connections between switches. For example, you may use two patch cables to create two connections between a pair of switches.

Don't chain more than two switches together. If you do, the network may not transmit your data reliably. However, you can get around this rule by using *stackable switches* (switches with a special cable connector that connects two or more switches so that they function as a single switch). Stackable switches are musts for large networks.

If your building is prewired and has a network jack near each desk, you can use a small switch to connect two or more computers to the network by using a single jack. Just use one cable to plug the daisy-chain port of the hub into the wall jack and then plug each computer into one of the hub's ports.

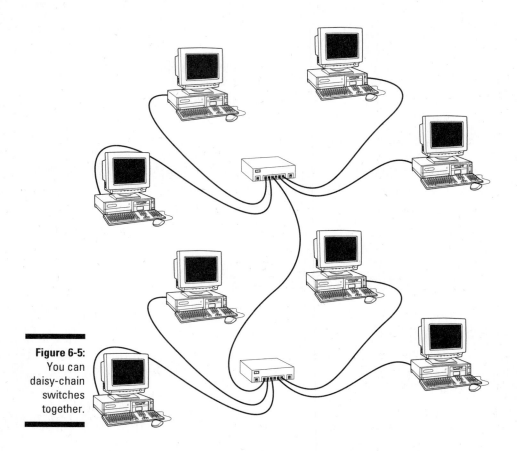

Figure 6-5:
You can
daisy-chain
switches
together.

Using a Router

A *router* is a device that is capable of passing data between two networks. The most common reason for using a router is to connect a LAN to the Internet. However, routers can perform many other functions as well. For example, a router can filter data based on its content, allowing some types of data to pass through while blocking other types.

You can configure a network with several routers that can work cooperatively. For example, some routers can monitor the network to determine the most efficient path for sending a message to its ultimate destination. If a part of the network is extremely busy, a router can automatically route messages along a less-busy route. In this respect, the router is kind of like a traffic reporter flying in a helicopter. The router knows that the 101 is bumper to bumper all the way through Sunnyvale, so it sends the message on the 280 instead.

Here's some additional information about routers:

- ✔ Routers used to be expensive and used only on large networks. However, the price of small routers has dropped substantially in recent years, so they're now becoming common even on small networks.

- ✔ The functional distinctions between bridges and routers — and switches and hubs, for that matter — get blurrier all the time. *Multifunction routers* (which combine the functions of routers, bridges, hubs, and switches) are often used to handle some chores that used to require separate devices.

- ✔ A pair of routers can be used to create a secure connection between two locations that are geographically distant from each other.

- ✔ One of the main reasons for using routers is to connect a LAN to the Internet. Figure 6-6 shows a router used for this purpose.

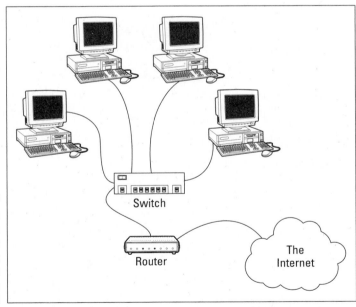

Figure 6-6:
Using a
router to
connect a
LAN to the
Internet.

Chapter 7

Configuring Windows Clients

*B*efore your network setup is complete, you must configure the network's client computers. In particular, you have to configure each client computer's network interface card (NIC) so that it works properly, and you have to install the right protocols so that the clients can communicate with other computers on the network.

Fortunately, the task of configuring client computers for the network is child's play in Windows. For starters, Windows automatically recognizes your network interface card when you start up your computer. All that remains is to make sure that Windows properly installed the network protocols and client software.

With each version of Windows, Microsoft has simplified the process of configuring client network support. In this chapter, I describe the steps for configuring networking for Windows XP, Windows Vista, Windows 7, and Windows 8.

Configuring Network Connections

Windows usually detects the presence of a network adapter automatically; typically, you don't have to install device drivers manually for the adapter. When Windows detects a network adapter, it automatically creates a network connection and configures it to support basic networking protocols. You may need to change the configuration of a network connection manually, however. The procedures for Windows XP and Vista are described in the following sections.

Configuring Windows XP network connections

The following steps show how to configure your network connection on a Windows XP system:

1. **Choose Start⇨Control Panel to open the Control Panel.**

2. **Double-click the Network Connections icon.**

   The Network Connections folder appears, as shown in Figure 7-1.

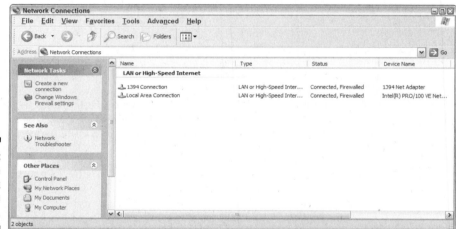

Figure 7-1: The Network Connections folder.

3. **Right-click the connection that you want to configure and then choose Properties from the contextual menu that appears.**

   Either way, the Properties dialog box for the network connection appears, as shown in Figure 7-2.

4. **To configure the network adapter settings, click Configure.**

   This action summons the Properties dialog box for the network adapter, as shown in Figure 7-3. This dialog box has five tabs that let you configure the NIC:

   • *General:* This tab shows basic information about the NIC, such as the device type and status. For example, the device shown in Figure 7-3 is an Intel Pro 100 network interface.

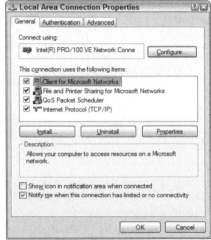

Figure 7-2:
The
Properties
dialog
box for a
network
connection.

- *Advanced:* From this tab, you can set a variety of device-specific parameters that affect the operation of the NIC. In most cases, you should leave the options on this tab alone.

- *Driver:* This tab displays information about the device driver that's bound to the NIC and lets you update the driver to a newer version, roll back the driver to a previously working version, or uninstall the driver.

Figure 7-3:
The
Properties
dialog
box for a
network
adapter.

- *Resources:* From this tab, you can use manual settings to limit the system resources used by the card. In most cases, you can leave the settings on this tab alone.

In the old days, before Plug and Play cards, you had to configure these settings whenever you installed a card, and it was easy to create resource conflicts. Windows configures these settings automatically so that you should rarely need to fiddle with them.

- *Power Management:* From this tab, you set power-management options. You can specify that the network card be shut down whenever the computer goes into sleep mode and that the computer wake up periodically to refresh its network state.

When you click OK to dismiss the network adapter's Properties dialog box, the network connection's Properties dialog box closes. Select the Change Settings of This Connection option again to continue the procedure.

5. **Click Internet Protocol (TCP/IP) and then click Properties to display the TCP/IP Properties dialog box. Adjust the settings and then click OK.**

The TCP/IP Properties dialog box, shown in Figure 7-4, lets you choose among these options:

- *Obtain an IP Address Automatically:* Choose this option if your network has a DHCP server that assigns IP addresses automatically. Choosing this option dramatically simplifies administering TCP/IP on your network. (See Chapter 5 for more information about DHCP.)

- *Use the Following IP Address:* If your computer must have a specific IP address, choose this option and then type the computer's IP address, subnet mask, and default gateway address. (For more information about these settings, see Chapter 5.)

- *Obtain DNS Server Address Automatically:* The DHCP server can also provide the address of the Domain Name System (DNS) server that the computer should use. Choose this option if your network has a DHCP server. (See Chapter 5.)

- *Use the Following DNS Server Addresses:* Choose this option if a DNS server isn't available. Then type the IP addresses of the primary and secondary DNS servers.

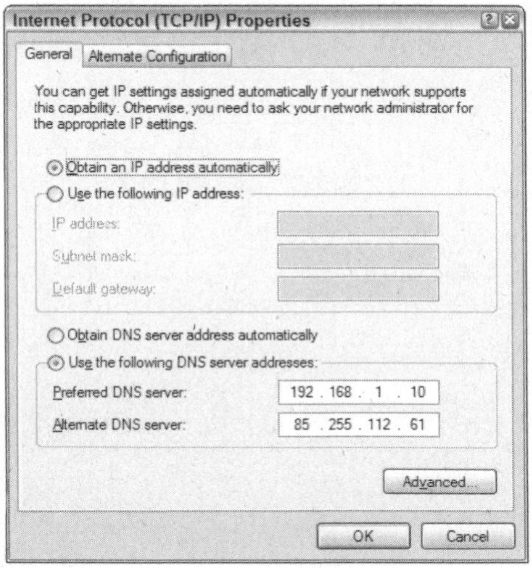

Figure 7-4:
Configuring
TCP/IP.

Configuring Windows Vista network connections

The procedure for configuring a network connection on Windows Vista is similar to the procedure for Windows XP, except that Microsoft decided to bury the configuration dialog boxes a little deeper in the bowels of Windows.

To find the settings you need, follow these steps:

1. **Choose Start⇨Control Panel.**

2. **Choose View Network Status and Tasks under the Network and Internet heading.**

   This step opens the Network and Sharing Center, shown in Figure 7-5.

3. **Click Manage Network Connections.**

   The Network Connections folder appears, as shown in Figure 7-6.

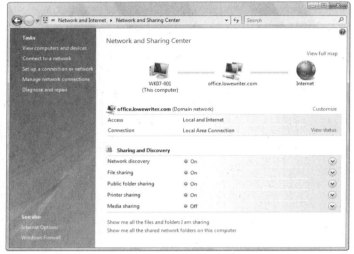

Figure 7-5:
The
Network
and Sharing
Center
(Windows
Vista).

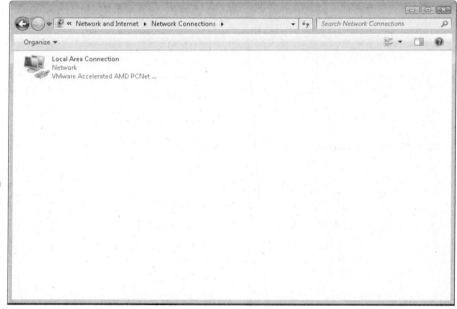

Figure 7-6:
The
Network
Connections
folder
(Windows
Vista).

4. **Right-click the connection that you want to configure and then choose Properties from the contextual menu that appears.**

The Properties dialog box for the network connection appears, as shown in Figure 7-7. If you compare this dialog box with the dialog box shown earlier, in Figure 7-2, you see that they are similar.

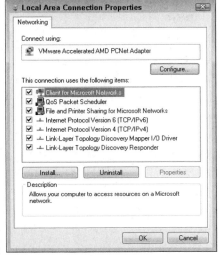

Figure 7-7:
The
Properties
dialog
box for a
network
connection
(Windows
Vista).

5. **Click Configure to configure the network connection.**

   From this point, the steps for configuring the network connection are the same as they are for Windows XP. As a result, you can continue by beginning with Step 4 in the preceding section, "Configuring Windows XP network connections."

Configuring Windows 7 and Windows 8 network connections

The procedure for configuring a Windows 7 network connection is similar to the Windows Vista procedure, with just a few minor variations. Here are the steps:

1. **Open the Control Panel.**

   - *Windows 7:* Choose Start⇨Control Panel.

   - *Windows 8:* Right-click the bottom-left corner of the screen and then choose Control Panel from the contextual menu.

2. **Choose Network and Sharing Center.**

   This step opens the Network and Sharing Center, shown in Figure 7-8.

The Change Adapter Settings link

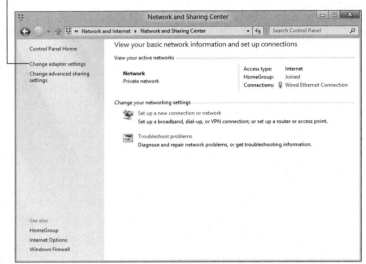

Figure 7-8:
The
Network
and Sharing
Center
(Windows 8).

3. **Click the Change Adapter Settings link on the left.**

   The Network Connections folder appears, as shown in Figure 7-9.

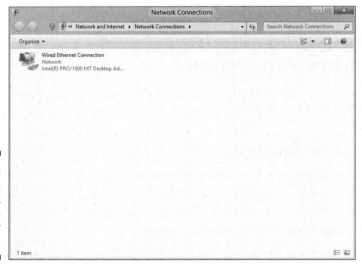

Figure 7-9:
The
Network
Connections
folder
(Windows 8).

4. **Right-click the connection that you want to configure and then choose Properties from the contextual menu that appears.**

   The Properties dialog box for the network connection appears, as shown in Figure 7-10. If you compare this dialog box with the dialog box shown earlier, in Figure 7-2, you see that they're very similar.

Figure 7-10:
The Properties dialog box for a network connection (Windows 8).

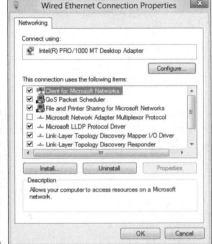

5. **Click Configure to configure the network connection.**

   From this point, the steps for configuring the network connection are the same as they are for Windows XP. As a result, you can continue by beginning with Step 4 in the earlier section "Configuring Windows XP network connections."

Configuring Client Computer Identification

Every client computer must identify itself to participate in the network. The computer identification consists of the computer's name, an optional description, and the name of either the workgroup or the domain to which the computer belongs.

The computer name must follow certain rules: It may be 1 to 15 characters long and may contain letters, numbers, or hyphens but no spaces or periods. For small networks, it's common to make the computer name the same as the username. For larger networks, you may want to develop a naming scheme that identifies the computer's location. A name such as C-305-1 may be assigned to the first computer in Room 305 of Building C, for example, or MKTG010 may be a computer in the Marketing department.

If the computer will join a domain, you need to have access to an Administrator account on the domain unless the administrator has already created a computer account on the domain. Note that only the following versions of Windows have the capability to join a domain:

- ✔ Windows 8 Professional and Enterprise
- ✔ Windows 7 Professional, Enterprise, and Ultimate
- ✔ Windows Vista Business, Enterprise, and Ultimate
- ✔ Windows XP Professional

When you install Windows on the client system, the Setup program asks for the computer name and workstation or domain information. You can change this information later, if you want. The procedure varies depending on the Windows version you're using.

Configuring Windows XP computer identification

To change the computer identification in Windows XP, follow these steps:

1. **Open the Control Panel (Start➪Control Panel) and then double-click the System icon to open the System Properties dialog box.**

2. **Click the Computer Name tab.**

   The computer identification information is displayed.

3. **Click the Change button.**

   This step displays the Computer Name Changes dialog box, as shown in Figure 7-11.

4. **Type the new computer name and then specify the workgroup or domain information.**

   To join a domain, select the Domain radio button and type the domain name in the appropriate text box. To join a workgroup, select the Workgroup radio button and type the workgroup name in the corresponding text box.

5. **Click OK.**

Figure 7-11:
The
Computer
Name
Changes
dialog box
(Windows
XP).

6. **If you're prompted, enter the username and password for an Administrator account.**

   You're asked to provide this information only if a computer account hasn't already been created for the client computer.

7. **When a dialog box appears, informing you that you need to restart the computer, click OK; then restart the computer.**

   You're done!

Configuring computer identification on Windows Vista, Windows 7, or Windows 8

To change the computer identification in Windows Vista, Windows 7, or Windows 8, follow these steps:

1. **Open the Control Panel.**

   - *Windows Vista or Windows 7:* Choose Start⇨Control Panel.
   - *Windows 8:* Right-click the bottom-left corner of the screen and then choose Control Panel from the contextual menu.

2. **Double-click the System icon.**

   This step displays the System information window. Figure 7-12 shows the Windows 8 version, but the Windows Vista and Windows 7 versions are similar. Notice the section that lists computer name, domain, and workgroup settings.

The Change Settings link

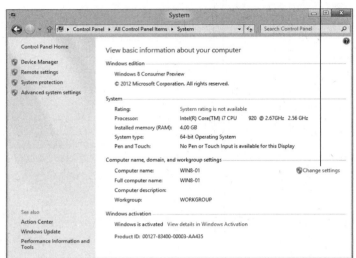

Figure 7-12:
The System
information
window
(Windows 8).

3. **Click the Change Settings link in the bottom-right corner.**

   If a dialog box appears and asks for your permission to continue, click
   Continue. The System Properties dialog box appears, as shown in
   Figure 7-13.

Figure 7-13:
The System
Properties
dialog box
(Windows 8).

4. **Click the Change button.**

   This step displays the Computer Name/Domain Changes dialog box, as shown in Figure 7-14.

Figure 7-14:
The
Computer
Name/
Domain
Changes
dialog box
(Windows 8).

5. **Enter the computer name and the workgroup or domain name.**

   If you want to join a domain, select the Domain radio button and type the domain name. If your network does not use domains, choose the Workgroup option button, and type the workgroup name.

6. **Click OK.**

7. **Enter the username and password for an Administrator account when prompted.**

   You're asked to provide this information only if a computer account hasn't already been created for the client computer.

8. **When a dialog box appears, informing you that you need to restart the computer, click OK; then restart the computer.**

   The computer is added to the domain or workgroup.

Configuring Network Logon

Every user who wants to access a domain-based network must log on to the domain by using a valid user account. The user account is created on the domain controller — not on the client computer.

Network logon isn't required to access workgroup resources. Instead, workgroup resources can be password-protected to restrict access.

When you start a Windows computer that's been configured to join a domain, as described in the section "Configuring Client Computer Identification," earlier in this chapter, the Log on to Windows dialog box is displayed. The user can use this dialog box to log on to a domain by entering a domain username and password and then selecting the domain that she wants to log on to (from the Log on To drop-down list).

You can create local user accounts in Windows that allow users to access resources on the local computer. To log on to the local computer, the user selects This Computer from the Log on To drop-down list and enters the username and password for a local user account. When a user logs on by using a local account, he isn't connected to a network domain. To log on to a domain, the user must select the domain from the Log on To drop-down list.

If the computer isn't part of a domain, Windows can display a friendly logon screen that displays an icon for each of the computer's local users. The user can log on simply by clicking the appropriate icon and entering a password. (This feature isn't available for computers that have joined a domain.)

Note that if the user logs on by using a local computer account rather than a domain account, she can still access domain resources. A Connect To dialog box appears whenever the user attempts to access a domain resource. Then the user can enter a domain username and password to connect to the domain.

Chapter 8

Connecting Your Network to the Internet

So you decided to connect your network to the Internet. All you have to do is call the cable company and have them send someone out, right? Wrong. Unfortunately, connecting to the Internet involves more than just calling the cable company. For starters, you have to make sure that cable is the right way to connect. Then you have to select and configure the software you use to access the Internet. Finally, you have to lie awake at night worrying whether hackers are breaking into your network via its Internet connection.

Not to worry. The advice in this chapter helps you decide how to connect to the Internet and, once the decision is made, how to do it safely.

Connecting to the Internet

Connecting to the Internet isn't free. For starters, you have to purchase the computer equipment necessary to make the connection. Then you have to obtain a connection from an Internet service provider (ISP). The ISP charges you a monthly fee that depends on the speed and capacity of the connection.

The following sections describe the most commonly used methods of connecting network users to the Internet.

Connecting with cable or DSL

For small and home offices, the two most popular methods of connecting to the Internet are cable and digital subscriber line (DSL). Cable and DSL connections are often called *broadband connections* for technical reasons you don't really want to know.

Cable Internet access works over the same cable that brings 40 billion TV channels into your home, whereas DSL is a digital phone service that works over a standard phone line. Both offer three major advantages over old-fashioned dialup connections:

- ✔ **Cable and DSL are much faster than dialup connections.**

  A cable connection can be anywhere from 10 to 200 times faster than a dialup connection, depending on the service you get. And the speed of a DSL line is comparable with cable. (Although DSL is a dedicated connection, cable connections are shared among several subscribers. The speed of a cable connection may slow down when several subscribers use the connection simultaneously.)

- ✔ **With cable and DSL, you're always connected to the Internet.**

  You don't have to connect and disconnect each time you want to go online like you would if you use a modem. No more waiting for the modem to dial your service provider and listening to the annoying modem shriek while it attempts to establish a connection.

- ✔ **Cable and DSL don't tie up a phone line while you're online.**

  With cable, your Internet connection works over TV cables, not over phone cables. With DSL, the phone company installs a separate phone line for the DSL service, so your regular phone line isn't affected.

Unfortunately, there's no such thing as a free lunch, and the high-speed, always-on connections offered by cable and DSL don't come without a price. For starters, you can expect to pay a higher monthly access fee for cable or DSL. In most areas of the United States, cable runs about $50 per month for residential users; business users can expect to pay more, especially if more than one user will be connected to the Internet via the cable.

The cost for DSL service depends on the access speed you choose. In some areas, residential users can get a relatively slow DSL connection for as little as $30 per month. For higher access speeds or for business users, DSL can cost substantially more.

Too, cable and DSL access aren't available everywhere. But if you live in an area where cable or DSL isn't available, you can still get high-speed Internet access by using a satellite hookup or a cellular network.

Connecting with high-speed private lines

If your network is large and high-speed Internet access is a high priority, contact your local phone company (or companies) about installing a dedicated high-speed digital line. These lines can cost you plenty (on the order of hundreds of dollars per month), so they're best suited for large networks in which 20 or more users are accessing the Internet simultaneously.

The following paragraphs describe three basic options for high-speed private lines:

✔ **T1 and T3 lines:** T1 and T3 lines run over standard copper phone lines. A T1 line has a connection speed of up to 1.544 Mbps. A T3 line is faster yet: It transmits data at an amazing 44.184 Mbps. Of course, T3 lines are also considerably more expensive than T1 lines.

If you don't have enough users to justify the expense of an entire T1 or T3 line, you can lease just a portion of the line. With a fractional T1 line, you can get connections with speeds of 128 Kbps to 768 Kbps; with a fractional T3 line, you can choose speeds ranging from 4.6 Mbps to 32 Mbps.

You may be wondering whether T1 or T3 lines are really any faster than cable or DSL connections. After all, T1 runs at 1.544 Mbps and T3 runs at 44.184 Mbps, and cable and DSL claim to run at comparable speeds. But there are many differences that justify the substantial extra cost of a T1 or T3 line. In particular, a T1 or T3 line is a *dedicated* line — not shared by any other users. T1 and T3 are higher-quality connections, so you actually get the 1.544 or 44.184 connection speeds. In contrast, both cable and DSL connections usually run at substantially less than their advertised maximum speeds because of poor-quality connections and because the connections are often shared with other users.

✔ **Business-class cable:** Cable TV providers (such as Comcast) offer business-class service on their cable network. The price and speed depends on your area. For example, where I live, I can get 100Mbps service for about $400/month.

One drawback of business-class cable service is that upload speeds are usually much slower than download speeds. For example, a typical plan that allows 100Mbps for downloads can support only 10Mbps for uploads. Thus, if you need to upload large amounts of data, you'll notice the performance drop.

Another drawback of business-class cable service is that it is, well, cable service. Your Internet connection is service by the same people who service cable TV in your community. Although business-class customers get priority service over residential customers, business-class service usually does not include response-time guarantees the way T1/T3 or fiber service does. So if your connection goes down, you might find yourself down for hours or even a few days instead of minutes or, at worse, a few hours.

✔ **Fiber optic:** The fastest, most reliable, and most expensive form of Internet connection is fiber optic. Fiber optic cable uses strands of glass to transmit data over light signals at very high speeds. Because the light signals traveling within the fiber cables are not subject to electromagnetic interference, fiber connections are extremely reliable; about the only thing that can interrupt a fiber connection is if someone physically cuts the wire.

Fiber is also very expensive. A 20 Mbps fiber connection can cost well over $1,000 per month. However, the connection is extremely reliable, and response time to service interruptions is measured in minutes instead of hours.

Sharing an Internet connection

After you choose a method to connect to the Internet, you can turn your attention to setting up the connection so that more than one user on your network can share it. The best way to do that is by using a separate device called a *router*. You can pick up an inexpensive router for a small network for less than $100. Routers suitable for larger networks will, naturally, cost a bit more.

Because all communications between your network and the Internet must go through the router, the router is a natural place to provide the security measures necessary to keep your network safe from the many perils of the Internet. As a result, a router used for Internet connections often doubles as a firewall, as described in the section "Using a firewall," later in this chapter.

Securing Your Connection with a Firewall

If your network is connected to the Internet, a whole host of security issues bubbles to the surface. You probably connected your network to the Internet so that your network's users could get out to the Internet. Unfortunately, however, your Internet connection is a two-way street. It not only enables your network's users to step outside the bounds of your network to access the Internet, but it also enables others to step in and access your network.

And step in they will. The world is filled with hackers who are looking for networks like yours to break into. They may do it just for the fun of it, or they may do it to steal your customers' credit card numbers or to coerce your mail server into sending thousands of spam messages on behalf of the bad guys. Whatever their motive, rest assured that your network will be broken into if you leave it unprotected.

Using a firewall

A *firewall* is a security-conscious router that sits between the Internet and your network with a single-minded task: preventing *them* from getting to *us*. The firewall acts as a security guard between the Internet and your local area network (LAN). All network traffic into and out of the LAN must pass through the firewall, which prevents unauthorized access to the network.

Some type of firewall is a must-have if your network has a connection to the Internet, whether that connection is broadband (cable modem or DSL), T1, or some other high-speed connection. Without it, sooner or later a hacker will discover your unprotected network and tell his friends about it, and within a few hours, your network will be toast.

You can set up a firewall in two basic ways:

- **Firewall appliance:** The easiest way, and usually the best choice. A firewall appliance is basically a self-contained router with built-in firewall features.

  Most firewall appliances include web-based interfaces that enable you to connect to the firewall from any computer on your network by using a browser. You can then customize the firewall settings to suit your needs.

- **Server computer:** Can be set up to function as a firewall computer.

  The server can run just about any network operating system, but most dedicated firewall systems run Linux.

Whether you use a firewall appliance or a firewall computer, the firewall must be located between your network and the Internet, as shown in Figure 8-1. Here, one end of the firewall is connected to a network hub, which is, in turn, connected to the other computers on the network. The other end of the firewall is connected to the Internet. As a result, all traffic from the LAN to the Internet (and vice versa) must travel through the firewall.

The term *perimeter* is sometimes used to describe the location of a firewall on your network. In short, a firewall is like a perimeter fence that completely surrounds your property and forces all visitors to enter through the front gate.

In large networks, figuring out exactly where the perimeter is located can be a little difficult. If your network has two or more Internet connections, make sure that every one of those connections connects to a firewall — and not directly to the network. You can do this by providing a separate firewall for each Internet connection or by using a firewall with more than one Internet port.

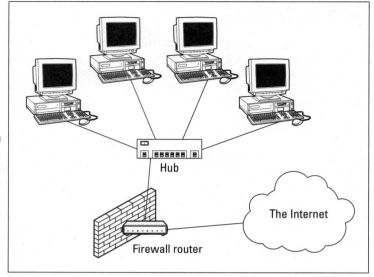

Figure 8-1:
A firewall
router
creates a
secure link
between a
network and
the Internet.

Hub

The Internet

Firewall router

Some firewall routers can also enforce virus protection for your network. For more information about virus protection, see Chapter 22.

The built-in Windows firewall

Windows includes a built-in firewall that provides basic packet-filtering firewall protection. In most cases, you're better off using a dedicated firewall router because these devices provide better security features than the built-in Windows firewall does. Still, the built-in firewall is suitable for home networks or very small office networks.

Here are the steps that activate the built-in firewall in Windows XP or Vista:

1. **Choose Start⇨Control Panel.**

2. **In the Control Panel, click the Windows Firewall icon.**

   This step opens the Windows Firewall dialog box. Figure 8-2 shows the Windows Vista version.

3. **Select the On (Recommended) option.**

   This option enables the firewall.

4. **Click OK.**

   That's all there is to it.

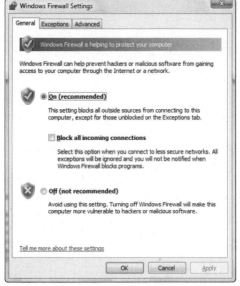

Figure 8-2:
The
Windows
Vista
Firewall
dialog box.

For Windows 7 or 8, the procedure is a bit different:

1. **Open the Control Panel.**

   - *Windows 7:* Choose Start⇨Control Panel.
   - *Windows 8:* Choose Settings⇨Control Panel from the Charms bar.

2. **Click the System and Security link.**

   The System and Security page appears.

3. **Click the Windows Firewall link.**

   The Windows Firewall page appears.

4. **Click the Turn Windows Firewall On or Off link.**

   The page shown in Figure 8-3 appears.

5. **Select the Turn on Windows Firewall option.**

   Note that you can independently turn the firewall on or off for public
   network — that is, for your connection to the Internet — and for your
   home or work network — that is, if you have a network that connects
   other computers in your home or office. I recommend you either turn
   the firewall on for both or turn it off for both. Turn the firewall off if
   you're using a separate firewall built into the router that connects your
   computer or home or work network to the Internet. Turn the firewall on
   if you don't have a separate firewall.

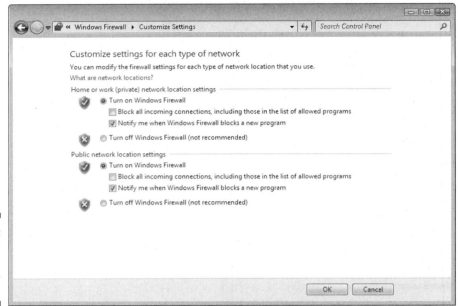

Figure 8-3:
Activating
the firewall
in Windows
7 and 8.

I also recommend leaving the Notify Me When Windows Firewall Blocks a New Program option enabled. That way, you'll be notified when the firewall blocks a suspicious program.

6. **Click OK.**

The firewall is enabled.

Note that the firewalls included with Windows Vista and Windows 7 have additional options you can configure. However, I recommend against fiddling with those options unless you've taken an upper-division college course in computer security.

Do *not* enable the Windows Internet firewall if you're using a separate firewall router to protect your network. Because the other computers on the network are connected directly to the router and not to your computer, the firewall doesn't protect the rest of the network. Additionally, as an unwanted side effect, the rest of the network will lose the capability of accessing your computer.

Chapter 9

Setting Up a Wireless Network

· ·

In This Chapter

▶ Understanding wireless network standards

▶ Reviewing basic radio terms

▶ Considering infrastructure and ad-hoc networks

▶ Working with a wireless access point

▶ Configuring Windows for wireless networking

· ·

Since the beginning of Ethernet networking, cable has been getting smaller and easier to work with. The original Ethernet cable was about as thick as your thumb, weighed a ton, and was difficult to bend around tight corners. Then came coaxial cable, which was lighter and easier to work with. Coaxial cable was supplanted by unshielded twisted-pair (UTP) cable, which is the cable used for most networks today.

Although cable through the years has become smaller, cheaper, and easier to work with, it is still *cable.* So you have to drill holes in walls, pull cable through ceilings, and get insulation in your hair to wire your entire home or office.

The alternative to networking with cables is, of course, networking *without* cables . . . also known as *wireless networking.* Wireless networks use radio waves to send and receive network signals. As a result, a computer can connect to a wireless network at any location in your home or office.

Wireless networks are especially useful for notebook computers. After all, the main benefit of a notebook computer is that you can carry it around with you wherever you go. At work, you can use your notebook computer at your desk, in the conference room, in the break room, or even out in the parking lot. At home, you can use it in the bedroom, kitchen, den, or game room, or out by the pool. With wireless networking, your notebook computer can be connected to the network no matter where you take it.

Wireless networks have also become extremely useful for other types of mobile devices, such as smartphones and tablet computers. Sure, these devices can connect via a cell network, but that can get real pricey real quick.

With a wireless network, though, you can connect your smart phone or tablet without having to pay your cellphone company for the connection time.

This chapter introduces you to the ins and outs of setting up a wireless network. I tell you what you need to know about wireless networking standards, how to plan your wireless network, and how to install and configure wireless network components. And if you end up with a hybrid network of wired and wireless, I show you how to create that, too.

Diving into Wireless Networking

As I mention earlier, a wireless network is just a network that uses radio signals rather than direct cable connections to exchange information. Simple as that. A computer with a wireless network connection is like a cellphone. Just as you don't have to be connected (tethered) to a phone line to use a cellphone, you don't have to be connected to a network cable to use a wireless networked computer.

Here are the key concepts and terms you need to understand to set up and use a basic wireless network:

- ✔ **WLAN:** A wireless network is often referred to as a wireless local area network (WLAN). Some people prefer to switch the acronym around to local area wireless network, or LAWN.

- ✔ **Wi-Fi:** The term *Wi-Fi* is often used to describe wireless networks although it technically refers to just one form of wireless network: the 802.11b standard. (See the section "Eight-Oh-Two-Dot-Eleventy Something?: Understanding Wireless Standards," later in this chapter for more information.)

- ✔ **SSID:** A wireless network has a name, known as a SSID. *SSID* stands for *service set identifier.* (Wouldn't that make a great *Jeopardy!* question? I'll take obscure four-letter acronyms for $400, please!) All the computers that belong to a single wireless network must have the same SSID.

- ✔ **Channels:** Wireless networks can transmit over any of several channels. For computers to talk to one another, though, they must be configured to transmit on the same channel.

- ✔ **Ad-hoc:** The simplest type of wireless network consists of two or more computers with wireless network adapters. This type of network is an *ad-hoc mode network.*

- ✔ **Infrastructure mode:** A more complex type of network is an infrastructure mode network. All this really means is that a group of wireless computers can be connected not only to one another, but also to an existing cabled network via a device called a *wireless access point* (WAP). (I tell you more about ad-hoc and infrastructure networks later in this chapter.)

A Little High School Electronics

I was a real nerd in high school: I took three years of electronics. The electronics class at my school was right next door to the auto shop. All the cool kids took auto shop, of course, and only nerds like me took electronics. We hung in there, though, and learned all about capacitors and diodes while the cool kids were learning how to raise their cars and install 2-gigawatt stereo systems.

It turns out that a little of that high school electronics information proves useful when it comes to wireless networking — not much, but a little. You'll understand wireless networking much better if you know the meanings of some basic radio terms.

Waves and frequencies

For starters, radio consists of electromagnetic waves sent through the atmosphere. You can't see or hear them, but radio receivers can pick them up and convert them to sounds, images, or — in the case of wireless networks — data. Radio waves are actually cyclical waves of electronic energy that repeat at a particular rate: the *frequency*.

Figure 9-1 shows two frequencies of radio waves. The first is one cycle per second; the second is two cycles per second. (Real radio doesn't operate at that low a frequency, but I figured that one and two cycles per second would be easier to draw than 680,000 and 2.4 million cycles per second.)

The measure of a frequency is *cycles per second,* which indicates how many complete cycles the wave makes in 1 second (duh). In honor of Heinrich Hertz — who didn't invent catsup, but was the first person to successfully send and receive radio waves (it happened in the 1880s) — cycles per second is usually referred to as *Hertz,* abbreviated *Hz.* Thus, 1 Hz is one cycle per second.

Incidentally, when the prefix *K* (for *kilo,* or 1,000), *M* (for *mega,* 1 million), or *G* (for *giga,* 1 billion) is added to the front of Hz, the *H* is still capitalized. Thus, 2.4 MHz is correct (not 2.4 Mhz).

So the beauty of radio frequencies is that transmitters can be tuned to broadcast radio waves at a precise frequency. Likewise, receivers can be tuned to receive radio waves at a precise frequency, ignoring waves at other frequencies. That's why you can tune the radio in your car to listen to dozens of radio stations: Each station broadcasts at its own frequency.

Cycles per second: 1

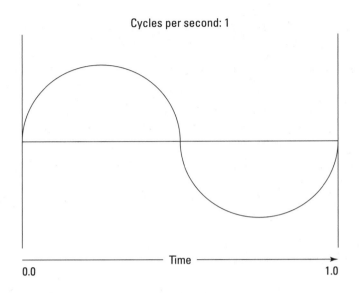

Time
0.0   1.0

Cycles per second: 2

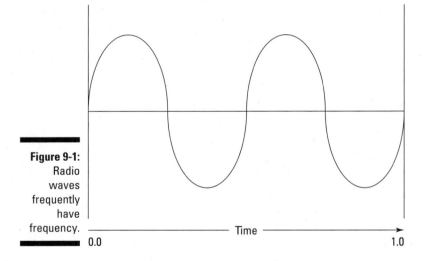

Time
0.0   1.0

Figure 9-1:
Radio
waves
frequently
have
frequency.

Wavelength and antennas

A term related to frequency is *wavelength.* Radio waves travel at the speed of light, and *wavelength* refers to how far the radio signal travels with each cycle. Because the speed of light is roughly 182,282 miles per second, for example, the wavelength of a 1 Hz radio wave is about 182,282 miles. The wavelength of a 2 Hz signal is about half that: a mere 91,141 miles.

As you can see, the wavelength decreases as the frequency increases. The wavelength of a typical AM radio station broadcasting at 580 KHz is about 522 yards. For a TV station broadcasting at 100 MHz, it's about 3 yards. For a wireless network broadcasting at 2.4 GHz, the wavelength is just shorter than 5 inches.

And the shorter the wavelength, the smaller the antenna needs to be to adequately receive the signal. As a result, higher-frequency transmissions need smaller antennas. You may have noticed that AM radio stations usually have huge antennas mounted on top of tall towers, but cellphone transmitters are much smaller, and their towers aren't nearly as tall because cellphones operate on a higher frequency than AM radio stations do. So who decides what type of radio gets to use specific frequencies? That's where spectrums and the FCC come in.

Spectrums and the FCC

Spectrum refers to a continuous range of frequencies on which radio can operate. In the United States, the Federal Communications Commission (FCC) regulates not only how much of Janet Jackson can be shown at the Super Bowl, but also how various portions of the radio spectrum can be used. Essentially, the FCC has divided the radio spectrum into dozens of small ranges — *bands* — and restricted certain uses to certain bands. AM radio, for example, operates in the band from 535 KHz to 1,700 KHz.

And now, a word from the irony department

I was an English-literature major in college, so I like to use literary devices such as irony. I don't get to use it much in the computer books I write, so when I get the chance to use irony, I like to jump on it like a hog out of water.

So here's my juicy bit of irony for today: The very first Ethernet system was actually a wireless network. Ethernet traces its roots to a network called AlohaNet, developed at the University of Hawaii in 1970. This network transmitted its data by using small radios. If two computers tried to broadcast data at the same time, the computers detected the collision and tried again after a short, random delay. This technique was the inspiration for the basic technique of Ethernet, now called "carrier sense multiple access with collision detection" or CSMA/CD. The wireless AlohaNet was the network that inspired Robert Metcalfe to develop his cabled network, which he called Ethernet, as his doctoral thesis at Harvard in 1973.

For the next 20 years or so, Ethernet was pretty much a cable-only network. It wasn't until the mid-1990s that Ethernet finally returned to its wireless roots.

Table 9-1 lists some of the most popular bands. Note that some of these bands are wide — UHF television begins at 470 MHz and ends at 806 MHz — but other bands are restricted to a specific frequency. The difference between the lowest and highest frequency within a band is the *bandwidth*.

Table 9-1	Popular Bands of the Radio Spectrum
Band	*Use*
535 KHz–1,700 KHz	AM radio
5.9 MHz–26.1 MHz	Shortwave radio
26.96 MHz–27.41 MHz	Citizens Band (CB) radio
54 MHz–88 MHz	Television (VHF channels 2–6)
88 MHz–108 MHz	FM radio
174 MHz–220 MHz	Television (VHF channels 7–13)
470 MHz–806 MHz	Television (UHF channels)
806 MHz–890 MHz	Cellular networks
900 MHz	Cordless phones
1850 MHz–1990 MHz	PCS cellular
2.4 GHz–2.4835 GHz	Cordless phones and wireless networks (802.11b and 802.11n)
4 GHz–5 GHz	Large-dish satellite TV
5 GHz	Wireless networks (802.11a)
11.7 GHz–12.7 GHz	Small-dish satellite TV

Two of the bands in the spectrum are allocated for use by wireless networks: 2.4 GHz and 5 GHz. Note that these bands aren't devoted exclusively to wireless networks. In particular, the 2.4 GHz band shares its space with cordless phones. As a result, cordless phones sometimes interfere with wireless networks.

Eight-Oh-Two-Dot-Eleventy Something?: Understanding Wireless Standards

The most popular standards for wireless networks are the IEEE 802.11 standards. These standards are essential wireless Ethernet standards and use many of the same networking techniques that the cabled Ethernet standards (in other words, 802.3) use. Most notably, 802.11 networks use the same CSMA/CD technique as cabled Ethernet to recover from network collisions.

The 802.11 standards address the bottom two layers of the IEEE seven-layer model: the Physical layer and the Media Access Control (MAC) layer. Note that TCP/IP protocols apply to higher layers of the model. As a result, TCP/IP runs just fine on 802.11 networks.

The original 802.11 standard was adopted in 1997. Two additions to the standard, 802.11a and 802.11b, were adopted in 1999. The latest and greatest versions are 802.11g and 802.11n.

Table 9-2 summarizes the basic characteristics of the four variants of 802.11.

Table 9-2		802.11 Variations	
Standard	*Speeds*	*Frequency*	*Typical Range (Indoors)*
802.11a	Up to 54 Mbps	5 GHz	150 feet
802.11b	Up to 11 Mbps	2.4 GHz	300 feet
802.11g	Up to 54 Mbps	2.4 GHz	300 feet
802.11n	Up to 600 Mbps (but most devices are in the 100 Mbps range)	2.4 GHz	230 feet

Currently, most wireless networks are based on the 802.11n standard.

Home on the Range

The maximum range of an 802.11g wireless device indoors is about 300 feet. This can have an interesting effect when you get a bunch of wireless computers together such that some of them are in range of one another but others are not. Suppose that Wally, Ward, and the Beaver all have wireless notebooks. Wally's computer is 200 feet away from Ward's computer, and Ward's computer is 200 feet away from Beaver's in the opposite direction (see Figure 9-2). In this case, Ward can access both Wally's and Beaver's computers, but Wally can access only Ward's computer, and Beaver can access only Ward's computer. In other words, Wally and Beaver won't be able to access each other's computers because they're outside the 300-feet range limit. (This is starting to sound suspiciously like an algebra problem. Now suppose that Wally starts walking toward Ward at 2 miles per hour, and Beaver starts running toward Ward at 4 miles per hour. . . .)

Note: Although the normal range for 802.11g is 300 feet, the range may be less in actual practice. Obstacles — solid walls, bad weather, cordless phones, microwave ovens, backyard nuclear reactors, and so on — can all conspire to reduce the effective range of a wireless adapter. If you're having trouble connecting to the network, sometimes just adjusting the antenna helps.

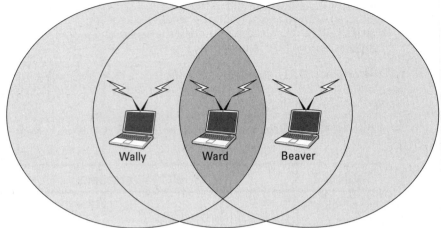

Figure 9-2:
Ward,
Wally, and
the Beaver
playing
with their
wireless
network.

Also, wireless networks tend to slow down when the distance increases. 802.11g network devices claim to operate at 54 Mbps, but they usually achieve that speed only at ranges of 100 feet or less. At 300 feet, they often slow to a crawl. You should also realize that when you're at the edge of the wireless device's range, you're more likely to lose your connection suddenly due to bad weather.

Using Wireless Network Adapters

Each computer that will connect to your wireless network needs a wireless network adapter, which is similar to the network interface card (NIC) used for a standard Ethernet connection. Instead of having a cable connector on the back, however, a wireless network adapter has an antenna.

Just about all notebook computers come with wireless networking built in, so you don't have to add a separate wireless network adapter to a notebook computer. Desktop computers, though, are a different story. They typically don't have built-in wireless networking, so you'll probably need to purchase one of two types of wireless adapters:

- ✓ **A wireless PCI card:** You install this wireless network adapter in an available slot inside your desktop computer. Yup, you need to take your computer apart, so use this type of card only if you have the expertise and the nerves to dig into your computer's guts.

✔ **A wireless USB adapter:** This gizmo is a separate box that plugs into a USB port on your computer. Because you can install this type of adapter without taking your computer apart, USB adapters are more readily available than PCI card adapters. Yea!

Setting Wireless Access Points

Unlike cabled networks, wireless networks don't need a hub or switch. If all you want to do is network a group of wireless computers, you just purchase a wireless adapter for each computer, put them all within 300 feet of one another, and *voilà!* — instant network.

But what if you already have an existing cabled network? Suppose that you work at an office with 15 computers all cabled up nicely, and you just want to add a couple of wireless notebook computers to the network. Or suppose that you have two computers in your den connected with network cable, but you want to link up a computer in your bedroom without pulling cable through the attic.

That's where a wireless access point (WAP) comes in. A WAP actually performs two functions:

✔ It acts as a central connection point for all your computers that have wireless network adapters. In effect, the WAP performs essentially the same function that a hub or switch performs for a wired network.

✔ It links your wireless network to your existing wired network so that your wired computer and your wireless computers get along like one big happy family. This sounds like the makings of a Dr. Seuss story. ("Now the wireless sneeches had hubs without wires. But the twisted-pair sneeches had cables to thires. . . .")

Wireless access points are sometimes just called access points (APs), which is basically a box with an antenna (or often a pair of antennae) and an RJ-45 Ethernet port. You plug the AP into a network cable and then plug the other end of the cable into a hub or switch, and your wireless network should be able to connect to your cabled network.

Figure 9-3 shows how an access point acts as a central connection point for wireless computers and also how it bridges your wireless network to your wired network.

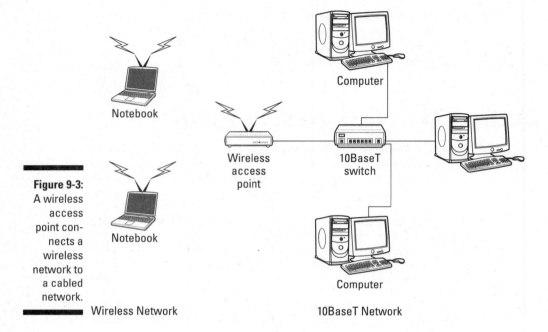

Figure 9-3:
A wireless
access
point con-
nects a
wireless
network to
a cabled
network.

Wireless Network   10BaseT Network

Infrastructure mode

When you set up a wireless network with an AP, you're creating an *infrastructure mode network:* The AP provides a permanent infrastructure for the network. The APs are installed at fixed physical locations, so the network has relatively stable boundaries. Whenever a mobile computer wanders into the range of one of the APs, it has come into the sphere of the network and can connect.

An AP and all the wireless computers that are connected to it are a Basic Service Set (BSS). Each BSS is identified by a SSID. When you configure an AP, you specify the SSID that you want to use. The SSID is often a generic name — such as *wireless* — or it can be a name that you create. Some access points use the MAC address of the WAP as the SSID.

Multifunction WAPs

Wireless access points often include other built-in features. Some APs double as Ethernet hubs or switches; in that case, the AP will have more than one RJ-45 port. In addition, some APs include broadband cable or DSL firewall routers that enable you to connect to the Internet. For example, I use a Linksys wireless router in my home. It includes the following features:

✔ A wireless access point that lets me connect a notebook computer and a computer located on the other side of the house

I didn't want to run cable through the attic.

✔ A four-port gigabit switch that I can use to connect up to four computers via twisted-pair cable

✔ A DSL/cable router that I connect to my cable modem

This router enables all the computers on the network (cabled and wireless) to access the Internet.

A multifunction AP designed to serve as an Internet gateway for home networks is sometimes called a *residential gateway*.

Roaming Capabilities

You can use two or more WAPs to create a large wireless network in which computer users can roam from area to area and still be connected to the wireless network. As the user moves out of the range of one AP, another AP automatically picks up the user and takes over without interrupting the user's network service.

To set up two or more APs for roaming, you must carefully place the WAPs so that all areas of the office or building that are being networked are in range of at least one of the WAPs. Then just make sure that all the computers and APs use the same SSID.

Two or more APs joined for roaming, along with all the wireless computers connected to any of the access points, form an Extended Service Set (ESS). The access points in the ESS are usually connected to a wired network.

One of the current limitations of roaming is that each AP in an ESS must be on the same TCP/IP subnet. That way, a computer that roams from one AP to another within the ESS retains the same IP address. If the APs had a different subnet, a roaming computer would have to change IP addresses when it moved from one AP to another.

Wireless bridging

Another use for wireless APs is to bridge separate subnets that can't easily be connected by cable. Suppose that you have two office buildings that are only about 50 feet apart. To run cable from one building to the other, you'd have to bury conduit — a potentially expensive job. Because the buildings are so close, though, you can probably connect them with a pair of WAPs that function as a wireless bridge between the two networks. Connect one of the APs to the first network and the other AP to the second network. Then configure both APs to use the same SSID and channel.

Ad-hoc networks

A WAP isn't necessary to set up a wireless network. Any time two or more wireless devices come within range of each other, they can link up to form an ad-hoc network. If you and a few of your friends all have notebook computers with wireless adapters, for example, you can meet anywhere and form an ad-hoc network.

All the computers within range of one another in an ad-hoc network are an Independent Basic Service Set (IBSS).

Configuring a Wireless Access Point

The physical setup for a WAP is pretty simple: You take it out of the box, put it on a shelf or on top of a bookcase near a network jack and a power outlet, plug in the power cable, and plug in the network cable.

The software configuration for an AP is a little more involved but still not very complicated. It's usually done via a web interface. To get to the configuration page for the AP, you need to know its IP address. Then you just type that address in the address bar of a browser on any computer on the network.

Multifunction APs usually provide DHCP and NAT services for the networks and double as the network's gateway router. As a result, they typically have a private IP address that's at the beginning of one of the Internet's private IP address ranges, such as `192.168.0.1` or. Consult the documentation that came with the AP to find out more.

 If you use a multifunction AP that serves as both your wireless AP and your Internet router, and you can't remember the IP address, run the `IPCONFIG` command at a command prompt on any computer on the network. The Default Gateway IP address should be the IP address of the access point.

Basic configuration options

Figure 9-4 shows the main configuration screen for a typical router. I called up this configuration page by entering `192.168.1.1` in the address bar of a web browser and then supplying the login password when prompted.

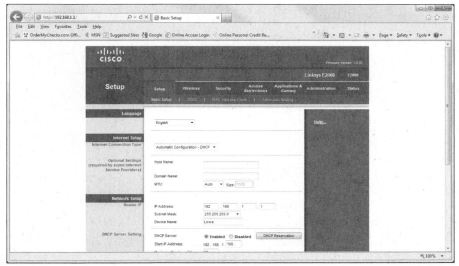

Figure 9-4:
The main configuration page for a Linksys wireless router.

On the main setup page of this router, you configure information such as the hostname and IP address of the router and whether the router's DHCP server should be enabled. Options found on additional tabs allow you to configure wireless settings, such as the network name (SSID), the type of security to enforce, and a variety of other settings.

DHCP configuration

You can configure most multifunction APs to operate as a DHCP server. For small networks, the AP is commonly the DHCP server for the entire network. In that case, you need to configure the AP's DHCP server. Figure 9-5 shows the DHCP configuration page for a Linksys WAP router. To enable DHCP, you select the Enable option and then specify the other configuration options to use for the DHCP server.

Larger networks with more demanding DHCP requirements are likely to have a separate DHCP server running on another computer. In that case, you can defer to the existing server by disabling the DHCP server in the AP.

For more information on configuring a DHCP server, please refer to Chapter 5.

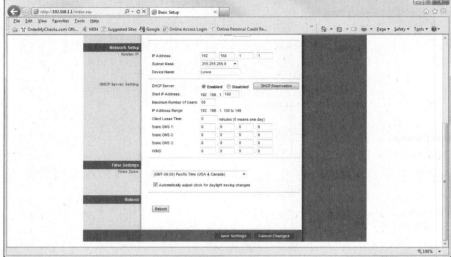

Figure 9-5:
Configuring
DHCP for
a Linksys
wireless
router.

Connecting to a Wireless Network with Windows Vista, 7, or 8

When Windows Vista, 7, or 8 detects that a wireless network is within range, a balloon notification appears onscreen to indicate that one or more wireless networks are available. Click this balloon to summon the dialog box shown in Figure 9-6 and then choose the network you want to connect to.

Figure 9-6:
Choosing
a wireless
network.

Configuring Windows XP for Wireless Networking

If you need to configure an older Windows XP computer for wireless networking, you must first install the appropriate device driver for your wireless network adapter. To do that, you need the installation CD that came with the adapter. Follow the instructions that came with the adapter to install the drivers.

Windows XP has some nice built-in features for working with wireless networks. Follow these steps to access the features:

1. **Open the Network Connections folder.**

   Choose Start⇨Control Panel and then double-click the Network Connections icon.

2. **Right-click the wireless network connection and choose Properties to open the Properties dialog box.**

3. **Click the Wireless Networks tab (see Figure 9-7).**

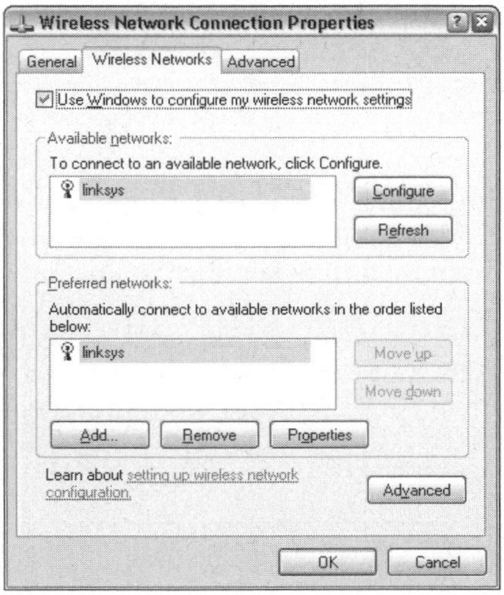

Figure 9-7: Configuring wireless networking in Windows XP.

Each time you connect to a wireless network, Windows XP adds that network to this dialog box. Then you can juggle the order of the networks in the Preferred Networks section to indicate which network you prefer to join if you find yourself within range of two or more networks at the same time. You can use the Move Up and Move Down buttons next to the Preferred Networks list to change your preferences.

To add a network that you haven't yet joined, click the Add button. This action opens the dialog box shown in Figure 9-8. Here, you can type the SSID value for the network that you want to add. You can also specify other information, such as whether to use data encryption, how to authenticate yourself, and whether the network is an ad hoc rather than an infrastructure network.

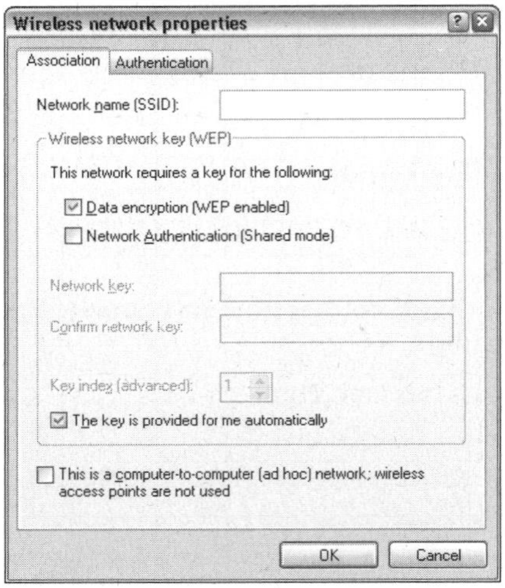

Figure 9-8:
Adding a
wireless
network in
Windows
XP.

When your computer comes within range of a wireless network, a pop-up balloon appears on the taskbar, indicating that a network is available. If one of your preferred networks is within range, clicking the balloon automatically connects you to that network. If Windows XP doesn't recognize any of the networks, clicking the balloon displays the Wireless Network Connection dialog box. From there, you can choose the network that you want to join (if more than one network is listed) and then click Connect to join the selected network.

Part III
Working with Servers

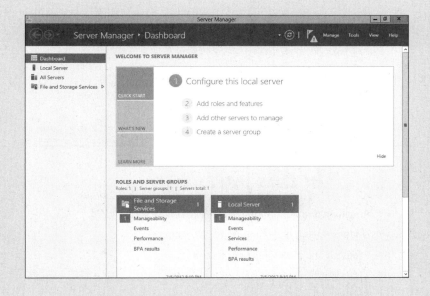

See how to manage a server remotely at www.dummies.com/extras/networking

In this part...

- ✔ Installing and configuring Windows Server 2012
- ✔ Understanding and using Active Director
- ✔ Creating and managing user accounts
- ✔ Managing file servers and e-mail servers
- ✔ Setting up a company Intranet

Chapter 10

Setting Up a Server

*O*ne of the basic choices that you must make before you proceed any further in building your network is to decide which network operating system (NOS) to use as the foundation for your network. This chapter begins with a description of several important features found in all network operating systems. Next, it provides an overview of the advantages and disadvantages of the most popular NOSes.

Of course, your work doesn't end with the selection of an NOS. You must then install and configure the operating system to get it working. This chapter provides an overview of what's involved with installing and configuring Microsoft's latest and greatest server operating system, Windows Server 2012.

Network Operating System Features

All NOSes must provide certain core functions, such as connecting to other computers on the network, sharing files and other resources, and providing for security. In the following sections, I describe some core NOS features in general terms.

Network support

It goes without saying that an NOS should support networks. That requires a range of technical capabilities:

- An NOS must support a wide variety of networking protocols to meet the needs of its users.

  A large network typically consists of a mixture of various versions of Windows as well as Macintosh and Linux computers. As a result, the server may need to simultaneously support TCP/IP, NetBIOS, and AppleTalk protocols.

- Many servers have more than one network interface card (NIC) installed. In that case, the NOS must be able to support multiple network connections:

  - Ideally, the NOS should be able to balance the network load among its network interfaces.

  - If one of the connections fails, the NOS should be able to seamlessly switch to another connection.

- Most NOSes include a built-in capability to function as a router that connects two networks.

  The NOS router functions should also include firewall features to keep unauthorized packets from entering the local network.

File-sharing services

One of the most important functions of an NOS is to share resources with other network users. The most common resource that's shared is the server's *file system* — organized disk space that a network server must be able to share (in whole or in part) with other users. In effect, those users can treat the server's disk space as an extension of their own computers' disk space.

The NOS allows the system administrator to determine which portions of the server's file system to share.

Although an entire hard drive can be shared, it isn't commonly done. Instead, individual folders are shared. The administrator can control which users are allowed to access each shared folder.

Because file sharing is the reason why many network servers exist, NOSes have more sophisticated disk management features than are found in desktop OSes. For example, most NOSes can manage two or more hard drives as though they were a single drive. In addition, most can create a *mirror* — an automatic backup copy of a drive — on a second drive.

Multitasking

Only one user at a time uses a desktop computer; however, multiple users simultaneously use server computers. As a result, an NOS must provide support for multiple users who access the server remotely via the network.

At the heart of multiuser support is *multitasking* — a technique that slices processing time microthin and juggles the pieces lightning fast among running programs. It's how an OS can execute more than one program (a task or a process) at a time. Multitasking operating systems are like the guy who used to spin plates balanced on sticks on the old *Ed Sullivan Show:* running from plate to plate, trying to keep them all spinning so that they don't fall off the sticks. To make it challenging, he'd do it blindfolded or riding on a unicycle. Substitute programs for the plates and file management for the unicycle, and there you are.

Although multitasking creates the appearance that two or more programs execute on the computer at the same time, in reality, a computer with a single processor can execute only one program at a time. The OS switches the CPU from one program to another to create the appearance that several programs execute simultaneously, but at any given moment, only one program processes commands. The others are patiently waiting their turns. (However, if the computer has more than one CPU core, the CPU cores *can* execute programs simultaneously — but that's another kettle of fish.)

Directory services

Directories are everywhere — and were, even in the days when they were all hard copy. When you needed to make a phone call, you looked up the number in a phone directory. When you needed to find the address of a client, you looked her up in your Rolodex. And then there were the nonbook versions: When you needed to find the Sam Goody store at a shopping mall (for example), you looked for the mall directory — usually, a lighted sign showing what was where.

Networks have directories, too, providing information about the resources that are available on the network: users, computers, printers, shared folders, and files. Directories are essential parts of any NOS.

In early NOSes (such as Windows NT 3.1 and NetWare 3.*x*), each server computer maintained its own *directory database* — a file that contained an organized list of the resources available just on that server. The problem with that approach was that network administrators had to maintain each directory database separately. That wasn't too bad for networks with just a few servers, but maintaining the directory on a network with dozens or even hundreds of servers was next to impossible.

In addition, early *directory services* (programs that made the directory databases usable) were application-specific. For example, a server had one directory database for user logons, another for file sharing, and yet another for e-mail addresses. Each directory had its own tools for adding, updating, and deleting directory entries.

The most popular modern directory service is Active Directory (AD), which is standard with Windows-based server OSes. Active Directory provides a single directory of all network resources. It drops the old-style 15-character domain and computer names used by Windows NT Server in favor of Internet-style DNS-style names, such as `Marketing.MyCompany.com` or `Sales.YourCompany.com`. Figure 10-1 shows the Active Directory Users and Computers tool, which manages Active Directory user and computer accounts on Windows Server 2008.

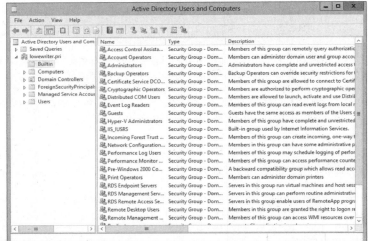

Figure 10-1:
Active
Directory
Users and
Computers.

Security services

All NOSes must provide some measure of security to protect the network from unauthorized access. Hacking seems to be the national pastime these days. With most computer networks connected to the Internet, anyone anywhere in the world can — and probably will — try to break into your network.

The most basic type of security is handled through user accounts, which grant individual users the right to access the network resources and govern which resources the user can access. User accounts are secured by passwords; therefore, good password policy is a cornerstone of any security system. Most NOSes give you some standard tools for maintaining network security:

✔ **Establish password policies.** For example, you can mandate that passwords have a minimum length and include a mix of letters and numerals.

✔ **Set passwords to expire after a certain number of days.** Network users must change their passwords frequently.

✔ **Encrypt network data.** A data-encryption capability scrambles data before it's sent over the network or saved on disk, making unauthorized use a lot more difficult.

Good encryption is the key to setting up a virtual private network (VPN), which enables network users to securely access a network from a remote location by using an Internet connection.

✔ **Issue digital certificates.** These special codes are used to ensure that users are who they say they are and files are what they claim to be.

Microsoft's Server Operating Systems

Over the years, Microsoft has released several versions of its Windows-based server OS: Windows NT Server 4, Windows 2000 Server, Windows 2003 Server, and Windows Server 2008 — and now Windows Server 2012. Most organizations are still using Windows Server 2008 or 2003. In fact, plenty of organizations still use Windows 2000 Server, and a few (mostly on deserted islands cut off from civilization) run Windows NT Server 4.

NTFS drives

All server versions of Windows use a special type of formatting for hard drives, different from the standard FAT system used by MS-DOS since the early 1980s. (*FAT* stands for File Allocation Table, in case you're interested.) The file system, called *NTFS* (for NT File System), offers many advantages over FAT drives:

✔ NTFS is much more efficient at using the space on your hard drive. As a result, NTFS can cram more data onto a given hard drive than FAT.

✔ NTFS drives provide better security features than FAT drives. NTFS stores security information on disk for each file and directory.

In contrast, FAT has only rudimentary security features.

✔ NTFS drives are more reliable because NTFS keeps duplicate copies of important information, such as the location of each file on the hard drive. If a problem develops on an NTFS drive, Windows NT Server can probably correct the problem without losing any data. In contrast, FAT drives are prone to losing information.

Note that Windows Server 2012 introduces a new file system called ReFS that will eventually replace NTFS. However, it will probably be several years before ReFS gains wide acceptance.

Each new version builds on the previous version by introducing new and improved features. However, keep in mind as you read the following sections that Windows NT Server 4, Windows 2000 Server, and Windows 2003 Server are considered obsolete.

Windows NT Server 4

Windows NT Server was the last in a long series of Windows servers dubbed *NT,* which stood for New Technology. The "new technology" that got everyone so excited about Windows NT in the first place was 32-bit processing, which was a huge step from the 16-bit processing of earlier versions of Windows. Windows NT was the first Microsoft OS that was reliable enough to work as a network server on large networks. At more than 16 years old, Windows NT 4 is hopelessly obsolete, but it's still important because of its legacy. Many OS features that were first introduced as part of Windows NT 4 are still in use today.

Probably the most important feature of Windows NT is its directory model, which is based on the concept of *domains,* which are groups of computers managed by a single directory database. To access shared resources within a domain, you must have a valid user account within the domain and be granted rights to access the resources in which you're interested. The domain system uses 15-character NetBIOS names to access individual computers within a domain and to name the domain itself.

Windows 2000 Server

Windows 2000 Server, built on the strengths of Windows NT Server 4, was faster, easier to manage, more reliable, and easier to use for large and small networks alike.

The most significant new feature offered by Windows 2000 Server was Active Directory (AD), which provides a single directory of all network resources and enables program developers to incorporate the directory into their programs. Active Directory drops the 15-character domain and computer names in favor of Internet-style DNS names, such as `Marketing.MyCompany.com` or `Sales.YourCompany.com`. (However, it still supports the old-style names for older clients that don't deal well with DNS names.)

Windows 2000 Server came in three versions:

- **Windows 2000 Server** was the basic server, designed for small to medium-sized networks. It included all the basic server features, including file and printer sharing, and acted as a web and e-mail server.

✔ **Windows 2000 Advanced Server** was the next step up, designed for larger networks. Advanced Server could support server computers that had up to 8GB of memory (not hard drive — RAM!) and four integrated processors instead of the single processor that desktop computers and most server computers had.

✔ **Windows 2000 Datacenter Server** supported servers that had as many as 32 processors with up to 64GB of RAM and was specially designed for large database applications.

For small networks with 50 or fewer computers, Microsoft offered a special Small Business Server bundle, which included the following components for one low, low price:

✔ **Windows Server 2003:** The OS for your network server

✔ **Exchange Server 2003:** For e-mail and instant messaging

✔ **SQL Server 2000:** A database server

✔ **FrontPage 2000:** For building websites

✔ **Outlook 2000:** For reading e-mail

Windows 2003 Server

The next server version of Windows was Windows 2003 Server, which was built on Windows 2000 Server, with the following added features:

✔ A new-and-improved version of AD with tighter security, an easier-to-use interface, and better performance.

✔ A better and easier-to-use system management interface: the Manage My Server window. On the flip side, for those who prefer brute-force commands, Windows 2003 Server includes a more comprehensive set of command line management tools than is offered by Windows 2000 Server. Of course, the familiar Microsoft Management Console tools from Windows 2000 Server are still there.

✔ A major change in the application-programming interface for Windows programs, known as the .NET Framework.

✔ Support for ever-larger clusters of computers. A *cluster* is a set of computers that work together as if they were a single server. Windows 2000 Server Datacenter Edition and previous versions supported clusters of four servers; Windows 2003 Server Enterprise and Datacenter Editions support clusters of eight servers. (Obviously, this is a benefit only for very large networks. The rest of us should just grin and say, "Cool!")

✔ An enhanced distributed file system that lets you combine drives on several servers to create one shared volume.

✔ Support for storage area networks (SANs).

✔ A built-in Internet firewall to secure your Internet connection.

✔ A new version of Microsoft's web server, Internet Information Services (IIS) 6.0.

Like its predecessor, Windows 2003 Server shipped in several versions:

✔ **Windows 2003 Server, Standard Edition:** This is the basic version of Windows 2003. If you're using Windows Server 2003 as a file server or to provide other basic network services, this is the version you'll use. Standard Edition can support servers with up to four processors and 4GB of RAM.

✔ **Windows 2003 Server, Web Edition:** A version of Windows 2003 optimized for use as a web server.

✔ **Windows 2003 Server, Enterprise Edition:** Designed for larger networks, this version can support servers with up to eight processors, 32GB of RAM, server clusters, and advanced features designed for high performance and reliability.

✔ **Windows 2003 Server, Datacenter Edition:** The most powerful version of Windows 2003, with support for servers with 64 processors, 64GB of RAM, and server clusters, as well as advanced fault-tolerance features designed to keep the server running for mission-critical applications.

Windows Server 2008

In February of 2008, Microsoft released the successor to Windows 2003 Server, not surprisingly known as Windows Server 2008. Windows Server 2008 added many new features, including the following:

✔ Even more enhancements to AD, including the ability to manage digital certificates, a new type of domain controller (a read-only domain controller), and the ability to stop and restart AD services without shutting down the entire server.

✔ A new graphical user interface (GUI) based on Windows Vista, including a new all-in-one management tool: Server Manager.

✔ A new version of the OS called Server Core, which has no GUI. Server Core is run entirely from the command line or by a remote computer that connects to the server via Microsoft Management Console. Server Core is designed to provide efficient file servers, domain controllers, or DNS and DHCP servers.

✔ Remote connection enhancements that enable computers to establish web-based connections to the server using the HTTPS protocol without having to establish a virtual private network (VPN) connection.

✔ Yet another new version of the Internet Information Services (IIS) web server (7.0).

Windows Server 2008 R2

In the fall of 2009, Microsoft issued an update to Windows Server 2008, officially called Windows Server 2008 R2. Network administrators the world over rejoiced, in part because most of them are also *Star Wars* fans and they can now refer to their favorite operating system as "R2."

R2 builds on Windows Server 2008 with a variety of new features, including virtualization features that let you run more than one instance of the OS on a single server computer, a new version of IIS (7.5), and support for up to 256 processors.

Also, R2 officially drops support for 32-bit processors. In other words, R2 runs only on server-class 64-bit processors, such as Intel Itanium and Xeon.

Windows Server 2012

The newest version of Windows Server, officially known as Windows Server 2012, offers many significant improvements over Windows Server 2008, the most notable being the new Metro user interface (UI), which is designed for use with touch-sensitive displays.

Other new features of Windows Server 2012 include

✔ A new file system – ReFS – that replaces NTFS, providing better performance and reliability

✔ A redesigned Task Manager designed to highlight which system tasks are drawing more of the server's CPU, memory, and disk and network I/O capacity

✔ IP *Address Management,* which is a feature designed to automatically discover what IP addresses are being used by computers and other devices on the network

✔ The ability to support servers with as many as 640 processors and 4TB of RAM

Seeing Other Server Operating Systems

Although Windows Server is the most popular choice of NOS, you have other choices. The following sections briefly describe two other server choices: Linux and Macintosh OS X Server.

Linux

Perhaps the most interesting OS now available is Linux. The free Linux OS is based on Unix, which is a powerful NOS often used on large networks. Linux was started by Linus Torvalds, who thought it'd be fun to write a version of Unix in his free time — as a hobby. He enlisted help from hundreds of programmers throughout the world, who volunteered their time and efforts via the Internet. Today, Linux is a full-featured version of Unix; its users consider it to be as good as or better than Windows.

Linux offers the same networking benefits of Unix and can be an excellent choice as a server OS.

Mac OS X Server

All the other server OSes I describe in this chapter run on Intel-based PCs with Pentium or Pentium-compatible processors. But what about Macintosh computers? After all, Macintosh users need networks, too. For Macintosh networks, Apple offers a special NOS — Mac OS X Server — which has all the features you expect, including file and printer sharing, Internet features, e-mail, and more.

Novell NetWare

NetWare was once the king of network operating systems. Today, NetWare networks are rare, but you can still find them if you look hard enough. NetWare has always had an excellent reputation for reliability. In fact, some network administrators swear that they have NetWare servers on their networks that have been running continuously, without a single reboot, since Ronald Reagan was president. (Unfortunately, there hasn't been a major upgrade to NetWare since George W. Bush's first term.)

Novell released the first version of NetWare in 1983, two years before the first version of Windows and four years before Microsoft's first network operating system, the now defunct LAN Manager. Over the years, NetWare has gone through many versions. The most important versions were

- ✔ NetWare version 3.*x,* the version that made NetWare famous. NetWare 3.*x* used a now-outdated directory scheme called the *bindery.* Each NetWare 3.*x* server has a bindery file that contains information about the resources on that particular server. With the bindery, you had to log on separately to each server that contained resources you wanted to use.

- ✔ NetWare 4.*x,* in which NetWare Directory Service (NDS) replaced the bindery. NDS is similar to AD. It provides a single directory for the entire network rather than separate directories for each server.

- ✔ NetWare 5.*x* was the next step, with a new UI based on Java for easier administration, improved support for Internet protocols, multiprocessing with up to 32 processors, and many other features.

- ✔ NetWare 6.0 introduced a variety of new features, including a new disk management system (Novell Storage Services); web-based access to network folders and printers; and built-in support for Windows, Linux, Unix, and Macintosh file systems.

- ✔ Novell released its last major version of NetWare (6.5) in summer 2003. It included improvements to its browser-based management tools and was bundled with open source servers, such as Apache and MySQL.

Beginning in 2005, NetWare has transformed itself into a Linux-based system: Open Enterprise System (OES). In OES, the core of the OS is actually Linux, with added applications that run the traditional NetWare services such as directory services. (For more information, see "Linux," earlier in this chapter.)

The Many Ways to Install a Network Operating System

Regardless of which NOS you choose to use for your network servers, you can use any of several common ways to actually install the NOS software on the server computer. The following sections describe these alternatives.

Full install versus upgrade

One of the basic NOS installation choices is whether you want to perform a full installation or an upgrade installation. In some cases, you may be better off performing a full installation even if you're installing the NOS on a computer with an earlier version of the NOS installed:

✔ If you're installing the NOS on a new server, you'll be performing a full installation that installs the OS and configures it with default settings.

✔ If you're installing the NOS on a server computer that already has a server OS installed, you can perform an upgrade installation to replace the existing OS with the new one, yet retain as many of the settings from the existing OS as possible.

✔ You can also perform a full installation on a computer that already has an OS installed. In that case, you have the option of deleting the existing OS or performing a multiboot installation that installs the new server OS alongside the existing OS. Then, when you restart the computer, you can choose which OS you want to run.

✔ Although multiboot installation may sound like a good idea, it's fraught with peril. Avoid multiboot unless you have a specific reason to use it.

✔ You can't upgrade a client version of Windows to a server version. Instead, you must perform a full installation, which deletes the existing Windows OS, or a multiboot installation, which leaves the existing client Windows intact. Either way, however, you can preserve existing data on the Windows computer when you install the server version.

Installing over the network

Typically, you install the NOS directly from the CD-ROM distribution discs on the server's CD-ROM drive. However, you can also install the OS from a shared drive located on another computer — provided that the server computer already has access to the network. You can either use a shared CD-ROM drive or copy the entire contents of the distribution CD-ROM disc onto a shared hard drive.

If you're going to install the NOS onto more than one server, save time by first copying the distribution CD onto a shared hard drive. That's because even the fastest CD-ROM drives are slower than the network. Even with a slow 100 Mbps network, access to hard drive data over the network is much faster than access to a local CD-ROM drive.

Gathering Your Stuff

Before you install an NOS, gather everything you need so you don't have to look for something in the middle of the setup. The following sections describe the items you're most likely to need.

A capable server computer

Obviously, you have to have a server computer on which to install the NOS. Each NOS has a list of minimum hardware requirements supported by the OS. For example, Table 10-1 summarizes the minimum requirements for Windows Server 2012.

My suggestion is that you take these minimums with a grain of salt. Windows Server 2012 will crawl like a snail with 512MB of RAM; I wouldn't bother with less than 4GB, and 16GB is a more appropriate minimum for most purposes.

Table 10-1	Minimum Hardware Requirements for Windows Server 2012
Item	*Windows Server 2012*
CPU	1.4 GHz
RAM	512MB
Free disk space	32GB

Also check your server hardware against the list of compatible hardware published by the maker of your NOS. For example, Microsoft publishes a list of hardware that it has tested and certified as compatible with Windows servers. You can find this list at www.windowsservercatalog.com.

The server OS

You also need a server OS to install. You need the distribution CDs or DVDs or access to copies of them over the network. In addition to the discs, you should have the following:

- **The product key:** The installation program will ask you to prove that you have a legal copy of the software. If you have the actual CDs or DVDs, the product key should be on a sticker attached to the case.

- **Manuals:** If the OS came with printed manuals, you should keep them handy. If the manuals are in PDF form, keep the PDFs handy.

- **Your license type:** You can purchase Microsoft OSes on a per-server or a per-user/per-device basis. You need to know which plan you have when you install the NOS.

Check the CD or DVD distribution disc for product documentation and additional last-minute information. For example, Windows servers have a \docs folder that contains several files that have useful setup information.

Other software

In most cases, the installation program should be able to automatically configure your server's hardware devices and install appropriate drivers. Just in case, though, you should dig out the driver disks/discs that came with your devices, such as network interface cards (NICs), SCSI devices, DVD drives, printers, scanners, and so on.

A working Internet connection

Online connectivity isn't an absolute requirement, but the installation will go much smoother if you have a working Internet connection before you start. The installation process may use this Internet connection for several things:

- **Downloading late-breaking updates or fixes to the OS:** This can eliminate the need to install a Service Pack after you finish installing the NOS.

- **Locating drivers for nonstandard devices:** This can be a big plus if you can't find the driver disk for an obscure SCSI card.

- **Activating the product after you complete the installation (for Microsoft OSes)**

A good book

You'll spend lots of time watching progress bars during installation, so you may as well have something to do while you wait. I recommend *Les Miserables*.

Making Informed Decisions

When you install a NOS, you have to make some decisions about how you want the OS and its servers configured. Most of these decisions aren't cast in stone, so don't worry if you're not 100 percent sure how you want everything configured. You can always go back and reconfigure things. However, you'll save yourself time if you make the right decisions up front rather than just guess when the setup program starts asking you questions.

The following list details most of the decisions that you'll need to make. (This list is for Windows Server 2012 installations. For other network OSes, the decisions may vary slightly.)

- ✔ **The existing OS:** If you want to retain the existing OS, the installation program can perform a multiboot setup, which allows you to choose which OS to boot to each time you start the computer. This is rarely a good idea for server computers, so I recommend that you elect to delete the existing OS.

- ✔ **Partition structure:** Most of the time, you'll want to treat the entire server disk as a single partition. However, if you want to divide the disk into two or more partitions, you should do so during setup. (Unlike most of the other setup decisions, this one is hard to change later.)

- ✔ **Computer name:** During the OS setup, you'll be asked to provide the computer name used to identify the server on the network. If your network has only a few servers, you can just pick a name such as Server01 or MyServer. If your network has more than a few servers, you'll want to establish a naming convention you can follow for naming your servers.

- ✔ **Administrator password:** Okay, this one is tough. You don't want to pick something obvious, like Password, Administrator, or your last name. On the other hand, you don't want to type in something random that you'll later forget because you'll find yourself in a big pickle if you forget the administrator password. I suggest that you make up a complex password with uppercase and lowercase letters, some numerals, and a special symbol or two; *then write it down and keep it in a secure location* where you know it won't get lost.

- ✔ **Networking protocols:** You'll almost always need to install the TCP/IP protocol, the Microsoft network client protocol, and file and printer sharing. Depending on how the server will be used, you may want to install other protocols as well.

- ✔ **TCP/IP configuration:** You'll need to know what IP address to use for the server. Even if your network has a DHCP server to dynamically assign IP addresses to clients, most servers use static IP addresses.

- ✔ **Workgroup or domain:** You'll need to decide whether the server will join a domain or just be a member of a workgroup. In either case, you need to know the domain name or the workgroup name. (In most cases, if you are installing Windows Server, you'll be using a domain. Workgroups are mostly used for peer-to-peer networks that do not have dedicated servers.)

Final Preparations

Before you begin the actual installation, take a few more steps:

✔ **Tidy up.** Clean up the server's disk by uninstalling any software that you don't need and removing any old data that is no longer needed. This cleanup is especially important if you're converting a computer that's been in use as a client computer to a server. You probably don't need Microsoft Office or a bunch of games on the computer after it becomes a server.

✔ **Backup.** Do a complete backup of the computer. Operating system setup programs are almost flawless, so the chances of losing data during installation are minimal, but you still face the chance that something may go wrong.

✔ **Disconnect serial and USB connection.** If the computer is connected to an uninterruptible power supply (UPS) that has a serial or USB connection to the computer, unplug the serial or USB connection. In some cases, this control connection can confuse the OS's setup program when it tries to determine which devices are attached to the computer.

✔ **Uncompress drives.** If the computer has hard drives compressed with DriveSpace or DoubleSpace, uncompress the drives before you begin.

✔ **Chill out.** Light some votive candles, take two acetaminophen, and put on a pot of coffee.

Installing a Network Operating System

The following sections present an overview of a typical installation of Windows Server 2012. Although the details vary, the overall installation process for other NOSes is similar.

In most cases, the best way to install Windows Server 2012 is to perform a new install directly from the DVD installation media. Although upgrade installs are possible, your server will be more stable if you perform a new install. (For this reason, most network administrators avoid upgrading to Windows Server 2012 until it's time to replace the server hardware.)

To begin the installation, insert the DVD distribution media in the server's DVD drive and then restart the server. This causes the server to boot directly from the distribution media, which initiates the setup program.

As the setup program proceeds, it leads you through two distinct installation phases: Collecting Information and Installing Windows. The following sections describe these installation phases in greater detail.

Phase 1: Collecting Information

In the first installation phase, the setup program asks for the preliminary information that it needs to begin the installation. A setup wizard prompts you for the following information:

- ✔ **Language:** Select your language, time zone, and keyboard type.

- ✔ **Product Key:** Enter the 25-character product key that came with the installation media. If setup says that you entered an invalid product key, double-check it carefully. You probably just made a typo.

- ✔ **Operating System Type:** Select Windows Server 2012 Standard Edition or Core.

    - *Standard Edition:* Install the full server OS.

    - *Core:* Install the new text-only version. Use this version only if you are a master of the Windows Server command-line interface known as PowerShell.

- ✔ **License Agreement:** The official license agreement is displayed. You have to agree to its terms to proceed.

- ✔ **Install Type:** Choose an Upgrade or Clean Install type.

- ✔ **Disk Location:** Choose the partition in which you want to install Windows.

Phase 2: Installing Windows

In this phase, Windows setup begins the actual process of installing Windows. The following steps are performed in sequence:

1. Copying Files: Compressed versions of the installation files are copied to the server computer.

2. Expanding Files: The compressed installation files are expanded.

3. Installing Features: Windows server features are installed.

4. Installing Updates: The setup program checks the Microsoft website and downloads any critical updates to the OS.

5. Completing Installation: When the updates are installed, the setup program reboots so it can complete the installation.

Configuring Your Server

After you install Windows Server 2012, the computer automatically reboots, and you're presented with the Server Manager program as shown in Figure 10-2.

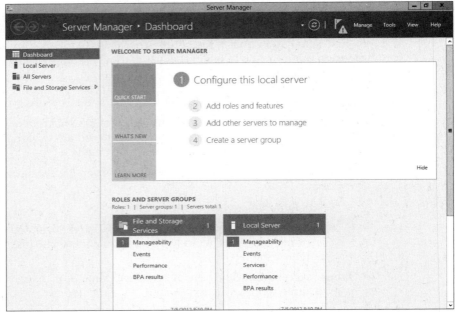

Figure 10-2:
The
Windows
2012 Server
Manager.

From Server Manager, you can perform a number of tasks that are necessary to configure the server for production use. Specifically, you can configure the server roles: the networking features that the server will provide, such as file server, web server, DHCP server, and DNS server.

Chapter 11

Managing Windows User Accounts

*E*very user who accesses a network must have a user account. User accounts allow you — as network administrator — to control who can access the network and who can't. In addition, user accounts let you specify what network resources each user can use. Without user accounts, all your resources would be open to anyone who casually dropped by your network.

Understanding Windows User Accounts

User accounts are among the basic tools for managing a Windows server. As a network administrator, you'll spend a large percentage of your time dealing with user accounts — creating new ones, deleting expired ones, resetting passwords for forgetful users, granting new access rights, and so on. Before I get into the specific procedures of creating and managing user accounts, this section presents an overview of user accounts and how they work.

Local accounts versus domain accounts

A *local account* is a user account stored on a particular computer, applicable to that computer only. Typically, each computer on your network has a local account for each person who uses that computer.

By contrast, a *domain account* is a user account that's stored by Active Directory (AD) and can be accessed from any computer that's a part of the domain. Domain accounts are centrally managed. This chapter deals primarily with setting up and maintaining domain accounts.

User account properties

Every user account has several important account properties that specify the characteristics of the account. The three most important account properties are

- **Username:** A unique name that identifies the account. The user must enter the username when logging on to the network. The username is public information. In other words, other network users can (and often should) find out your username.

- **Password:** A secret word that must be entered to gain access to the account. You can set up Windows so that it enforces password policies, such as the minimum length of the password, whether the password must contain a mixture of letters and numerals, and how long the password remains current before the user must change it.

- **Group membership:** The group(s) to which the user account belongs. Group memberships are the key to granting access rights to users so that they can access various network resources (such as file shares or printers) or perform certain network tasks (such as creating new user accounts or backing up the server).

Many other account properties record information about the user, such as the user's contact information, whether the user is allowed to access the system only at certain times or from certain computers, and so on.

Creating a New User

To create a new domain user account in Windows Server 2012, follow these steps:

1. **Choose Start⇨Administrative Tools⇨Active Directory Users and Computers.**

   This command fires up the Active Directory Users and Computers management console, as shown in Figure 11-1.

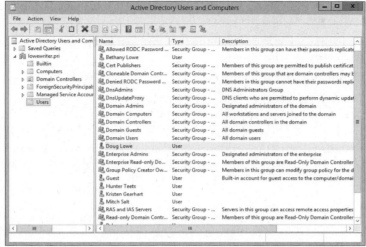

Figure 11-1:
The Active
Directory
Users and
Computers
management
console.

2. **Right-click the domain that you want to add the user to and then choose New▷User from the contextual menu.**

   This command summons the New Object – User Wizard, as shown in Figure 11-2.

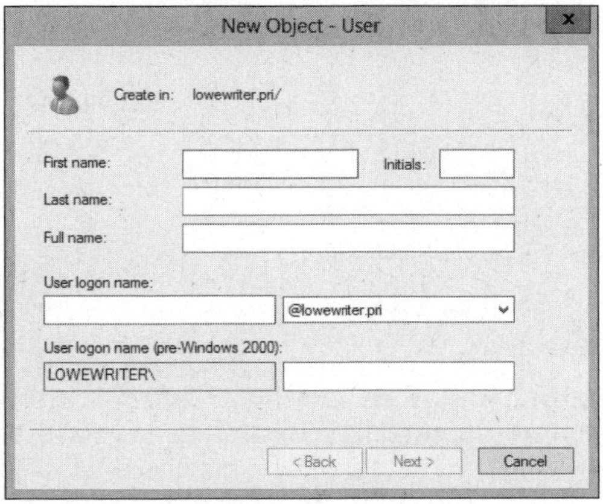

Figure 11-2:
Use the
wizard to
create a
new user.

3. **Enter the user's first name, middle initial, and last name.**

   As you fill in these fields, the New Object Wizard automatically fills in the Full Name field.

4. **Change the Full Name field if you want it to appear different from what the wizard proposes.**

   You may want to reverse the first and last names so the last name appears first, for example.

5. **Enter the user logon name.**

   This name must be unique within the domain. (Don't worry, if you try to use a name that isn't unique, you'll get an error message.)

   Pick a naming scheme to follow when creating user logon names. You can use the first letter of the first name followed by the complete last name, the complete first name followed by the first letter of the last name, or any other scheme that suits your fancy.

6. **Click Next.**

   The second page of the New Object – User Wizard appears, as shown in Figure 11-3.

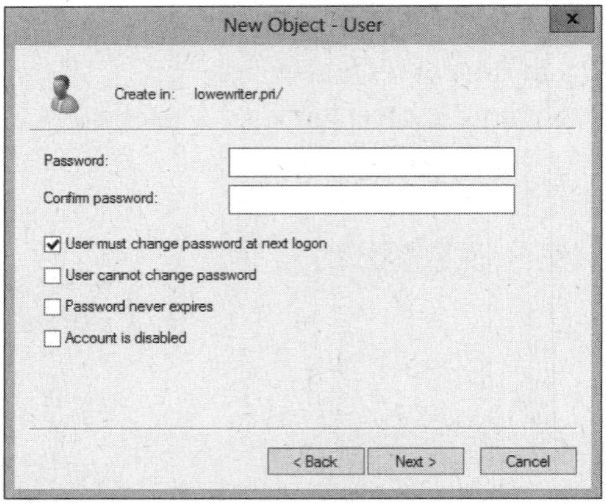

New Object - User

Create in: lowewriter.pri/

Password:

Confirm password:

☑ User must change password at next logon
☐ User cannot change password
☐ Password never expires
☐ Account is disabled

< Back   Next >   Cancel

Figure 11-3: Set the user's password.

---

7. **Enter the password twice.**

   You're asked to enter the password and then confirm it, so type it correctly. If you don't enter it identically in both boxes, you're asked to correct your mistake.

8. **Specify the password options that you want to apply.**

   The following password options are available:

   - User Must Change Password at Next Logon
   - User Cannot Change Password
   - Password Never Expires
   - Account Is Disabled

For more information about these options, see the section "Setting account options," later in this chapter.

9. **Click Next.**

   You're taken to the final page of the New Object – User Wizard, as shown in Figure 11-4.

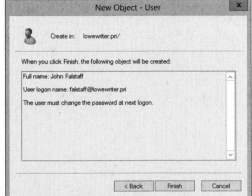

Figure 11-4:
Verifying
the user
account
information.

10. **Verify that the information is correct and then click Finish to create the account.**

    If the account information isn't correct, click the Back button, and correct the error.

You're done! Now you can customize the user's account settings. At minimum, you'll probably want to add the user to one or more groups. You may also want to add contact information for the user or set up other account options.

Setting User Properties

After you create a user account, you can set additional properties for the user by right-clicking the new user and choosing Properties from the contextual menu. This command brings up the User Properties dialog box, which has about a million tabs that you can use to set various properties for the user. Figure 11-5 shows the General tab, which lists basic information about the user, such as the user's name, office location, and phone number.

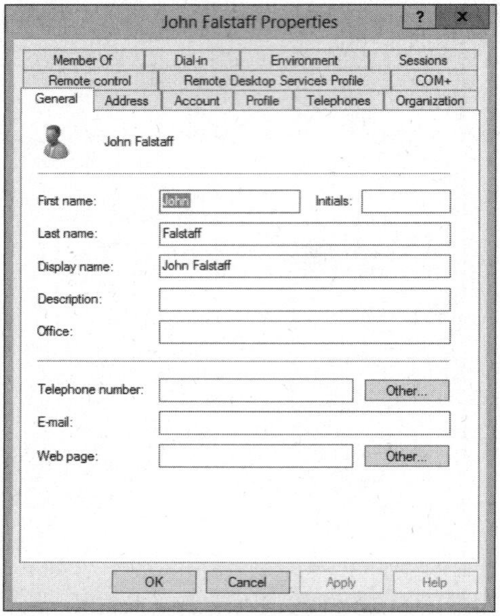

Figure 11-5:
The General
tab.

The following sections describe some of the administrative tasks that you can perform via the various tabs of the User Properties dialog box.

Changing the user's contact information

Several tabs of the User Properties dialog box contain contact information for the user, such as

- **Address:** Change the user's street address, post office box, city, state, zip code, and so on.
- **Telephones:** Specify the user's phone numbers.
- **Organization:** Record the user's job title and the name of his boss.

Setting account options

The Account tab of the User Properties dialog box, shown in Figure 11-6, features a variety of interesting options that you can set for the user. You can change the user's logon name, change the password options that you set when you created the account, and set an expiration date for the account.

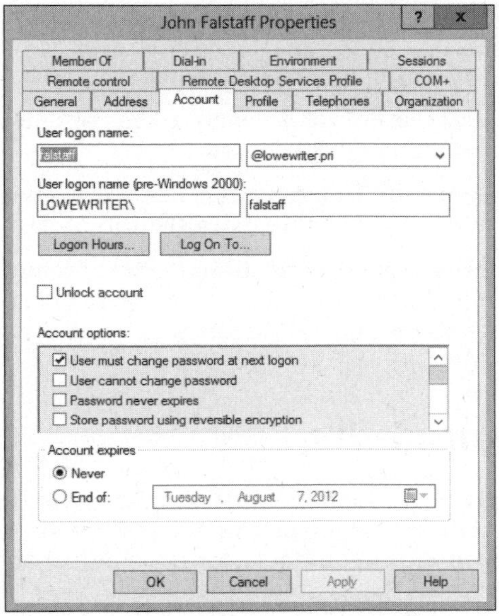

Figure 11-6:
Set user
account info
here.

The following account options are available in the Account Options list box:

- **User Must Change Password at Next Logon:** This default option allows you to create a one-time-only password that can get the user started with the network. The first time the user logs on to the network, he is asked to change the password.

- **User Cannot Change Password:** Use this option if you don't want to allow users to change their passwords. (Obviously, you can't use this option and the preceding one at the same time.)

- **Password Never Expires:** Use this option to bypass the password-expiration policy for this user so that the user will never have to change her password.

- **Store Password Using Reversible Encryption:** This option stores passwords by using an encryption scheme that hackers can easily break, so you should avoid it like the plague.

- **Account Is Disabled:** This option allows you to create an account that you don't yet need. As long as the account remains disabled, the user won't be able to log on. See the upcoming section, "Disabling and Enabling User Accounts," to find out how to enable a disabled account.

- **Smart Card Is Required for Interactive Logon:** If the user's computer has a smart card reader to read security cards automatically, select this option to require the user to use it.

✔ **Account Is Trusted for Delegation:** This option indicates that the account is trustworthy and can set up delegations. This advanced feature usually is reserved for Administrator accounts.

✔ **Account Is Sensitive and Cannot Be Delegated:** This option prevents other users from impersonating this account.

✔ **Use DES Encryption Types for This Account:** This option beefs up the encryption for applications that require extra security.

✔ **Do Not Require Kerberos Preauthentication:** *Kerberos* refers to a common security protocol used to authenticate users. Select this option only if you are using a different type of security.

Specifying logon hours

You can restrict the hours during which the user is allowed to log on to the system. Click the Logon Hours button on the Account tab of the User Properties dialog box to open the Logon Hours for [User] dialog box, as shown in Figure 11-7.

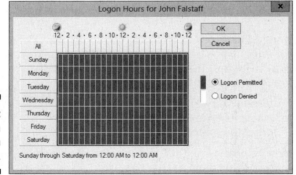

Figure 11-7:
Restrict a user's logon hours.

Initially, the Logon Hours dialog box is set to allow the user to log on at any time of day or night. To change the hours that you want the user to have access, click a day and time or a range of days and times, select Logon Permitted or Logon Denied, and then click OK.

Restricting access to certain computers

Typically, a user can use his user account to log on to any computer that's part of the user's domain. You can restrict a user to certain computers, however, by clicking the Log On To button on the Account tab of the User Properties dialog box. This button brings up the Logon Workstations dialog box, as shown in Figure 11-8.

Figure 11-8:
Restricting
the user
to certain
computers.

To restrict the user to certain computers, select the The Following Computers radio button. Then, for each computer you want to allow the user to log on from, enter the computer's name in the text box and click Add.

If you make a mistake, you can select the incorrect computer name and then click Edit to change the name. or click Remove to delete the name.

Setting the user's profile information

From the Profile tab, as shown in Figure 11-9, you can configure three bits of information about the user's profile information:

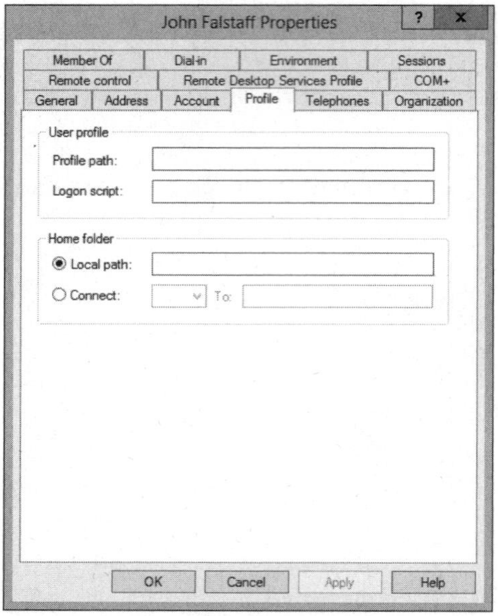

Figure 11-9:
The Profile
tab.

John Falstaff Properties	? X

Member Of	Dial-in	Environment		Sessions
Remote control		Remote Desktop Services Profile		COM+
General	Address	Account	Profile	Telephones	Organization

User profile

Profile path: _____

Logon script: _____

Home folder

◉ Local path: _____

○ Connect: ▽ To: _____

OK	Cancel	Apply	Help

✔ **Profile Path:** This field specifies the location of the user's roaming profile.

✔ **Logon Script:** This field is the name of the user's logon script. A *logon script* is a batch file that's run whenever the user logs on. The main purpose of the logon script is to map the network shares that the user requires access to. Logon scripts are carryovers from early versions of Windows NT Server. In Windows Server 2012, profiles are the preferred way to configure the user's computer when the user logs on, including setting up network shares. Many administrators still like the simplicity of logon scripts, however. For more information, see the section "Creating a Logon Script," later in this chapter.

✔ **Home Folder:** This section is where you specify the default storage location for the user.

From the Profile tab, you can specify the location of an existing profile for the user, but it doesn't actually let you set up the profile.

Resetting User Passwords

By some estimates, the single most time-consuming task of most network administrators is resetting user passwords. Lest you assume that all users are forgetful idiots, put yourself in their shoes, being made to set their passwords to something incomprehensible (94kD82leL384K) that they have change a week later to something more unmemorable (dJUQ63DWd8331) that they don't write down. Then network admins get mad when they forget their passwords.

Sooo, when a user calls and says that she forgot her password, the least you can do is (appear to) be cheerful when you reset it. After all, the user probably spent 15 minutes trying to remember it before finally giving up and admitting failure.

Here's the procedure to reset the password for a user domain account:

1. **Log on as an administrator.**

   You must have administrator privileges to perform this procedure.

2. **Choose Start⇨Administrative Tools⇨Active Directory Users and Computers.**

   The Active Directory Users and Computers management console appears.

3. **In the Active Directory Users and Computers management console, click Users in the console tree.**

   Refer back to Figure 11-1.

4. **In the Details pane, right-click the user who forgot her password and then choose Reset Password from the contextual menu.**

   A dialog box appears allowing you to change the password.

5. **Enter the new password in both password boxes.**

   Enter the password twice to ensure that you input it correctly.

6. **(Optional) Select the User Must Change Password at Next Logon option.**

   If you select this option, the password that you assign will work for only one logon. As soon as the user logs on, she will be required to change the password.

7. **Click OK.**

   That's all there is to it! The user's password is reset.

Disabling and Enabling User Accounts

To temporarily prevent a user from accessing the network, you can disable his account. You can always enable the account later, when you're ready to restore the user to full access. Here's the procedure:

1. **Log on as an administrator.**

   You must have administrator privileges to perform this procedure.

2. **From Server Manager, choose Tools⇨Active Directory Users and Computers.**

3. **In the Active Directory Users and Computers management console that appears, click Users in the console tree.**

4. **In the Details pane, right-click the user that you want to enable or disable; then choose either Enable Account or Disable Account from the contextual menu to enable or disable the user, respectively.**

Deleting a User

People come, and people go. And when they go, so should their user account. Deleting a user account is surprisingly easy. Just follow these steps:

1. **Log on as an administrator.**

   You must have administrator privileges to perform this procedure.

2. **Choose Start⇨Administrative Tools⇨Active Directory Users and Computers.**

3. **In the Active Directory Users and Computers management console that appears, click Users in the console tree.**

4. **In the Details pane, right-click the user that you want to delete and then choose Delete from the contextual menu.**

   Windows asks whether you really want to delete the user, just in case you're kidding.

5. **Click Yes.**

   Poof! The user account is deleted.

Deleting a user account is a permanent, nonreversible action. Do it only if you're absolutely sure that you never ever want to restore the user's account. If there's any possibility of restoring the account later, disable the account instead of deleting it. (See the preceding section.)

Working with Groups

A *group* is a special type of account that represents a set of users who have common network access needs. Groups can dramatically simplify the task of assigning network access rights to users. Rather than assign access rights to each user individually, you can assign rights to the group itself. Then those rights automatically extend to any user you add to the group.

The following sections describe some of the key concepts that you need to understand to use groups, along with some of the most common procedures you'll employ when setting up groups for your server.

Creating a group

Here's how to create a group:

1. **Log on as an administrator.**

   You must have administrator privileges to perform this procedure.

2. **From Server Manager, choose Tools⇨Active Directory Users and Computers.**

   The Active Directory Users and Computers management console appears.

3. **Right-click the domain to which you want to add the group and then choose New⇨Group from the contextual menu.**

4. **In the New Object – Group dialog box that appears, as shown in Figure 11-10, enter the name for the new group.**

   Enter the name in both text boxes.

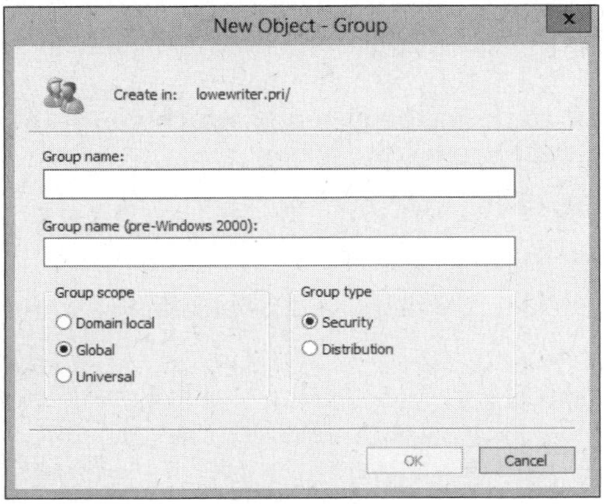

Figure 11-10:
Create a
new group.

5. **Choose the group scope.**

   The choices are

   - *Domain Local:* For groups that will be granted access rights to network resources

   - *Global:* For groups to which you'll add users and Domain Local groups

   - *Universal:* If you have a large network with multiple domains

6. **Choose the group type.**

   The choices are Security and Distribution. In most cases, choose Security.

7. **Click OK.**

   The group is created. However, at this point, it has no members. To remedy that, keep reading.

Adding a member to a group

Groups are collections of objects called *members*. The members of a group can be user accounts or other groups. A newly created group (see the preceding section) has no members. As you can see, a group isn't useful until you add at least one member.

Follow these steps to add a member to a group:

1. **Log on as an administrator.**

   You must have administrator privileges to perform this procedure.

2. **Choose Start↪Administrative Tools↪Active Directory Users and Computers.**

   The Active Directory Users and Computers management console appears.

3. **Open the folder that contains the group to which you want to add members and then double-click the group.**

   The Group Properties dialog box appears.

4. **Click the Members tab.**

   The members of the group are displayed, as shown in Figure 11-11.

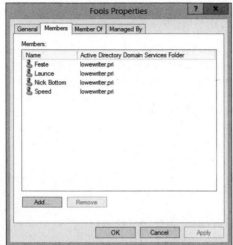

Figure 11-11:
Adding
members to
a group.

5. **Click Add, type the name of a user or other group that you want to add to this group, and then click OK.**

   The member is added to the list.

6. **Repeat Step 5 for each user that you want to add.**

   Keep going until you add everyone!

7. **Click OK.**

That's all there is to it.

On the Member Of tab of the Group Properties dialog box, you can see a list of each group that the current group is a member of.

Creating a Logon Script

A *logon script* is a batch file that's run automatically whenever a user logs on. The most common reason for using a logon script is to map the network shares that the user needs access to. Here's a simple logon script that maps three network shares:

```
echo off
net use m: \\server1\shares\admin
net use n: \\server1\shares\mktg
net use o: \\server2\archives
```

Here, two shares on server1 are mapped to drives M: and N:, and a share on server2 is mapped as drive O:.

If you want, you can use the special variable %username% to get the user's username. This variable is useful if you created a folder for each user, and you want to map a drive to each user's folder, as follows:

```
net use u: \\server1\users\%username%
```

If a user logs on with the username dlowe, for example, drive U: is mapped to \\server1\users\dlowe.

Scripts should be saved in the Scripts folder, which is buried deep in the bowels of the SYSVOL folder — typically, here:

```
c:\Windows\SYSVOL\Sysvol\domainname\Scripts
```

where *domainname* is your domain name. Because you need to access this folder frequently, I suggest creating a shortcut to it on your desktop.

After you create a logon script, you can assign it to a user by using the Profile tab of the User Properties dialog box. For more information, see the section "Setting the user's profile information," earlier in this chapter.

Chapter 12

Managing Network Storage

In This Chapter
▶ Understanding network storage
▶ Setting permissions
▶ Sharing folders
▶ Configuring and managing a file server

*O*ne key purpose of most computer networks is to provide shared access to disk storage. In this chapter, you find out about several ways that a network can provide shared disk storage. Then you discover how to configure Windows Server 2012 to operate as a file server.

Understanding Network Storage

Many network servers exist solely for the purpose of making disk space available to network users. As networks grow to support more users and as users require more disk space, network administrators are continually finding ways to add more storage to their networks. The following sections describe some key concepts for providing network storage.

File servers

A *file server* is simply a network server whose primary role is to share its disk drives. Using a file server is the most common way to provide shared network storage.

A file server can be anything from a simple desktop computer that has been pressed into service as a file server to an expensive ($25,000 or more) server with redundant components so that the server can continue to run when a component fails. A file server can even consist of advanced disk subsystems with racks of disk drives that can be replaced without shutting down the server.

One of the most common advanced disk subsystems for file servers is Redundant Array of Inexpensive Disks (RAID). A *RAID* system, which is a type of disk storage that hardly ever fails, works by lumping together several disk drives and treating them as though they're a single humongous drive. RAID uses some fancy techniques devised by computer nerds at Berkeley. These techniques ensure that if one of the disk drives in the RAID system fails, no data is lost. The disk drive that failed can be removed and repaired, and the data that was on it can be reconstructed from the other drives.

Most of this chapter is devoted to showing you how to configure Windows Server 2012 to run as a file server.

Storage appliances

A *storage appliance* is a device specifically designed for providing shared network storage. Also known as Network Attached Storage (NAS), it's a self-contained file server that's preconfigured and ready to run. All you have to do to set it up is take it out of the box, plug it in, and turn it on. Storage appliances are easy to set up and configure, easy to maintain, and less expensive than traditional file servers.

A typical entry-level storage appliance is the Dell PowerVault NX300. This self-contained file server is built into a small rack-mount chassis. It supports up to four hard drives with a total capacity of up to 12 terabytes (TB; that's 12,000GB). The Dell NX300 runs a special version of Windows Server: Windows Storage Server. This version of Windows, designed specifically for NAS devices, allows you to configure the network storage from any computer on the network by using a web browser.

Note that some storage appliances use customized versions of Linux rather than Windows Storage Server. Also, in some systems, the operating system (OS) resides on a separate hard drive that's isolated from the shared disks so users are prevented from inadvertently damaging the OS.

Understanding Permissions

Before I get into the details of setting up a file server, you need to have a solid understanding of the concept of permissions. *Permissions* allow users to access shared resources on a network. Simply sharing a resource, such as a disk folder or a printer, doesn't guarantee that a given user is able to access that resource. Windows makes this decision based on the permissions that have been assigned to various groups for the resource and group memberships of the user. For example, if the user belongs to a group that has been granted permission to access the resource, the access is allowed. If not, access is denied.

In theory, permissions sound pretty simple. In practice, however, they can get pretty complicated. The following paragraphs explain some of the nuances of how access control and permissions work:

- ✔ Every object — that is, every file and folder — on an NTFS volume has a set of permissions — the Access Control List (ACL) — associated with it.

- ✔ The ACL identifies which users and groups can access the object and specifies what level of access each user or group has. A folder's ACL may specify that one group of users can read files in the folder, whereas another group can read and write files in the folder, and a third group is denied access to the folder.

- ✔ Container objects — files and volumes — allow their ACLs to be inherited by the objects that they contain. As a result, if you specify permissions for a folder, those permissions extend to the files and child folders that appear within it.

Table 12-1 lists the six permissions that can be applied to files and folders on an NTFS volume.

Table 12-1	File and Folder Permissions
Permission	*Description*
Full Control	The user has unrestricted access to the file or folder.
Modify	The user can change the file or folder's contents, delete the file or folder, read the file or folder, or change the attributes of the file or folder. For a folder, this permission allows you to create new files or subfolders within the folder.
Read & Execute	For a file, this permission grants the right to read or execute the file. For a folder, this permission grants the right to list the contents of the folder or to read or execute any of the files in the folder.
List Folder Contents	This permission applies only to folders; it grants the right to list the contents of the folder.
Read	This permission grants the right to read the contents of a file or folder.
Write	This permission grants the right to change the contents of a file or its attributes. For a folder, this permission grants the right to create new files and subfolders within the folder.

Actually, the six file and folder permissions comprise various combinations of special permissions that grant more detailed access to files or folders. Table 12-2 lists the special permissions that apply to each of the six file and folder permissions.

Assign permissions to groups rather than to individual users. that way, if a particular user needs access to a particular resource, add that user to a group that has permission to use the resource.

Table 12-2	Special Permissions					
Special Permission	*Full Control*	*Modify*	*Read & Execute*	*List Folder Contents*	*Read*	*Write*
Traverse Folder/ Execute File	*	*	*	*		
List Folder/Read Data	*	*	*	*	*	
Read Extended Attributes	*	*	*	*	*	
Create Files/ Write Data	*	*				*
Create Folders/ Append Data	*	*				*
Write Attributes	*	*				*
Write Extended Attributes	*	*				*
Delete Subfolders and Files	*					
Delete	*	*				
Read Permissions	*	*	*	*	*	*
Change Permissions	*					
Take Ownership	*					
Synchronize	*	*	*	*	*	*

Understanding Shares

A *share* is simply a folder that is made available to other users via the network. Each share has the following elements:

- **Share name:** The name by which the share is known over the network
- **Path:** The path to the folder on the local computer that's being shared, such as `C:\Accounting`

  ✔ **Description:** A one-line description of the share

  ✔ **Permissions:** A list of users or groups who have been granted access to the share

When you install Windows and configure various server roles, special shared resources are created to support those roles. You shouldn't disturb these special shares unless you know what you're doing. Table 12-3 lists some of the most common special shares.

Table 12-3	Special Shares
Share Name	*Description*
drive$	The root directory of a drive.
ADMIN$	Used for remote administration of a computer. This share points to the OS folder (usually, C: \Windows).
IPC$	Used by named pipes, a programming feature that lets processes communicate with one another.
NETLOGON	Required for domain controllers to function.
SYSVOL	Another required domain controller share.
PRINT$	Used for remote administration of printers.
FAX$	Used by fax clients.

Notice that some of the special shares end with a dollar sign ($). These shares are hidden shares, not visible to users. You can still access them, however, by typing the complete share name (including the dollar sign) when the share is needed. The special share C$, for example, is created to allow you to connect to the root directory of the C: drive from a network client. You wouldn't want your users to see this share, would you? (Shares such as C$ are also protected by privileges, of course, so if an ordinary user finds out that C$ is the root directory of the server's C: drive, he still can't access it.)

Managing Your File Server

To manage shares on a Windows Server 2012 system, open the Server Manager, and select File and Storage Services in the task pane on the left side of the window. Then click Shares to reveal the management console shown in Figure 12-1.

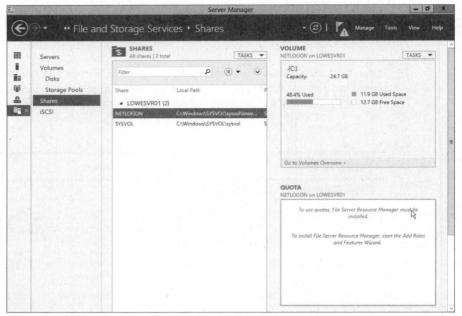

Figure 12-1:
Managing
shares in
Windows
Server 2012.

The following sections describe some of the most common procedures that you'll use when managing your file server.

Using the New Share Wizard

To be useful, a file server should offer one or more *shares* — folders that have been designated as publicly accessible via the network. To create a new share, use the New Share Wizard:

1. **In Server Manager, select File and Storage Services, click Shares and then choose New Share from the Tasks drop-down menu.**

    The opening screen of the New Share Wizard appears, as shown in Figure 12-2. Here, the wizard asks you what folder you want to share.

2. **Select SMB Share – Quick in the list of profiles and then click Next.**

    The New Share Wizard asks for the location of the share, as shown in Figure 12-3.

Figure 12-2:
The New
Share
Wizard
comes to
life.

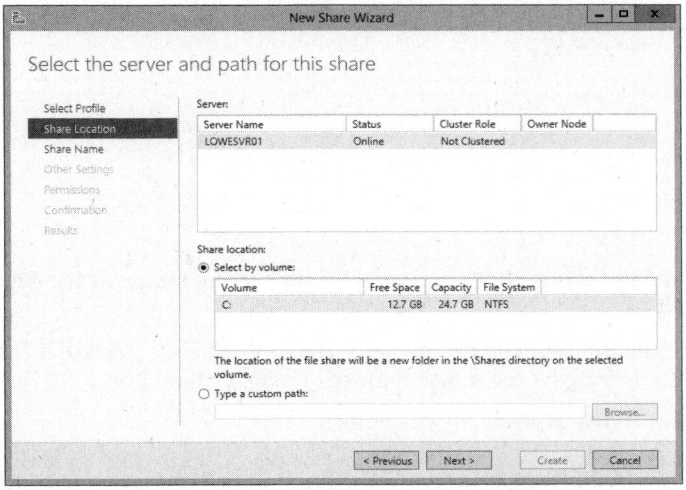

Figure 12-3:
The wizard
asks where
you'd like to
locate the
share.

3. **Select the server where you want the share to reside.**

4. **Select the location of the share by choosing one of these two options:**

   - *Select by Volume:* This option selects the volume on which the shared folder will reside while letting the New Share Wizard create a folder for you. If you select this option, the wizard will create the shared folder on the designated volume. Use this option if the folder doesn't yet exist and you don't mind Windows placing it in the default location, which is inside a folder called `Shares` on the volume you specify.

- *Type a Custom Path:* Use this option if the folder exists or if you want to create one in a location other than the `Shares` folder.

5. **Click Next.**

The dialog box shown in Figure 12-4 appears.

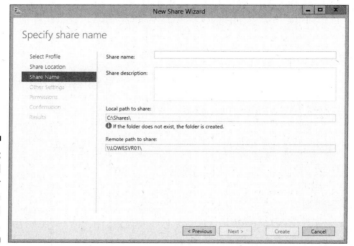

Figure 12-4:
The wizard asks for the share name and description.

6. **Enter the name that you want to use for the share in the Share Name field.**

The default name is the name of the folder being shared. If the folder name is long, you can use a more succinct name here.

7. **Enter a description for the share.**

8. **Click Next.**

The dialog box shown in Figure 12-5 appears.

9. **Select the share settings you'd like to use:**

- *Enable Access-Based Enumeration:* Hides files that the user does not have permission to access

- *Allow Caching of Share:* Makes the files available to offline users

- *Encrypt Data Access:* Encrypts files accessed via the share

10. **Click Next.**

The wizard displays the default permissions that will be used for the new share, as shown in Figure 12-6.

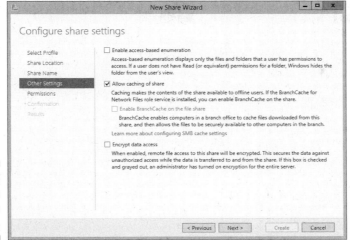

Figure 12-5:
Specify the
share
settings.

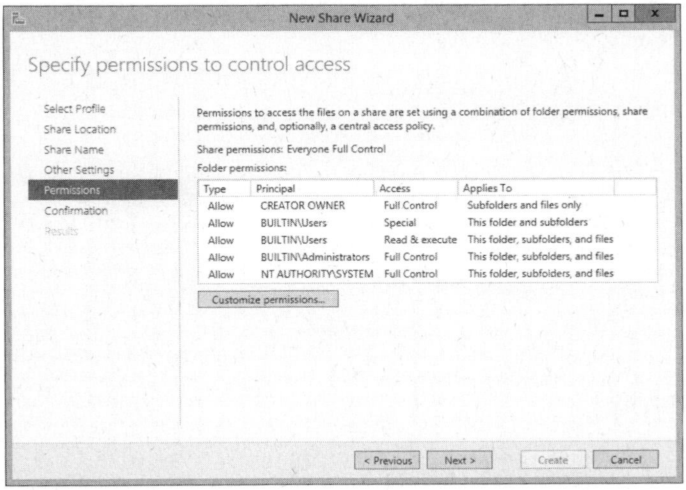

Figure 12-6:
Setting the
share
permissions.

11. **(Optional) If you want to customize the permissions, click the Customize Permissions button.**

Clicking this button summons the Advanced Security Settings for Data dialog box, where you can customize both the NTFS and the share permissions.

12. **Click Next.**

The confirmation page appears, as shown in Figure 12-7.

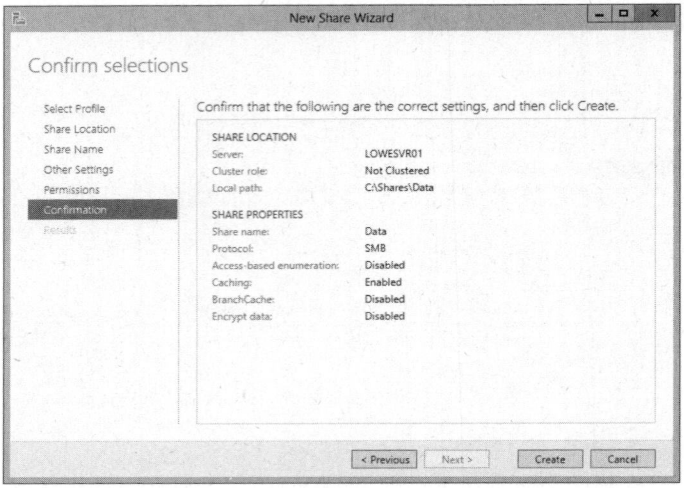

Figure 12-7:
Confirming
your share
settings.

13. **Verify that all the settings are correct and then click the Create button.**

    The share is created, and a results dialog box is displayed, as shown in Figure 12-8.

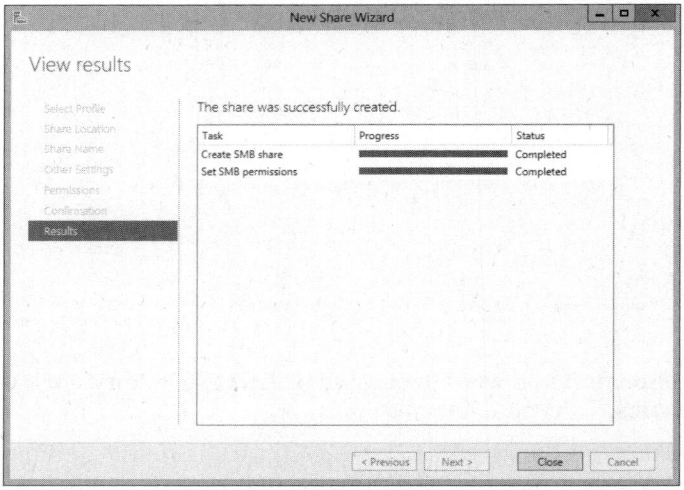

Figure 12-8:
You're
done!

Sharing a folder without the wizard

If you think wizards should be confined to *Harry Potter* movies, you can set up a share without bothering with the wizard. Just follow these steps:

1. **Press the Windows key, click Computer, and navigate to the folder that you want to share.**

2. **Right-click the folder and choose Properties from the contextual menu.**

   This action brings up the Properties dialog box for the folder.

3. **Click the Sharing tab.**

   The Sharing tab comes to the front, as shown in Figure 12-9.

Figure 12-9: Manually share a folder.

4. **Click the Advanced Sharing button.**

   The dialog box shown in Figure 12-10 appears.

5. **Select the Share This Folder check box to designate the folder as shared.**

   The rest of the controls in this dialog box are unavailable until you select this check box.

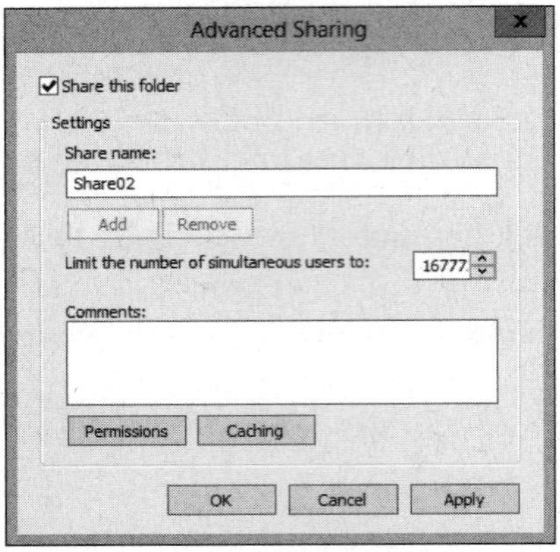

Figure 12-10:
Set the
share name.

6. **Enter the name that you want to use for the share in the Share Name field and then enter a description of the share in the Comments field.**

   The default name is the name of the folder being shared. If the folder name is long, you can use a more succinct name here.

   The description is strictly optional but sometimes helps users determine the intended contents of the folder.

7. **Click the Permissions button and then set the permissions you want to apply to the share.**

   For more information, see the next section.

8. **Click OK.**

   The folder is now shared.

Granting permissions

When you first create a file share, all users are granted read-only access to the share. If you want to allow users to modify files in the share or allow them to create new files, you need to add permissions. Here's how to do this via the Share and Storage Management console:

1. **Open Windows Explorer by pressing the Windows key and clicking Computer; then browse to the folder whose permissions you want to manage.**

2. **Right-click the folder you want to manage and then choose Properties from the contextual menu.**

   The Properties dialog box for the folder appears.

3. Click the Sharing tab; then click Advanced Sharing.

The Advanced Sharing dialog box appears.

4. Click Permissions.

The dialog box shown in Figure 12-11 appears. This dialog box lists all the users and groups to whom you've granted permission for the folder. Initially, read permissions are granted to a group called Everyone, which means that anyone can view files in the share but no one can create, modify, or delete files in the share.

When you select a user or group from the list, the check boxes at the bottom of the list change to indicate which specific permissions you've assigned to each user or group.

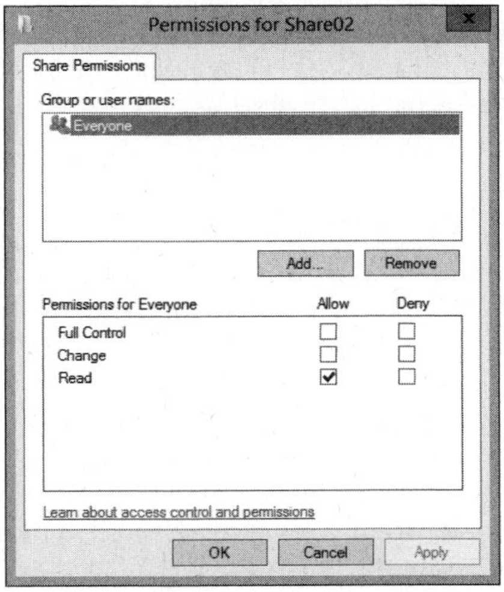

Figure 12-11:
Set the
share
permissions.

5. Click the Add button.

The dialog box shown in Figure 12-12 appears.

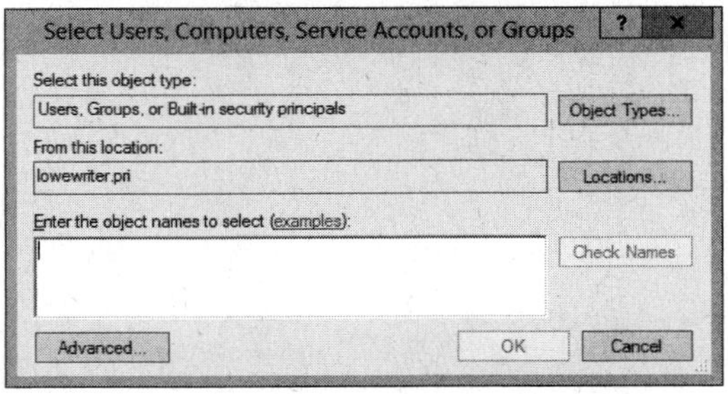

Figure 12-12:
Adding
permissions.

6. **Enter the name of the user or group to whom you want to grant permission and then click OK.**

   If you're not sure of the name, click the Advanced button. This action brings up a dialog box from which you can search for existing users.

   When you click OK, you return to the Share Permissions tab (refer to Figure 12-11), with the new user or group added.

7. **Select the appropriate Allow and Deny check boxes to specify which permissions to allow for the user or group.**

8. **Repeat Steps 5–7 for any other permissions that you want to add.**

9. **When you're done, click OK.**

Here are a few other thoughts to ponder concerning adding permissions:

- ✔ If you want to grant full access to everyone for this folder, don't bother adding another permission. Instead, select the Everyone group and then select the Allow check box for each permission type.

- ✔ You can remove a permission by selecting the permission and then clicking the Remove button.

- ✔ If you'd rather not fuss with the Share and Storage Management console, you can set the permissions from My Computer. Right-click the shared folder, choose Sharing and Security from the contextual menu, and then click Permissions. Then you can follow the preceding procedure, picking up at Step 5.

- ✔ The permissions assigned in this procedure apply only to the share itself. The underlying folder can also have permissions assigned to it. If that's the case, whichever of the restrictions is most restrictive always applies. If the share permissions grant a user Full Control permission but the folder permission grants the user only Read permission, for example, the user has only Read permission for the folder.

Chapter 13

Managing Exchange Server 2010

*A*lthough not strictly a part of Windows Server 2012, Exchange Server 2010 is the mail server software that's used on most Windows networks. Yes, I know Microsoft doesn't call Exchange Server a "mail server." It's a "messaging and collaboration server." But the basic reason for Exchange Server's existence is e-mail. The other messaging and collaboration features are just icing on the cake.

In this chapter, you discover how to perform the most commonly requested maintenance chores for Exchange Server, such as how to create a new mailbox, grant a user access to an additional mailbox, and deal with mailbox size limits.

Creating a Mailbox

In previous versions of Exchange, you created user mailboxes using Active Directory Users and Computers (ADUC). With Exchange 2010, however, Microsoft has removed the Exchange management features of ADUC. So instead, you create and manage user mailboxes using Exchange Management Console, which you can find in Server Manager on the Tools menu.

The Exchange Management Console lets you create a mailbox for an existing Active Directory (AD) user. (Refer to Chapter 11 for information about creating Active Directory users.) Or you can use Exchange Management Console to create a new user with a mailbox. Because that's the most likely case, the following procedure describes the steps you should follow to create a new AD user with a mailbox:

1. **From Server Manager, choose Tools➪Microsoft Exchange Server 2010➪Exchange Management Console.**

   This fires up the Exchange Management Console, as shown in Figure 13-1.

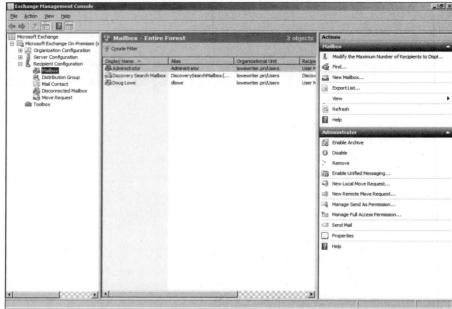

Figure 13-1:
The
Exchange
Management
Console.

2. In the Navigation pane (left side of the window), navigate to Microsoft Exchange⇨Microsoft Exchange On-Premises⇨Recipient Configuration.

If you have more than one Exchange server, pick the Microsoft Exchange On-Premises node for the server you want to add the user to.

3. Right-click the Mailbox node in the navigation pane and choose New Mailbox.

This summons the New Mailbox Wizard, as shown in Figure 13-2. From here, the first page of the wizard, you choose among several different types of mailbox accounts you can create.

4. Select the User Mailbox radio button and then click Next.

This brings up the User Type page, as shown in Figure 13-3. Here, you indicate whether you want to create a new user account or add a mailbox for an existing AD user.

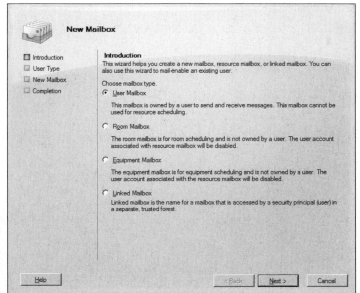

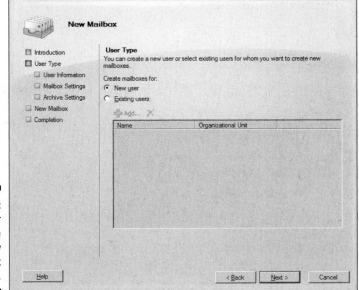

5. **Select the New User radio button and then click Next.**

   The User Information page is displayed, as shown in Figure 13-4.

6. **Enter the user's first name, middle initial, and last name.**

   As you type the name, the New Mailbox Wizard automatically fills in the Name field.

7. **(Optional) Change the Name field if you want it to appear different from what was proposed.**

   You may want to reverse the first and last names so the last name appears first, for example.

8. **Enter the user logon name.**

   This name must be unique within the domain and will be used to form the user's e-mail address.

9. **Enter the password twice.**

   You're asked to type the password twice, so type it correctly. If you don't type it identically in both boxes, you're asked to correct your mistake.

10. **If the password is temporary, select the User Must Change Password at Next Logon check box.**

    This setting requires the user to change the temporary password the first time he logs on.

11. **Click Next.**

    The Mailbox Settings page is displayed, as shown in Figure 13-5, where you can create an alias for the user's account name and also set several Exchange options for the user's mailbox.

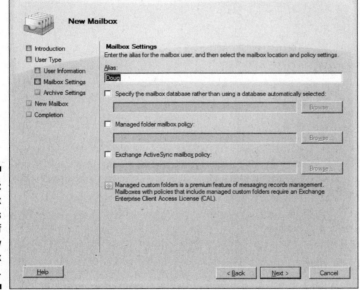

Figure 13-5:
The Mailbox Settings page of the New Mailbox Wizard.

12. **Enter an alias for the user and then click Next.**

    The alias can be the same as the name that was used in the Name field on the previous page of the wizard, or you can type a different name if you want.

    When you click Next, the page shown in Figure 13-6 is displayed.

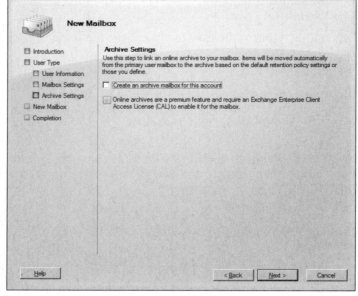

13. If you want to create an archive mailbox for the user, select the Create an Archive Mailbox for This Account check box; otherwise, leave the option deselected.

Archive mailboxes are available only with the Enterprise Edition of Exchange Server 2010, so don't even think about this option unless you've shelled out the money for Enterprise Edition.

14. Click Next.

You're taken to the final page of the New Mailbox Wizard, as shown in Figure 13-7.

15. Verify that the information is correct and then click New to create the mailbox.

If the account information is not correct, click the Back button and correct the error.

When you click Next, Exchange Management Console displays various and sundry messages and progress bars as it creates the user account and its mailbox. When it's finished, the Completion page shown in Figure 13-8 is displayed.

16. Pat yourself on the back; then click Finish.

You're done!

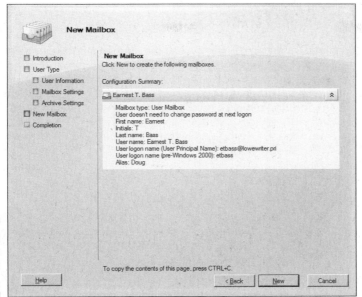

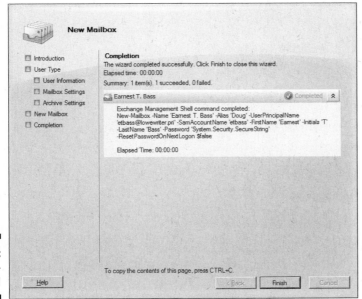

Managing Mailboxes

After you set up a mailbox, you can use the Exchange Management Console to manage the basic settings of the mailbox. To do that, right-click the mailbox you want to manage and choose the Properties command from the contextual menu. This action brings up the Properties dialog box, which is the portal that grants access to many of the most frequently used features of Exchange.

The following sections describe several commonly used features that are controlled via this dialog box.

Enabling mailbox features

Exchange Mailbox Features refers to several features of Exchange mailboxes that are controlled via the Mailbox Features tab of the mailbox Properties dialog box. This tab is shown in Figure 13-9.

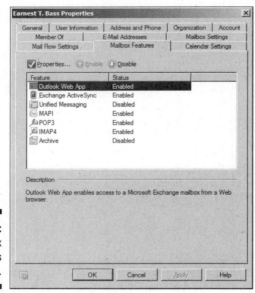

Figure 13-9:
The Mailbox
Features
tab.

The following paragraphs describe the features that are controlled from this tab:

- ✔ **Outlook Web App:** Lets the user access her Exchange mailbox from a web browser rather than from an Outlook client. With this feature enabled, the user can read e-mail from any computer that has an Internet connection. This feature used to be called Outlook Web Access.

- ✔ **Exchange ActiveSync:** Activates the ActiveSync feature, which allows Exchange data to synchronize with mobile devices, such as iPhones or Windows Mobile phones.

- ✔ **Unified Messaging:** Enables a premium feature (available only with Enterprise Edition) that integrates voice mail and fax messages with Exchange mailboxes.

- ✔ **MAPI:** Enables e-mail using the MAPI protocol. This protocol is enabled by default and is the most common way to access e-mail with Microsoft Outlook.

- ✔ **POP3:** Enables e-mail using the POP3 protocol. POP3 is disabled by default and should be enabled only if the user will need to access e-mail using an e-mail client that requires the POP3 protocol.

- ✔ **IMAP4:** Enables e-mail using the IMAP4 protocol. IMAP4 is disabled by default and should be enabled only if required to support an IMAP4 e-mail client.

- ✔ **Archive:** Enables the Exchange Archive feature, which (as I mention earlier) is available only with the Enterprise edition of Exchange.

Creating a forwarder

A *forwarder* is a feature that automatically forwards any incoming e-mail to another e-mail address. This feature is most often used when an employee is on vacation or leave, and the employee's manager requests that someone else temporarily handle the absent employee's e-mail.

To configure a forwarder, follow these steps:

1. **In Server Manager, choose Tools⇨Microsoft Exchange Server 2010⇨ Exchange Management Console.**

   This command fires up the Exchange Management Console (refer to Figure 13-1).

2. **In the Navigation pane, navigate to Microsoft Exchange⇨Microsoft Exchange On-Premises⇨Recipient Configuration.**

3. **Right-click the mailbox for the user whose e-mail you want to forward and then choose Properties from the contextual menu.**

   This summons the mailbox Properties dialog box.

4. **Click the Mail Flow Settings tab.**

   The Mail Flow settings are displayed, as shown in Figure 13-10.

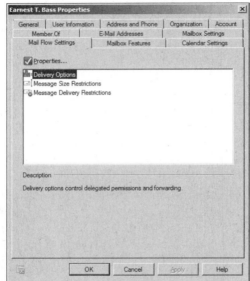

5. **Double-click Delivery Options.**

   The Delivery Options dialog box appears.

6. **Select the Forward To check box.**

7. **Click the Browse button.**

   The Select Recipient dialog box appears.

8. **Select the recipient you want to forward the e-mail to and then click OK.**

   The name you selected is displayed in the text box next to the Browse button in the Delivery Options dialog box.

9. **(Optional) If you want the e-mail to be delivered to this user's mailbox in addition to the forwarding address, select the Deliver Message to Both Forwarding Address and Mailbox check box.**

   If you leave this option deselected, only the forwarding address will receive the e-mail; the mail won't be delivered to this user's mailbox.

10. **Click OK to close the Delivery Options dialog box.**

    You return to the mailbox Properties dialog box.

11. **Click OK to dismiss the Properties dialog box.**

Setting mailbox storage limits

Exchange lets you set a limit on the size of each user's mailbox. In a very small organization, you can probably get away without imposing strict mailbox size limits. If your organization has 20 or more users, though, you need to limit the size of each user's mailbox to prevent the Exchange private mail store from getting out of hand.

Exchange provides three kinds of storage limits for user mailboxes:

✔ **Issue Warning At:** When this limit is exceeded, an e-mail warning is sent to the user to let him know that his mailbox is getting large.

✔ **Prohibit Send At:** When this limit is reached, the user can't send e-mail, but the mailbox continues to receive e-mail. The user won't be able to send e-mails again until she deletes enough e-mails to reduce the mailbox size below the limit.

✔ **Prohibit Send and Receive At:** When this limit is reached, the mailbox shuts down and can neither send nor receive e-mails.

You can (and should) set a default storage limit that applies to all mailboxes in your organization. You can also override these limits for specific users. The limits you set will depend on many factors, including the number of users in your organization, the type of e-mail they typically use (for example, do they require large attachments?), and the amount of disk space available on your Exchange server.

To configure the default storage limits for all mailboxes, follow these steps:

1. **In Server Manager, choose Tools➪Microsoft Exchange Server 2010➪ Exchange Management Console.**

   This command fires up the Exchange Management Console (refer to Figure 13-1).

2. **In the Navigation pane, navigate to Microsoft Exchange➪Microsoft Exchange On-Premises➪Organization Configuration➪Mailbox.**

   The organization's mailbox configuration displays, as shown in Figure 13-11.

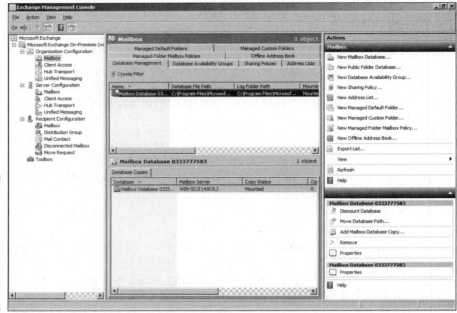

Figure 13-11:
The Orga-
nization
Mailbox
page of the
Exchange
Management
Console.

3. **In the list of mailbox databases, right-click the mailbox database and then choose Properties from the contextual menu.**

   Usually, only one mailbox database is listed; the mailbox database is highlighted in Figure 13-11.

   When you choose Properties, the Mailbox Database Properties dialog box is displayed.

4. **Click the Limits tab.**

   The Limits tab is displayed, as shown in Figure 13-12.

5. **Change the Storage Limits settings to meet your needs.**

   By default, the storage limits are set quite high: Warnings are issued at about 1.9GB, send permission is revoked at 2GB, and both send and receive permissions are revoked at about 2.4GB. A 2GB allowance for each user's mailbox is generous, but bear in mind that if you have 100 users, your mailbox database may grow to 200GB. You may want to set lower limits.

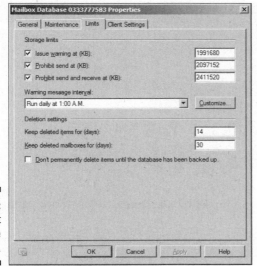

Figure 13-12:
Set default
storage
limits.

6. **Click OK.**

   The limits you set take effect immediately.

If you impose restrictive default storage limits for your users, you may want to relax the limits on a case-by-case basis. Some users may require a larger mailbox because of the type of work they do, and you probably don't want to impose a tight limit on your boss.

Fortunately, overriding the default limits for a specific user is easy. Here are the steps:

1. **In Exchange Management Console, navigate to Microsoft Exchange⇨ Microsoft Exchange On-Premises⇨Recipient Configuration⇨Mailbox.**

2. **Right-click the user for whom you want to override the limits and choose Properties.**

   This summons the Mailbox Properties dialog box.

3. **Click the Mailbox Settings tab.**

4. **Double-click Storage Quotas.**

   The Storage Quotas dialog box appears, as shown in Figure 13-13.

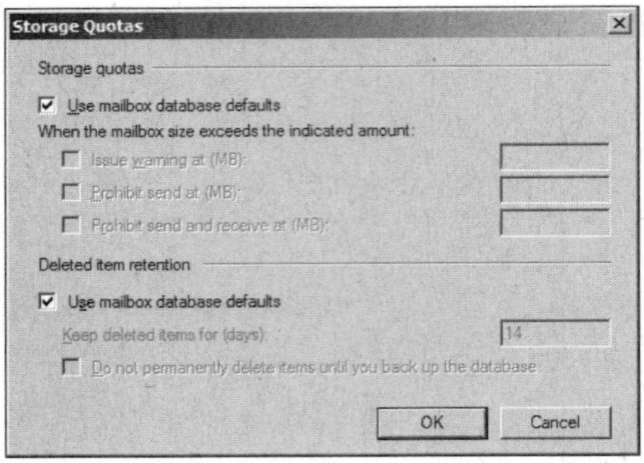

Figure 13-13:
Customize
storage
quotas here.

5. **Deselect the Use Mailbox Database Defaults check box in the Storage Quotas section.**

   This option enables the controls that let you set the Issue Warning, Prohibit Send, and Prohibit Send and Receive limits.

6. **Set the appropriate limits for the user.**

7. **Click OK.**

   The storage limits are configured.

You can configure many other features of Exchange via the Exchange Management Console. You should take some time to explore all the nodes in the navigation pane and to examine the Properties dialog boxes for the various types of Exchange objects that appear when you select each node.

Configuring Outlook for Exchange

After you create an Exchange mailbox for a user, you can configure that user's Outlook client software to connect to the user's account. Although you can do this configuration directly within Outlook, it's better to do it outside Outlook, using the Control Main Mail applet. Here are the steps:

1. **Open Control Panel and then open the Mail applet.**

   The dialog box shown in Figure 13-14 appears.

2. **Click the Show Profiles button.**

   The dialog box shown in Figure 13-15 appears, listing the mail profiles that already exist on the computer.

Figure 13-14:
The Mail
Setup
dialog box.

Figure 13-15:
Viewing
mail
profiles.

3. Double-click the user's profile.

The Mail Setup dialog box shown in Figure 13-16 appears.

Figure 13-16:
The Mail
Setup
dialog box.

4. **Click the E-mail Accounts button.**

   The Account Settings dialog box appears, as shown in Figure 13-17.

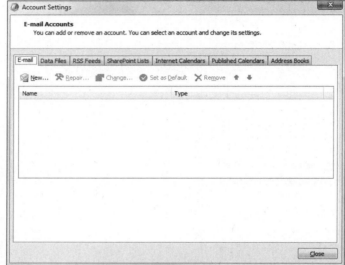

Figure 13-17:
The
Account
Settings
dialog box.

5. **Click the New icon.**

   An Add E-mail Account dialog box appears.

   Don't enter your e-mail address as prompted in this dialog box; instead, proceed to Step 6.

6. **Click the Manually Configure Server Settings or Additional Server Types option and then click Next.**

   A dialog box asks you what type of e-mail account you want to create. The choices are Internet E-mail, Microsoft Exchange, and Other.

7. **Select the Microsoft Exchange option and then click Next.**

   The dialog box shown in Figure 13-18 appears.

8. **Enter the name of the Exchange server and the username in the appropriate text boxes; then click Next.**

   A dialog box displays the following message:

   ```
   The E-Mail account you have just added will not start until you choose Exit
               from the File menu, and then restart Microsoft Outlook.
   ```

9. **Click OK.**

   The message dialog box disappears, and the last page of the E-Mail Accounts Wizard appears.

10. **Click the Finish button.**

    The wizard is dismissed.

11. **Choose File⇨Exit to close Outlook.**

12. **Restart Outlook.**

    The mailbox should be configured.

Chapter 14

Creating an Intranet

*N*o, I'm not mispronouncing *Internet,* although an intranet is similar to the Internet, but with a twist. Rather than connect your computer to millions of other computers around the world, an intranet connects your computer to other computers in your company or organization. How is an intranet different from your ordinary, run-of-the-mill network? Read on, and I'll explain.

Defining an Intranet

Everyone knows that the Internet, and especially the World Wide Web, is a phenomenon. Millions of computer users worldwide surf the web, sharing and downloading files.

Companies realized that such a platform would help employees share and access data and documents. But understandably, not many companies wanted their proprietary and private info all over the web. So ingenious network managers at large companies figured out that although "the" web is a great conduit for distributing public information around the world, "a" web — a private internal web — is even better for distributing sensitive information within a company. Thus, the idea of intranets was born. An *intranet* is simply a network that's built by using the same tools and protocols that are used by the global Internet but applied instead to an organization's internal network.

Think of an intranet as a small, private version of the World Wide Web. Anyone who connects to your local area network (LAN) can access your intranet. The intranet is accessed by using a web browser, such as Internet Explorer or Firefox. However, users don't need an Internet connection because the information on the intranet is stored on the company's server computers rather than on a computer that must be accessed from the Internet.

An intranet is analogous to a closed-circuit television system that can be viewed only by people within the organization that owns the system. In contrast, the Internet is more like cable television in that anyone who's willing to pay a monthly fee can watch.

Here are two interesting but contradictory points of view about the significance of intranets:

- ✔ Some computer industry pundits say that intranets are more popular than the Internet. For example, many companies that sell web development tools make more money selling software used for intranets than for the Internet.

- ✔ On the other hand, other industry pundits think that the intranet phenomenon is merely a fad that some other promising new technology, such as pet rocks or hula hoops, will replace in a few years. Only time will tell.

Identifying Intranet Uses

Intranets can distribute just about any type of information within a company. Intranets use two basic types of applications:

- ✔ **Publishing application:** Information is posted in the form of pages that you can view from any computer with access to the intranet. This type of intranet application is commonly used for company newsletters, policy manuals, and price lists, for example.

  Publishing applications are simple to set up. In fact, you may be able to set up one without a lot of outside help from highly paid computer consultants.

- ✔ **Transaction application:** Information is gathered from users of the intranet who file online expense reports, report problems to the help desk, or enroll in employee benefit programs, for example.

  Expect to spend big bucks on computer consulting to get an intranet transaction application set up.

A webless intranet

The correct way to set up a proper intranet is to set up a Windows-based server running IIS or a Linux-based server running Apache or some other web server. However, you can create a rudimentary intranet without going to the trouble of setting up an actual web server. Here's how:

1. **Set up a share on a file server that will hold the HTML files that make up your intranet.**

2. **Create an HTML file for the home page of your intranet, and save the file in the location you create in Step 1.**

   I recommend that you name it `index.html`.

3. **Create any other HTML files that your intranet needs.**

   The `index.html` file should include links to these pages.

4. **Point your web browser to the `index.html` file at the shared network location.**

   For example, if the server is named `iserver` and the share is named `intranet`, enter this information into your browser's address box: **\\iserver\ intranet\index.html**. *Voilà!* — you have an instant intranet without the fuss of a web server.

This rudimentary intranet works without a web server because a web browser can display HTML files directly, without the need for a web server. However, without a web server, your intranet is limited in what it can do. In particular, all its pages must be *static* (their content is fixed). For *dynamic* content, which users interact with, you need to set up a web server.

Here's the key difference between these two types of intranet applications:

- ✔ **In a publishing application, information flows in one direction.** It flows from the intranet to the user. The user requests some information, and the intranet system delivers it.

- ✔ **In a transaction application, information flows in both directions.** Not only does the user request information from the intranet system, but the intranet system itself also requests information from the user.

Setting Up an Intranet

To properly set up an intranet, you need the right tools. Here's a list of requirements:

- ✔ **A network:** An intranet doesn't require its own cabling; it can operate on your existing network.

- ✔ **A server computer that's dedicated to the intranet:** Make sure that this computer has plenty of RAM (at least 4GB) and gigabytes of disk space (at least 100GB). Of course, the more users your network has and the more information you intend to place on the server, the more RAM and disk storage you need.

✔ **Windows Server or a Linux operating system:** Web server software requires one or the other.

✔ **Web server software for the server computer:** You need to install a web server, such as IIS (for Windows servers) or Apache (for Linux servers).

✔ **Programs to help you create web pages:** If you're the type who dreams in binary, you can create web pages by typing HTML codes directly into text files. In that case, the only program you need is Notepad. Alternatively, you can use a program designed specifically for creating web pages, such as Microsoft FrontPage, or perhaps something fancier, such as Adobe Dreamweaver. If you're going to develop transaction-based applications, you need additional tools.

Setting Up an IIS Web Server

IIS is a free component of Windows Server 2012, but it's not installed by default. After you complete installing Windows Server, you must add the Web Server role to enable IIS. The following procedure is for Windows Server 2012, but the procedure for Windows 2008 Server (or 2003, for that matter) is similar:

1. **Open the Server Manager; then choose Add Roles and Features.**

   The Add Roles and Features Wizard comes to life.

2. **Follow the steps of the Add Roles and Features Wizard up to the Select Server Roles step.**

   The Select Server Roles page is shown in Figure 14-1.

3. **Select the Web Server (IIS) check box and then click Next.**

   The Add Roles and Features Wizard asks whether you want to install the related IIS Management Console, as shown in Figure 14-2.

4. **Click the Add Features button; then click Next.**

   The Select Features page appears.

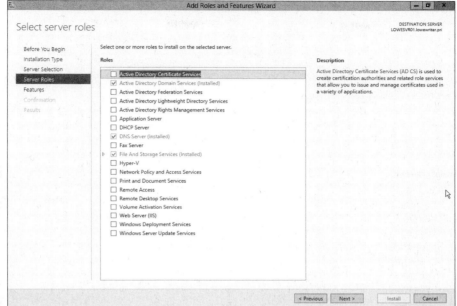

Figure 14-1:
The Select
Server
Roles page
of the Add
Roles and
Features
Wizard.

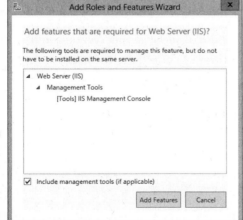

Figure 14-2:
Installing
the IIS
Management
Console.

5. **Click Next.**

   The Web Server Role (IIS) page appears, as shown in Figure 14-3.

Figure 14-3:
The Web
Server Role
(IIS) page
of the Add
Roles and
Features
Wizard.

6. Click Next.

The Select Role Services page appears, as shown in Figure 14-4. This page lists a variety of optional services that can be configured for IIS.

7. Select the services you want to configure for IIS.

If you want, you can study this list and try to anticipate which features you think you'll need. Or you can just leave the default options selected.

You can always return to the Add Roles and Features Wizard to add features you leave out here.

8. Click Next.

A confirmation page appears.

9. Click Install.

The features you selected are installed. This may take a few minutes, so now would be a good time to take a walk.

When the installation finishes, an Installation Results page is displayed to verify that IIS was properly installed.

10. Click Close.

IIS is now installed and ready to use!

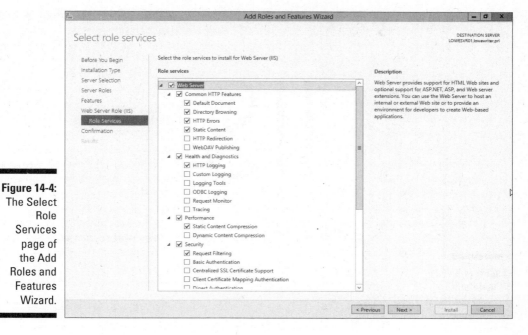

Figure 14-4:
The Select
Role
Services
page of
the Add
Roles and
Features
Wizard.

Understanding the Default Website

Initially, IIS is configured with a single website: the *default website*. You can test that IIS is up and running by opening a browser window on the server and typing **localhost** in the address bar. You can also reach this page by entering your local domain name in the address bar, such as **lowewriter.pri**. Figure 14-5 shows the standard welcome page that appears when you browse to the default site.

The actual files that make up the default website are stored on the server's C: drive in a folder named `\inetpub\wwwroot`. When you browse to the default website without requesting a specific file (simply by typing **localhost** in the address bar, for example), IIS looks for the following files, in this order:

- `default.htm`
- `default.asp`
- `index.htm`
- `index.html`
- `iisstart.htm`
- `default.aspx`

Figure 14-5:
The default
website.

Initially, `c:\inetpub\wwwroot` contains just two files: `iisstart.htm` and `welcome.png`. The `iisstart.htm` file is the file that's displayed when you browse to the website; it contains the HTML markup necessary to display the image contained in the `welcome.png` file, which is the image you actually see on the page.

You can preempt the standard page for the default website by providing your own file one of the preceding names. You can follow these steps, for example, to create a simple `default.htm` file that displays the words *Hello World!* as the start page for the default website:

1. **Open an Explorer window, and browse to `c:\inetpub\wwwroot`.**

2. **Choose File⇨New⇨Text Document, type** default.htm **for the filename, and press Enter.**

3. **Right-click the `default.htm` file you just created and choose Open With⇨Notepad from the contextual menu.**

4. **Enter the following text in the Notepad window:**

```
<HTML>
<BODY>
<H1>Hello World!</H1>
</BODY>
</HTML>
```

5. **Choose File⇨Save to save the file and then choose File⇨Exit to quit Notepad.**

6. **Open a browser window.**

7. **Type** localhost **in the address bar, and press Enter.**

   The page shown in Figure 14-6 appears.

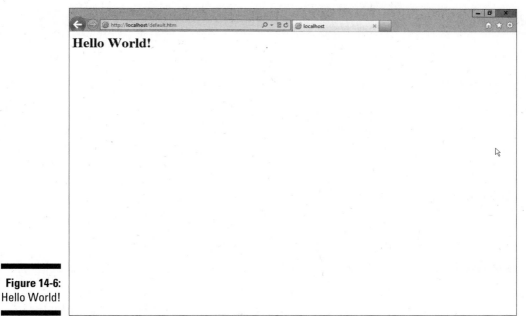

Figure 14-6:
Hello World!

Creating Websites

IIS has the ability to host multiple websites. This is an extremely useful feature not only for web servers that host public sites, but also for web servers that host internal (intranet) sites. You might create a separate intranet website for Human Resources and assign it the website name hr. Then, assuming that the domain name is lowewriter.pri, users can browse to the website by using the address hr.lowewriter.pri.

Here are the steps:

1. **Using Windows Explorer, create a folder in which you will save the files for the new website.**

   For this example, I created a folder named c:\HR-Web-Site.

2. **In Server Manager, choose Tools⇨Internet Information Services (IIS) Manager.**

   The IIS Manager springs to life, as shown in Figure 14-7.

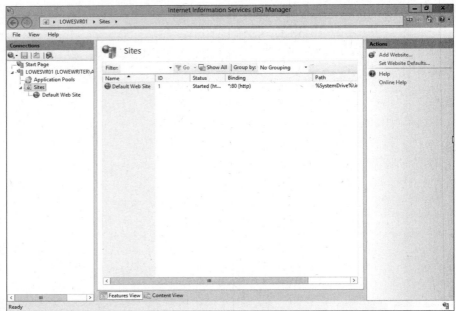

Figure 14-7:
The IIS
Manager.

3. **Right-click Sites and then choose Add Website from the contextual menu.**

   The Add Website dialog box appears, as shown in Figure 14-8.

4. **Enter a name for the website in the Site Name text box.**

   For this example, I used HR.

5. **Click the Browse button (the one with the ellipsis), browse to the folder you created in Step 1, and then click OK.**

   For this example, I browsed to C:\HR-Web-Site.

6. **In the Host Name text box, enter the exact DNS name you want to use for the site.**

   For this example, I entered **hr.lowewriter.pri**.

7. **Click OK.**

   The newly created website appears below the Sites node in the IIS Manager, as shown in Figure 14-9.

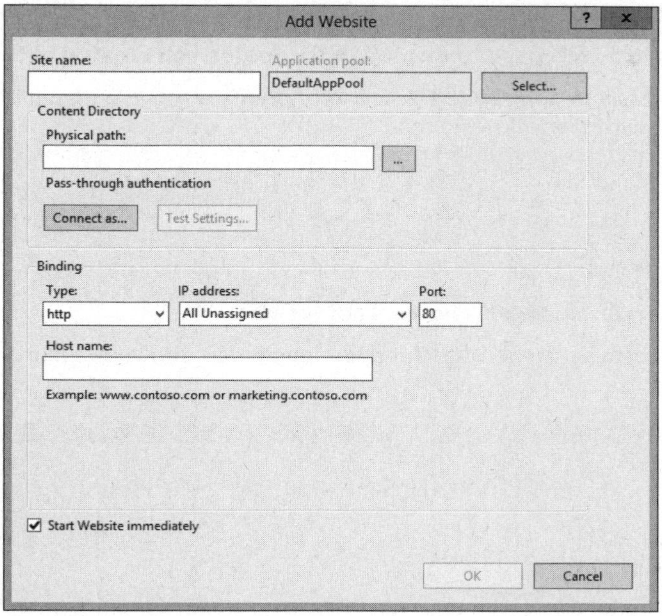

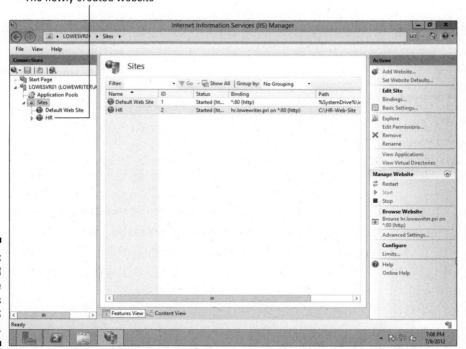

Figure 14-8: The Add Website dialog box.

The newly created website

Figure 14-9: The HR website appears in the IIS Manager.

8. **Close the IIS Manager.**

9. **Create a web page to display in the folder you created in Step 1.**

   For this example, I used Notepad to create a text file named `default.htm`, with the following text:

   ```
   <HTML>
   <BODY>
   <H1>Welcome to the HR Web Site!</H1>
   </BODY>
   </HTML>
   ```

10. **In Server Manager, choose Tools⇨DNS.**

    This brings up the DNS Manager console, as shown in Figure 14-10.

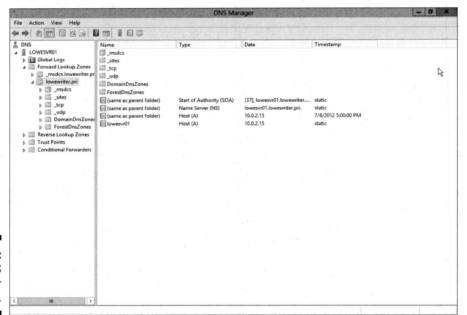

Figure 14-10:
The DNS
Manager
console.

11. **In the navigation pane, navigate to the node for your domain.**

    In this example, I navigated to `lowewriter.pri`.

12. **Choose Action⇨New Alias (CNAME).**

    The New Resource Record dialog box appears, as shown in Figure 14-11.

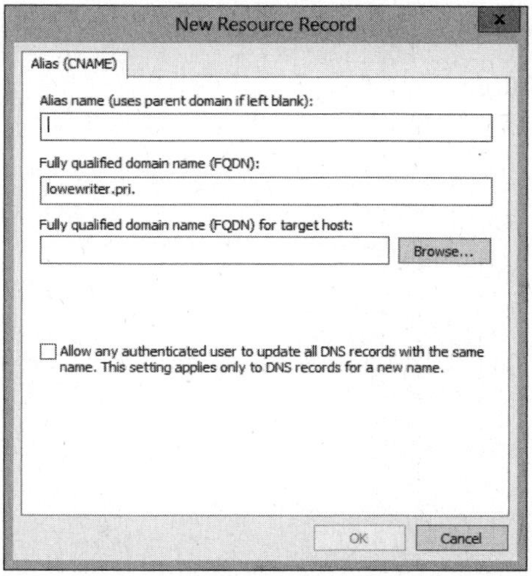

Figure 14-11:
Creating
a CNAME
record.

13. **Enter the alias name you want to use in the Alias Name text box.**

    For this example, I entered simply hr.

14. **Enter the computer name of your web server in the Fully Qualified Domain Name (FQDN) for Target Host text box.**

    For this example, I entered lserver01.

15. **Click OK.**

    The DNS alias is created.

16. **Close the DNS Manager console.**

17. **Open a browser window.**

18. **Browse to the alias address you just created.**

    For this example, I browsed to hr.lowewriter.pri. Figure 14-12 shows the resulting page.

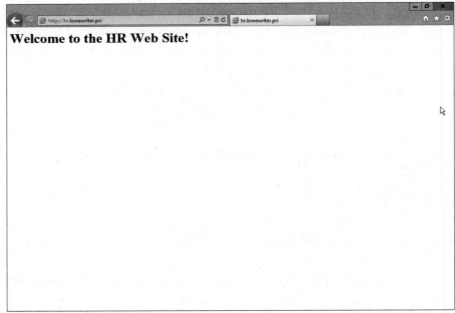

Figure 14-12:
Viewing a
website.

Part IV
Cloudy with a Chance of Gigabytes

See how to configure Outlook to work with cloud-based e-mail services like gmail at
www.dummies.com/extras/networking

In this part...

- ✔ Using cloud computing to move critical network functions out of your server room and onto the Internet

- ✔ Using the cloud to incorporate mobile devices such as smart phones and tablets into your network

- ✔ Using the cloud to connect to your work computer from home or on the road

Chapter 15

Life in Cloud City

* *

In This Chapter

▶ Examining the basics of cloud computing

▶ Looking at three kinds of cloud computing services

▶ Understanding the pros and cons of cloud computing

▶ Perusing a few major cloud computing service providers

* *

*T*wo of the world's great science fiction franchises — *Star Wars* and *Star Trek* — feature cities that are suspended in the clouds. In *Star Wars Episode V: The Empire Strikes Back,* Han takes the *Millennium Falcon* to Cloud City, hoping that his friend Lando Calrissian can help repair their damaged hyperdrive. And in the original *Star Trek* series episode "The Cloud Minders," the crew of the *Enterprise* visits a city named Stratos, which is suspended in the clouds.

Coincidence? Perhaps. Or maybe Gene Roddenberry and George Lucas both knew that the future would be in the clouds. At any rate, the future of computer networking is rapidly heading for the clouds. Cloud computing, to be specific. This chapter is a brief introduction to cloud computing. You discover what it is, the pros and cons of adopting it, and what services are provided by the major cloud computer providers.

Introducing Cloud Computing

The basic idea behind cloud computing is to outsource one or more of your networked computing resources to the Internet. "The cloud" represents a new way of handling common computer tasks. Following are a few examples of how the cloud way differs from the traditional way:

✔ **E-mail services**

- *Traditional:* Provide e-mail services is to install Microsoft Exchange on a local server computer. Then your clients can connect use Microsoft Outlook to connect to the Exchange server to send and receive e-mail.

- *Cloud:* Contract with an Internet-based e-mail provider, such as Google Mail (Gmail). Cloud-based e-mail services typically charge a low monthly per-user fee, so the amount you pay for your e-mail service depends solely on the number of e-mail users you have.

✔ **Disk storage**

- *Traditional:* Set up a local file server computer with a large amount of shared disk space.

- *Cloud:* Sign up for an Internet file storage service and then store your data on the Internet. Cloud-based file storage typically charges a small monthly per-gigabyte fee, so you pay only for the storage you use. The disk capacity of cloud-based storage is essentially unlimited.

✔ **Accounting services**

- *Traditional:* Purchase expensive accounting software and install it on a local server computer.

- *Cloud:* Sign up for a web-based accounting service. Then all your accounting data is saved and managed on the provider's servers, not on yours.

Looking at the Benefits of Cloud Computing

Cloud computing is a different — and, in many ways, better — approach to networking. Here are a few of the main benefits of moving to cloud-based networking:

✔ **Cost-effective:** Cloud-based computing typically is less expensive than traditional computing. Consider a typical file server application: To implement a file server, first you must purchase a file server computer with enough disk space to accommodate your users' needs, which amounts to 1TB of disk storage. You want the most reliable data storage possible, so you purchase a server-quality computer and fully redundant disk drives. For the sake of this discussion, figure that the total price of the server — including its disk drive, the operating system license, and the labor cost of setting it up — is about $10,000. Assuming that the server will last for four years, that totals about $2,500 per year.

If you instead acquire your disk storage from a cloud-based file sharing service, you can expect to pay about one fourth of that amount for an equivalent amount of storage.

The same economies apply to most other cloud-based solutions. Cloud-based e-mail solutions, for example, typically cost around $5 per month per user — well less than the cost of setting up and maintaining a Microsoft Exchange Server.

✔ **Scalable:** So what happens if you guess wrong about the storage requirements of your file server, and your users end up needing 2TB instead of just 1TB? With a traditional file server, you must purchase additional disk drives to accommodate the extra space. Sooner than you want, you'll run out of capacity in the server's cabinet. Then you'll have to purchase an external storage cabinet. Eventually, you'll fill that up, too.

Now suppose that after you expand your server capacity to 2TB, your users' needs contract to just 1TB. Unfortunately, you can't return disk drives for a refund.

With cloud computing, you pay only for the capacity you're actually using, and you can add capacity whenever you need it. In the file server example, you can write as much data as you need to the cloud storage. Each month, you're billed according to your actual usage. Thus, you don't have to purchase and install additional disk drives to add storage capacity.

✔ **Reliable:** Especially for smaller businesses, cloud services are much more reliable than in-house services. Just a week before I wrote this chapter, the tape drive that a friend uses to back up his company's data failed. As a result, he was unable to back up data for three days while the tape drive was repaired. Had he been using cloud-based backup, he could have restored his data immediately and wouldn't have been without backups for those four days.

The reason for the increased reliability of cloud services is simply a matter of scale. Most small businesses can't afford the redundancies needed to make their computer operations as reliable as possible. My friend's company can't afford to buy two tape drives so that an extra is available in case the main one fails.

By contrast, cloud services are usually provided by large companies such as Amazon, Google, Microsoft, and IBM. These companies have state-of-the-art data centers with multiple redundancies for their cloud services. Cloud storage may be kept on multiple servers so that if one server fails, others can take over the load. In some cases, these servers are in different data centers in different parts of the country. Thus, your data will still be available even in the event of a disaster that shuts down an entire data system.

✔ **Hassle-free:** Face it, IT can be a hassle. With cloud-based services, you basically outsource the job of complex system maintenance chores, such as software upgrade, patches, hardware maintenance, backup, and so on. You get to consume the services while someone else takes care of making sure that the services run properly.

- ✔ **Globally accessible:** One of the best things about cloud services is that they're available anywhere you have an Internet connection. Suppose that you have offices in five cities. Using traditional computing, each office would require its own servers, and you'd have to carefully design systems that allowed users in each of the offices to access shared data.

  With cloud computing, each office simply connects to the Internet to access the cloud applications. Cloud-based applications are also great if your users are mobile because they can access the applications anywhere they can find an Internet connection.

Detailing the Drawbacks of Cloud Computing

Although cloud computing has many advantages over traditional techniques, it isn't without its drawbacks. Here are some of the most significant roadblocks to adopting cloud computing:

- ✔ **Entrenched applications:** Your organization may depend on entrenched applications that don't lend themselves especially well to cloud computing — or that at least require significant conversion efforts to migrate to the cloud. For example, you might have use an accounting system that relies on local file storage.

  Fortunately, many cloud providers offer assistance with this migration. And in many cases, the same application that you run locally can be run in the cloud, so no conversion is necessary.

- ✔ **Internet connection speed:** Cloud computing shifts much of the burden of your network to your Internet connection. Your users used to access their data on local file servers over gigabit-speed connections; now they must access data over slower bandwidth Internet connections.

  Although you can upgrade your connection to higher speeds, doing so will cost money — money that may offset the money you otherwise save from migrating to the cloud.

- ✔ **Internet connection reliability:** The cloud resources you access may feature all the redundancy in the world, but if your users access the cloud through a single Internet connection, that connection becomes a key point of vulnerability. Should it fail, any applications that depend on the cloud will be unavailable. If those applications are mission-critical, business will come to a halt until the connection is restored.

Here are two ways to mitigate this risk:

- *Make sure that you're using an enterprise-class Internet connection.* Enterprise-class connections are more expensive but provide much better fault tolerance and repair service than consumer-class connections do.

- *Provide redundant connections if you can.* That way, if one connection fails, traffic can be rerouted through alternative connections.

✔ **Security threats:** You can bet your life that hackers throughout the world are continually probing for ways to break through the security perimeter of all the major cloud providers. When they do, your data may be exposed.

The best way to mitigate this threat is to ensure that strong password policies are enforced.

Examining Three Basic Kinds of Cloud Services

Three distinct kinds of services can be provided via the cloud: applications, platforms, and services (infrastructure). The following paragraphs describe these three types of cloud services in greater detail.

Applications

Most often referred to as *Software as a Service (SaaS),* fully functional applications can be delivered via the cloud. One of the best-known examples is *Google Apps,* which is a suite of cloud-based office applications designed to compete directly with Microsoft's traditional office applications, including Word, Excel, PowerPoint, Access, and Outlook. Google Apps can also replace the back-end software often used to support Microsoft Office, including Exchange and SharePoint.

When you use a cloud-based application, you don't have to worry about any of the details that are commonly associated with running an application on your network, such as deploying the application and applying product upgrades and software patches. Cloud-based applications usually charge a small monthly fee based on the number of users running the software, so costs are low.

Also, as a cloud-based application user, you don't have to worry about providing the hardware or operating system platform on which the application will run. The application provider takes care of that detail for you, so you can focus simply on developing the application to best serve your users' needs.

Platforms

Also referred to as *Platform as a Service (PaaS)*, this class of service refers to providers that give you access to a remote virtual operating platform on which you can build your own applications.

At the simplest level, a PaaS provider gives you a complete, functional remote virtual machine that's fully configured and ready for you to deploy your applications to. If you use a web provider to host your company's website, you're already using PaaS: Most web host providers give you a functioning Linux system, fully configured with all the necessary servers, such as Apache or MySQL. All you have to do is build and deploy your web application on the provider's server.

More-complex PaaS solutions include specialized software that your custom applications can tap to provide services such as data storage, online order processing, and credit card payments. One of the best-known examples of this type of PaaS provider is Amazon.

 When you use PaaS, you take on the responsibility of developing your own custom applications to run on the remote platform. The PaaS provider takes care of the details of maintaining the platform itself, including the base operating system and the hardware on which the platform runs.

Infrastructure

If you don't want to delegate the responsibility of maintaining operating systems and other elements of the platform, you can use *Infrastructure as a Service (IaaS)*. When you use IaaS, you're purchasing raw computing power that's accessible via the cloud. Typically, IaaS provides you access to a remote virtual machine. It's up to you to manage and configure the remote machine however you want.

Public Clouds versus Private Clouds

The most common form of cloud computing uses what is known as a *public cloud* — that is, cloud services that are available to anyone in the world via the Internet. Google Apps is an excellent example of a public cloud service. Anyone with access to the Internet can access the public cloud services of Google Apps: Just point your browser to http://apps.google.com.

A public cloud is like a public utility, in that anyone can subscribe to it on a pay-as-you-go basis. One of the drawbacks of public cloud services is that they're inherently insecure. When you use a public cloud service, you're entrusting your valuable data to a third party that you cannot control. Sure, you can protect your access to your public cloud services by using strong passwords, but if your account names and passwords are compromised, your public cloud services can be hacked into, and your data can be stolen. Every so often, we all hear news stories about how this company's or that company's back-door security has been compromised.

Besides security, another drawback of public cloud computing is that it's dependent on high-speed, reliable Internet connections. Your cloud service provider may have all the redundancy in the world, but if your connection to the Internet goes down, you won't be able to access your cloud services. And if your connection is slow, your cloud services will be slow.

A *private cloud* mimics many of the features of cloud computing but is implemented on a private hardware within a local network, so it isn't accessible to the general public. Private clouds are inherently more secure because the general public can't access them. Also, they're dependent only on private network connections, so they aren't subject to the limits of a public Internet connection.

As a rule, private clouds are implemented by large organizations that have the resources available to create and maintain their own cloud servers.

A relative newcomer to the cloud computing scene is the *hybrid cloud,* which combines the features of public and private clouds. Typically, a hybrid cloud system uses a small private cloud that provides local access to the some of the applications and the public cloud for others. You might maintain your most frequently used data on a private cloud for fast access via the local network and use the public cloud to store archives and other less frequently used data, for which performance isn't as much of an issue.

Introducing Some of the Major Cloud Providers

Hundreds, if not thousands, of companies provide cloud services. Most of the cloud computing done today, however, is provided by just a few providers, which are described in the following sections.

Amazon

By far the largest provider of cloud services in the world is Amazon. Amazon launched its cloud platform — Amazon Web Services (AWS) — in 2006. Since then, hundreds of thousands of customers have signed up. Some of the most notable users of AWS include Netflix, Pinterest, and Instagram.

AWS includes the following features:

- **Amazon CloudFront:** A PaaS content-delivery system designed to deliver web content to large numbers of users.

- **Amazon Elastic Compute Cloud:** Also called Amazon EC2. An IaaS system that provides access to raw computing power.

- **Amazon Simple Storage Service:** Also called Amazon S3. Provides web-based data storage for unlimited amounts of data.

- **Amazon Simple Queue Service:** Also called Amazon SQS. Provides a data transfer system that lets applications send messages to other applications. SQS enables you to build applications that work together.

- **Amazon Virtual Private Cloud:** Also called Amazon VPC. Uses virtual private network (VPN) connections to connect your local network to Amazon's cloud services.

Google

Google is also one of the largest providers of cloud services. Its offerings include the following:

- **Google Apps:** A replacement for Microsoft Office that provides basic e-mail, word processing, spreadsheet, and database functions via the cloud. Google Apps is free to the general public and can even be used free by small business (up to 50 users). For larger businesses, Google offers an advanced version, Google Apps for Business. For $5 per month per user, you get extra features, such as 25GB of e-mail data per user, archiving, and advanced options for customizing your account policies.

✔ **Google Cloud Connect:** A cloud-based solution that lets you work with Google cloud data directly from within Microsoft Office applications.

✔ **Google App Engine:** A PaaS interface that lets you develop your own applications that work with Google's cloud services.

✔ **Google Cloud Print:** Allows you to connect your printers to the cloud so that they can be accessed from anywhere.

✔ **Google Maps:** A Global Information System (GIS).

Microsoft

Microsoft has its own cloud strategy, designed in part to protect its core business of operating systems and Office applications against competition from other cloud providers, such as Google Apps.

The following paragraphs summarize several of Microsoft's cloud offerings:

✔ **Microsoft Office 365:** A cloud-based version of Microsoft Office. According to Microsoft's website, Office 365 provides "anywhere access to cloud-based email, web conferencing, file sharing, and Office Web Apps at a low predictable monthly cost." For more information, check out www. office365.com.

✔ **Windows Azure:** A PaaS offering that lets you build websites, deploy virtual machines that run Windows Server or Linux, or access cloud versions of server applications such as SQL Server.

✔ **Microsoft Business Productivity Suite:** A SaaS product that provides cloud-based access to two of Microsoft's most popular productivity servers: Microsoft Exchange and Microsoft SharePoint. The suite lets you deploy these servers without having to create and maintain your own local servers.

Getting Into the Cloud

After you wrap your head around just how cool cloud computing can be, what should you do to take your network toward the cloud? Allow me to make a few recommendations:

✔ **Don't depend on a poor Internet connection.** First and foremost, before you take any of your network operations to the cloud, make sure that you're *not* dependent on a consumer-grade Internet connection if you decide to adopt cloud computing. Consumer-grade Internet connections can be fast, but when an outage occurs, there's no telling how long you'll wait for the connection to be repaired. You definitely don't want to wait for hours or days while the cable company thinks about sending someone out to your site. Instead, spend the money for a high-speed enterprise-class connection that can scale as your dependence on it increases.

✔ **Assess what applications you may already have running on the cloud.** If you use Gmail rather than Exchange for your e-mail, congratulations! You're already a cloud user. Other examples of cloud services that you may already be using include a remote web or FTP host, Dropbox or another file sharing service, Carbonite or another online backup service, a payroll service, and so on.

✔ **Don't move to the cloud all at once.** Start by identifying a single application that lends itself to the cloud. If your engineering firm archives projects when they close and wants to get them off your primary file server but keep them readily available, look to the cloud for a file storage service.

✔ **Go with a reputable company.** Google, Amazon, and Microsoft are all huge companies with proven track records in cloud computing. Many other large and established companies also offer cloud services. Don't stake your company's future on a company that didn't exist six months ago.

✔ **Research, research, research.** Pour yourself into the web, and buy a few books. *Cloud Computing For Dummies,* by Judith Hurwitz, Robin Bloor, Marcia Kaufman, and Fern Halper (John Wiley & Sons, Inc.), is a good place to start.

Chapter 16

Managing Mobile Devices

A computer consultant once purchased a used BlackBerry device on eBay for $15.50. When he put in a new battery and turned on the device, he discovered that it contained confidential e-mails and personal contact information for executives of a well-known financial institution.

Oops!

It turns out that a former executive with the company sold his old BlackBerry on eBay a few months after he left the firm. He'd assumed that because he'd removed the battery, everything on the BlackBerry had been erased.

The point of this true story is that mobile devices such as smartphones and tablet computers pose a special set of challenges for network administrators. These challenges are now being faced even by administrators of small networks. Just a few years ago, only large companies had BlackBerry or other mobile devices that integrated with Exchange e-mail, for example. Now it isn't uncommon for companies with just a few employees to have mobile devices connected to the company network.

This chapter is a brief introduction to mobile devices and the operating systems they run, with an emphasis on iPhone and Android devices. You find out more about how these devices can interact with Exchange e-mail and the steps you can take to ensure their security.

The Many Types of Mobile Devices

Once upon a time, there were mobile phones and PDAs. A mobile phone was just that: a handheld telephone you could take with you. The good ones had nice features such as a call log, an address book, and perhaps a crude game, but not much else. PDAs — *Personal Digital Assistants* — were little handheld computers designed to replace the old-fashioned Day-Timer books people used to carry around with them to keep track of their appointment calendars and address books.

All that changed when cellular providers began adding data capabilities to their networks. Now cellphones can have complete mobile Internet access. This fact has resulted in the addition of sophisticated PDA features to mobile phones and phone features to PDAs so that the distinctions are blurred.

A *mobile device* can be any one of a wide assortment of devices that you can hold in one hand and that are connected through a wireless network. The term *handheld* is a similar generic name for such devices. The following list describes some of the most common specifics of mobile devices:

- ✔ **Mobile phone:** Primary purpose is to enable phone service. Most mobile phones also include text messaging, address books, appointment calendars, and games; they may also provide Internet access.

- ✔ **Smartphone:** A mobile phone with advanced features not typically found on mobile phones. There's no clearly drawn line between mobile phones and smartphones. One distinction is whether the phone can provide integrated access to corporate e-mail. The screen on a smartphone is typically bigger than the screen on a traditional cellphone, and most models (such as the iPhone and most Android devices) don't have hard keyboards.

- ✔ **BlackBerry:** BlackBerry devices are sophisticated PDAs that have cellphone capabilities. The most distinctive feature of BlackBerry devices is their capability to synchronize with Exchange e-mail servers to provide instant access to your corporate e-mail. Typically, this synchronization requires a special server — BlackBerry Enterprise Server (BES) — running on the corporate network. BlackBerry devices use a proprietary operating system (OS) developed by RIM.

- ✔ **iPhone and iPad:** Apple's iPhone has taken the smartphone market by storm. Although there are still more BlackBerry devices in use than iPhones, iPhone is gaining market share and may soon overtake BlackBerry. Unlike a BlackBerry, an iPhone doesn't require a separate server to enable full Exchange mailbox synchronization.

- ✔ **Android:** Android is an open source OS for smartphones, developed by Google. Android is designed in many ways to mimic the features of the iPhone, so experienced iPhone users will find Android phones to be very similar. At the time I wrote this chapter, the overwhelming majority of new smartphones being sold were Android devices.

Considering Security for Mobile Devices

As a network administrator, one of your main responsibilities regarding mobile devices is to keep them secure. Unfortunately, that's a significant challenge. Here are some reasons why:

- ✓ **Mobile devices connect to your network via other networks that are out of your control.** You can go to great lengths to set up firewalls, encryption, and a host of other security features, but mobile devices connect via public networks whose administrators may not be as conscientious as you.

- ✓ **Mobile devices are easy to lose.** A user might leave her smartphone at a restaurant or hotel, or it might fall out of her pocket on the subway.

- ✓ **Mobile devices run OSes that aren't as security conscious as Windows.**

- ✓ **Users who wouldn't dare install renegade software on their desktop computers think nothing of downloading free games or other applications to their handheld devices.** Who knows what kinds of viruses or Trojans these downloads carry?

- ✓ **Inevitably, someone will buy his own handheld device and connect it to your network without your knowledge or permission.**

Here are some recommendations for beefing up security for your mobile devices:

- ✓ Establish clear, consistent policies for mobile devices, and enforce them.

- ✓ Make sure employees understand that they aren't allowed to bring their own devices into your network. Allow only company-owned devices to connect.

- ✓ Train your users in the security risks associated with using mobile devices.

- ✓ Implement antivirus protection for your mobile devices.

Managing iOS Devices

In 2007, the Apple iPhone, one of the most innovative little gadgets in many, many years, hit the technology market. As a result, in just a few short years, the iPhone captured a huge slice of a market dominated almost exclusively by RIM and its BlackBerry devices. Since then, the iPhone's share of the mobile-phone market has grown beyond that of the former king, BlackBerry.

The success of the iPhone was due in large part to the genius of its OS: iOS. In 2010, Apple released the iPad, a tablet computer that runs the same iOS as the iPhone. And in 2012, Apple introduced a smaller version of the iPad: the iPad mini. Together, these devices are commonly known as *iOS devices*.

Understanding the iPhone

The iPhone is essentially a combination of four devices:

- A cellphone
- An iPod with a memory capacity of 8GB to 64GB
- A digital camera
- An Internet device with its own web browser (Safari) and applications, such as e-mail, calendar, and contact management

The most immediately noticeable feature of the iPhone is its lack of a keyboard. Instead, nearly the entire front surface of the iPhone is a high-resolution, touch-sensitive LCD display. The display is not only the main output device of the iPhone, but also its main input device. The display can become a keypad input for dialing a telephone number or a keyboard for entering text. You can also use various finger gestures, such as tapping icons to start programs or pinching to zoom in the display.

The iPhone has several other innovative features:

- An *accelerometer* tracks the motion of the iPhone in three directions. The main use of the accelerometer is to adjust the orientation of the display from landscape to portrait based on how the user is holding the phone. Some other applications — mostly games — use the accelerometer as well.
- A Wi-Fi interface lets the iPhone connect to local Wi-Fi networks for faster Internet access.
- GPS capability provides location awareness for many applications, including Google Maps.
- The virtual private network (VPN) client lets you connect to your internal network.

Of all the unique features of the iPhone, probably the most important is its huge collection of third-party applications that can be downloaded from a special web portal, the App Store. Many of these applications are free or cost just a few dollars. (Many are just 99 cents or $1.99.) As of this writing, more than 500,000 applications — everything from business productivity to games — were available from the App Store.

Understanding the iPad

The iPad is essentially an iPhone without the phone but with a larger screen. The iPhone comes with a 3.5" screen; the iPad has a 9.7" screen; and its smaller cousin, the iPad mini, has a 7.9" screen.

Apart from these basic differences, an iPad is nearly identical to an iPhone. Any application that can run on an iPhone can also run on an iPad, and many applications are designed to take special advantage of the iPad's larger screen.

All the information that follows in this chapter applies equally to iPhones and iPads.

Integrating iOS Devices with Exchange

An iOS device can integrate with Microsoft Exchange e-mail. You must follow three procedures to make that integration possible:

1. Enable the Mobile Services feature of Microsoft Exchange.

2. Enable ActiveSync for the user's mailbox.

3. Configure the iPhone to connect to the user's Exchange mailbox.

The following sections describe these procedures.

Enabling Exchange Mobile Services

To enable an Exchange mailbox for an iOS device, you must enable the Exchange Mobile Services feature on the Exchange server. You must complete this procedure just once for each Exchange server. Here are the steps:

1. **Log on to the Exchange server with an Exchange Administrator account.**

2. **Choose Start⇨Administrative Tools⇨Exchange System Manager.**

3. **In the navigation pane of Exchange System Manager, expand the Global Settings node.**

4. **Right-click Mobile Services and then choose Properties from the contextual menu.**

   The dialog box shown in Figure 16-1 appears.

5. **Select all the check boxes on the General tab.**

   This step enables all the capabilities of Outlook Mobile Access.

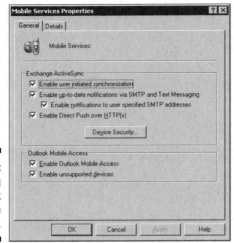

Figure 16-1:
Enabling
Outlook
Mobile
Access.

6. **Click OK.**

7. **Close Exchange System Manager.**

   You're done!

Enabling ActiveSync for a user's mailbox

After you enable Exchange Mobile Services for your Exchange server, you can enable ActiveSync for the user's Exchange mailbox. Enabling ActiveSync allows the mailbox to be synchronized with a remote mail client such as an iPhone. Here are the steps:

1. **Choose Start➪Administrative Tools➪Active Directory Users and Computers.**

   The Active Directory Users and Computers console opens.

2. **Expand the domain and then locate the user you want to enable mobile access for.**

3. **Right-click the user and then choose Properties from the contextual menu.**

4. **Click the Exchange Features tab.**

   The Exchange Features options are displayed, as shown in Figure 16-2.

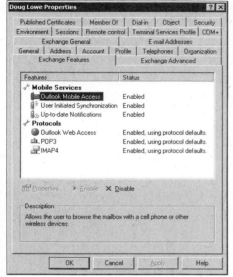

5. **Enable all three options listed under Mobile Services.**

   If the options aren't already enabled, right-click each option and choose Enable from the contextual menu.

6. **Click OK.**

7. **Repeat Steps 5 and 6 for any other users you want to enable mobile access for.**

8. **Close Active Directory Users and Computers.**

That's all there is to it. After you enable these features, any users running Windows Mobile can synchronize their handheld devices with their Exchange mailboxes.

Configuring an iOS device for Exchange e-mail

After ActiveSync is enabled for the mailbox, you can configure an iPhone or iPad to tap into the Exchange account by following these steps:

1. **On the iPhone or iPad, tap Settings; tap Mail, Contacts, Calendars; and then tap Add Account.**

   The screen shown in Figure 16-3 appears.

Figure 16-3:
Add an
e-mail
account.

2. **Tap Add Account.**

   The screen shown in Figure 16-4 appears, allowing you to choose the type of e-mail account you want to add.

Figure 16-4:
The iPhone can support many types of e-mail accounts.

3. **Tap Microsoft Exchange.**

The screen shown in Figure 16-5 appears, where you can enter basic information for your Exchange account.

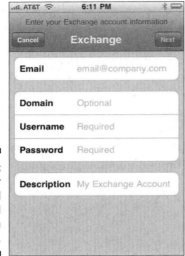

Figure 16-5: Enter your e-mail address and logon information.

4. **Enter your e-mail address, Windows username, and password.**

   For most installations, you should leave the Domain field empty. (If the e-mail configuration doesn't work, come back to this screen, and enter your domain name here.)

5. **Tap Next.**

   The screen shown in Figure 16-6 appears.

Figure 16-6: Enter your Exchange server information.

6. **Enter either the DNS name or the IP address of your Exchange server in the Server field.**

   For example, if your Exchange server uses the name **mail.mydomain. com**, enter that in the Server field.

7. **Tap Next.**

   The screen shown in Figure 16-7 appears. Here, you select which mailbox features you want to synchronize: Mail, Contacts, or Calendars.

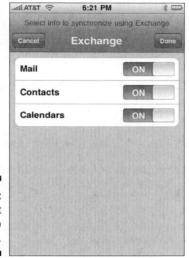

Figure 16-7:
Select
features to
synchronize.

8. **Select the features you want to synchronize and then tap Done.**

   The e-mail account is created.

After the e-mail account has been configured, the user can access it via the Mail icon on the iPhone's home screen.

Managing Android Devices

For the better part of a year, Apple had the touchscreen smartphone market all to itself. But in late 2008, T-Mobile released a touchscreen smartphone called the Dream, made by HTC. This smartphone was the first of many phones based on the Android OS developed by Google. Android-based phones are similar to iPhones in many ways, but they also have many differences. The most important difference is that the Android OS is available on many phones, whereas the iOS operating system is proprietary to Apple and available only on Apple devices.

This section is a brief introduction to the Android platform. You find out a bit about what Android actually is, and you discover the procedures for setting up Exchange e-mail access on an Android phone.

In many ways, Android phones are similar to iPhones. Like iPhones, Android phones feature a touchscreen display, have built-in MP3 music players, and provide access to a large library of downloadable third-party applications. In essence, Android phones are competitors with iPhones.

Crucial differences exist between Android phones and iPhones, however. The most important difference — in many ways, the *only* important difference — is that Android phones are based on an open source OS derived from Linux, which can be extended and adapted to work on a wide variety of hardware devices from different vendors. With the iPhone, you're locked into Apple hardware. With an Android phone, though, you can buy hardware from a variety of manufacturers.

Looking at the Android OS

Most people associate the Android OS with Google, and it's true that Google is the driving force behind Android. The Android OS is an open source OS managed by the Open Handset Alliance (OHA). Google still plays a major role in the development of Android, but more than 50 companies are involved in the OHA, including hardware manufacturers (such as HTC, Intel, and Motorola), software companies (such as Google and eBay), and mobile-phone operators (such as T-Mobile and Sprint-Nextel).

Technically speaking, Android is more than just an OS. It's also a complete *software stack,* which comprises several key components that work together to create the complete Android platform:

- ✔ **The OS core,** which is based on the popular Linux OS

- ✔ **A middleware layer,** which provides drivers and other support code to enable the OS core to work with the hardware devices that make up a complete phone, such as a touch-sensitive display, the cellphone radio, the speaker and microphone, Bluetooth or Wi-Fi networking components, and so on

- ✔ **A set of core applications** that the user interacts with to make phone calls, read e-mail, send text messages, take pictures, and so on

- ✔ **A Software Developers Kit (SDK)** that lets third-party software developers create their own applications to run on an Android phone, as well as a marketplace where the applications can be marketed and sold, much as the App Store lets iPhone developers market and sell applications for the iPhone

Besides the basic features provided by all OSes, here are a few bonus features of the Android software stack:

✔ An optimized graphical display engine that can produce sophisticated 2-D and 3-D graphics

✔ GPS capabilities that provide location awareness that can be integrated with applications such as Google Maps

✔ Compass and accelerometer capabilities that can determine whether the phone is in motion and in which direction it's pointed

✔ A built-in SQL database server for data storage

✔ Support for several network technologies, including 3G, 4G, Bluetooth, and Wi-Fi

✔ Built-in media support, including common formats for still images, audio, and video files

Perusing Android's core applications

The Android OS comes preconfigured with several standard applications, which provide the functionality that most people demand from a modern smartphone. These applications include

✔ **Dialer:** Provides the basic cellphone function that lets users make calls.

✔ **Browser:** A built-in web browser that's similar to Google's Chrome browser.

✔ **Messaging:** Provides text (SMS) and multimedia (MMS) messaging.

✔ **Email:** A basic e-mail client that works best with Google's Gmail but that can be configured to work with other e-mail servers, including Exchange.

✔ **Contacts:** Provides a contacts list that integrates with the Dialer and Email applications.

✔ **Camera:** Lets you use the phone's camera hardware (if any) to take pictures.

✔ **Calculator:** A simple calculator application.

✔ **Alarm Clock:** A basic alarm clock. You can set up to three different alarms.

✔ **Maps:** An integrated version of Google Maps.

✔ **YouTube:** An integrated version of YouTube.

✔ **Music:** An MP3 player similar to the iPod. You can purchase and download music files from Amazon.

✔ **Google Play:** Lets you purchase and download third-party applications for the Android phone.

✔ **Settings:** Lets you control various settings for the phone.

Integrating Android with Exchange

The Android's core Email application can integrate with Microsoft Exchange e-mail. To do that, you must enable Exchange Mobile Services and then enable ActiveSync for the user's mailbox. For more information, see the sections "Enabling Exchange Mobile Services" and "Enabling ActiveSync for a user's mailbox," earlier in this chapter.

After you enable Exchange Mobile Services and ActiveSync on your Exchange server, you can easily configure the Android phone for e-mail access. Just run the Email application on the Android phone, and follow the configuration steps, which ask you for basic information such as your e-mail address, username, password, and Exchange mail server.

Chapter 17

Connecting from Home

- -

In This Chapter

▶ Accessing your e-mail with Outlook Web Access

▶ Using a virtual private network

- -

A typical computer user takes work home to work on in the evening or over the weekend and bring back to the office the following weekday. This arrangement can work okay, except that exchanging information between your home computer and your office computer isn't easy.

One way to exchange files is to mark them for offline access, as I describe in Chapter 3. However, this approach has its drawbacks. What if someone goes to the office on Saturday and modifies the same file you're working on at home? What if you get home and discover that the file you need is on a folder you didn't mark for offline access?

What about e-mail? Offline access doesn't give you access to your company e-mail account, so you can't check whether you have mail in your Inbox or send mail from your company e-mail account.

This chapter introduces two features that can alleviate these problems. The first is Internet-based access to your e-mail via Outlook Web App (OWA) in Microsoft Exchange. The second is the *virtual private network* (VPN), which lets you connect to your network from home as though you were at work so that you can safely access all your network resources as though you were locally connected to the network.

Using Outlook Web App

Most people who connect to their office networks from home really just need their e-mail. If the only reason for accessing the office network is to get e-mail, try this simple, easy tool: Outlook Web App, also known as *OWA*. This Microsoft Exchange Server feature can access your company e-mail from any computer that has an Internet connection. The remote computer just needs a web browser and an Internet connection; no VPN or other special configuration is required.

The best part is that you don't have to do anything special to enable OWA; it's enabled by default when you install Microsoft Exchange. Although you can configure plenty of options to improve its use, OWA is functional right out of the box.

To access OWA from any web browser, just browse to the address designated for your organization's OWA. The default address is the DNS name of your mail server, followed by /exchange. For example, for the mail server smtp.low ewriter.com, the OWA address is smtp.lowewriter.com/exchange.

The connection must use the secure version of the normal HTTP web protocol. You must type **https://** before the OWA address. The complete address will be something like https://smtp.lowewriter.com/exchange.

When you browse to your OWA address, you're prompted to enter a name and password. Use your regular network logon name and password. OWA appears in the browser window, as shown in Figure 17-1.

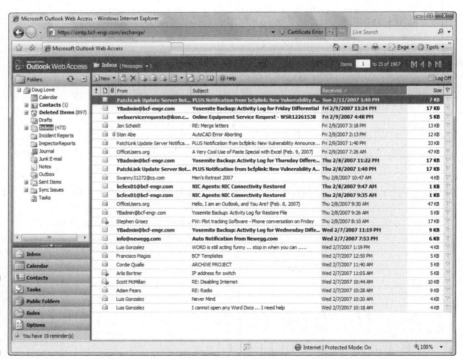

Figure 17-1:
OWA looks
a lot like
Outlook.

If you're familiar with Outlook, you'll have no trouble using OWA. Almost all Outlook features are available, including your inbox, calendar, contacts, tasks, reminders, and even public folders. You can even set up an Out of Office reply.

One difference between OWA and Outlook is that there's no menu bar across the top. However, most of the functions that are available from the menu bar are available elsewhere in OWA. If you can't find a feature, look in the Options page, which you can reach by clicking Options at the bottom left of the window. Figure 17-2 shows the Options page. From here, you can create an Out of Office reply, set your signature, and change a variety of other options.

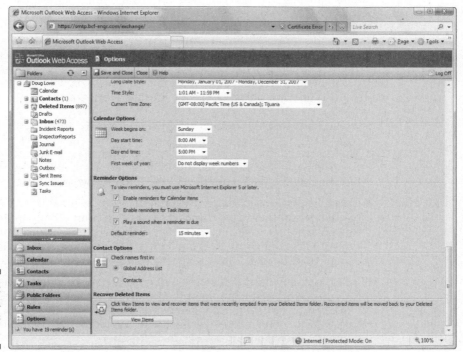

Figure 17-2: Set OWA options here.

Using a Virtual Private Network

A *virtual private network* (VPN) is a type of network connection that creates the illusion that you're directly connected to a network when in fact, you're not. For example, suppose you set up a LAN at your office, but you also occasionally work from home. But how will you access the files on your work computer from home?

- You could simply copy whatever files you need from your work computer onto a flash drive and take them home with you, work on the files, copy the updated files back to the flash drive, and take them back to work with you the next day.

- You could e-mail the files to your personal e-mail account, work on them at home, and then e-mail the changed files back to your work e-mail account.

- You could get a laptop and use the Windows Offline Files feature to automatically synchronize files from your work network with files on the laptop.

Or you could set up a VPN that allows you to log on to your work network from home. The VPN uses a secured Internet connection to connect you directly to your work network, so you can access your network files as if you had a really long Ethernet cable that ran from your home computer all the way to the office and plugged directly into the work network.

Here are at least three situations in which a VPN is the ideal solution:

- Workers need to occasionally work from home (as in the scenario just described). In this situation, a VPN connection establishes a connection between the home computer and the office network.

- Mobile users — who may not ever actually show up at the office — need to connect to the work network from mobile computers, often from locations like hotel rooms, clients' offices, airports, or coffee shops. This type of VPN configuration is similar to the home user's configuration except that the exact location of the remote user's computer is not fixed.

- Your company has offices in two or more locations, each with its own LAN, and you want to connect the locations so that users on either network can access each other's network resources. In this situation, the VPN doesn't connect a single user with a remote network; instead, it connects two remote networks to each other.

Looking at VPN security

The *V* in VPN stands for *virtual,* which means that a VPN creates the appearance of a local network connection when in fact the connection is made over a public network — the Internet. The term *tunnel* is sometimes used to describe a VPN because the VPN creates a tunnel between two locations, which can be entered only from either end. The data that travels through the tunnel from one end to the other is secure as long as it's within the tunnel — that is, within the protection provided by the VPN.

The *P* in VPN stands for *private,* which is the purpose of creating the tunnel. If the VPN didn't create effective security so that data can enter the tunnel only at one of the two ends, the VPN would be worthless; you may as well just open your network and your remote computer up to the Internet and let the hackers have their way.

Prior to VPN technology, the only way to provide private remote network connections was through actual private lines, which were (and still are) very expensive. For example, to set up a remote office, you could lease a private T1 line from the phone company to connect the two offices. This private T1 line provided excellent security because it physically connected the two offices and could be accessed only from the two endpoints.

VPN provides the same point-to-point connection as a private leased line, but does it over the Internet instead of through expensive dedicated lines. To create the tunnel that guarantees privacy of the data as it travels from one end of the VPN to the other, the data is encrypted using special security protocols.

The most important of the VPN security protocols is *Internet Protocol Security* (IPSec), which is a collection of standards for encrypting and authenticating packets that travel on the Internet. In other words, it provides a way to encrypt the contents of a data packet so that only a person who knows the secret encryption keys can decode the data. And it provides a way to reliably identify the source of a packet so that the parties at either end of the VPN tunnel can trust that the packets are authentic.

Another commonly used VPN protocol is Layer 2 Tunneling Protocol (L2TP). This protocol doesn't provide data encryption. Instead, it's designed to create end-to-end connections — *tunnels* — through which data can travel. L2TP is actually a combination of two older protocols: Layer 2 Forwarding Protocol (L2FP, from Cisco), and Point-to-Point Tunneling Protocol (PPTP, from Microsoft).

Many VPNs today use a combination of L2TP and IPSec: L2TP over IPSec. This type of VPN combines the best features of L2TP and IPSec to provide a high degree of security and reliability.

Understanding VPN servers and clients

A VPN connection requires a VPN *server* — the gatekeeper at one end of the tunnel — and a VPN client at the other end. The main difference between the server and the client is that the client initiates the connection with the server, and a VPN client can establish a connection with just one server at a time. However, a server can accept connections from many clients.

Typically, the VPN server is a separate hardware device, most often a security appliance such as a Cisco ASA security appliance. VPN servers can also be implemented in software. For example, Windows Server includes built-in VPN capabilities even though they're not easy to configure. And a VPN server can be implemented in Linux as well.

Figure 17-3 shows one of the many VPN configuration screens for a Cisco ASA appliance. This screen provides the configuration details for an IPSec VPN connection. The most important item of information on this screen is the Pre-Shared Key, which is used to encrypt the data sent over the VPN. The client will need to provide the identical key in order to participate in the VPN.

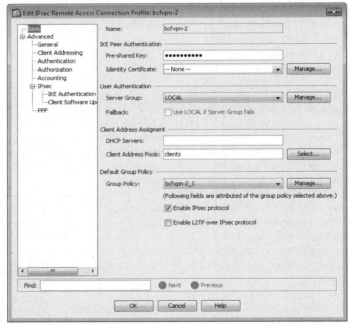

Figure 17-3:
An IPSec configuration page on a Cisco ASA security appliance.

A VPN client is usually software that runs on a client computer that wants to connect to the remote network. The VPN client software must be configured with the IP address of the VPN server as well as authentication information such as a username and the Pre-Shared Key that will be used to encrypt the data. If the key used by the client doesn't match the key used by the server, the VPN server will reject the connection request from the client.

Figure 17-4 shows a typical VPN software client. When the client is configured with the correct connection information (which you can do by clicking the New button), you just click Connect. After a few moments, the VPN client will announce that the connection has been established and the VPN is connected.

Figure 17-4:
A VPN
client.

A VPN client can also be a hardware device, like another security appliance. This is most common when the VPN is used to connect two networks at separate locations. For example, suppose your company has an office in Pixley and a second office in Hooterville. Each office has its own network with servers and client computers. The easiest way to connect these offices with a VPN would be to put an identical security appliance at each location. Then you could configure the security appliances to communicate with each other over a VPN.

Part V
Managing and Protecting Your Network

Get advice about preparing for network disasters at www.dummies.com/extras/networking

In this part...

- ✔ Learning what network management is all about
- ✔ Solving pesky networking problems
- ✔ Protecting your network data by backing it up
- ✔ Securing your network by enforcing user account policies
- ✔ Making your network even more secure by installing a firewall and using antivirus software

Chapter 18

Welcome to Network Management

*H*elp wanted. Network administrator to help small business get control of a network run amok. Must have sound organizational and management skills. Only moderate computer experience required. Part-time only.

Does this sound like an ad that your company should run? Every network needs a network administrator, whether the network has 2 computers or 2,000. Of course, managing a 2,000-computer network is a full-time job, whereas managing a 2-computer network isn't. At least, it shouldn't be.

This chapter introduces you to the boring job of network administration. Oops — you're probably reading this chapter because you've been elected to be the network manager, so I'd better rephrase that:

This chapter introduces you to the wonderful, exciting world of network management! Oh, boy! This is going to be fun!

What a Network Administrator Does

A network administrator "administers" a network: installing, configuring, expanding, protecting, upgrading, tuning, and repairing the network.

A network administrator takes care of the network hardware (such as cables, hubs, switches, routers, servers, and clients) and the network software (such as network operating systems, e-mail servers, backup software, database servers, and application software). Most important, the administrator takes care of network users by answering their questions, listening to their troubles, and solving their problems.

On a big network, these responsibilities constitute a full-time job. Large networks tend to be volatile: Users come and go, equipment fails, software chokes, and life in general seems to be one crisis after another.

Smaller networks are much more stable. After you get your network up and running, you probably won't have to spend much time managing its hardware and software. An occasional problem may pop up, but with only a few computers on the network, problems should be few and far between.

Regardless of the network's size, the administrator attends to common chores:

- **Get involved in every decision to purchase new computers, printers, or other equipment.**

- **Put on the pocket protector whenever a new computer is added to the network.** The network administrator's job includes considering changes in the cabling configuration, assigning a computer name to the new computer, integrating the new user into the security system, and granting user rights.

- **Whenever a software vendor releases a new version of its software, read about the new version and decide whether its new features warrant an upgrade.** In most cases, the hardest part of upgrading to new software is determining the *migration path* — that is, upgrading your entire network to the new version while disrupting the network and its users as little as possible. This statement is especially true if the software in question happens to be your network operating system because any change to the network operating system can potentially impact the entire network.

Between upgrades, software vendors periodically release patches and service packs that fix minor problems. For more information, see Chapter 22.

✔ **Perform routine chores, such as backing up the servers, archiving old data, and freeing up server disk space.** Much of the task of network administration involves making sure that things keep working by finding and correcting problems before users notice that something is wrong. In this sense, network administration can be a thankless job.

✔ **Gather, organize, and track the entire network's software inventory.** You never know when something will go haywire on the ancient Windows 95 computer that Joe in Marketing uses, and you have to reinstall that old copy of Lotus Approach. Do you have any idea where the installation disks are?

Choosing the Part-Time Administrator

The larger the network, the more technical support it needs. Most small networks — with just a dozen or so computers — can get by with a part-time network administrator. Ideally, this person should be a closet computer geek: someone who has a secret interest in computers but doesn't like to admit it. Someone who will take books home with him or her and read them over the weekend. Someone who enjoys solving computer problems just for the sake of solving them.

The job of managing a network requires some computer skills, but it isn't entirely a technical job. Much of the work that the network administrator does is routine housework. Basically, the network administrator dusts, vacuums, and mops the network periodically to keep it from becoming a mess.

Here are some additional ideas on picking a part-time network administrator:

✔ The network administrator needs to be an organized person. Conduct a surprise office inspection and place the person with the neatest desk in charge of the network. (Don't warn them in advance, or everyone may mess up their desks intentionally the night before the inspection.)

✔ Allow enough time for network administration. For a small network (say, no more than 20 or so computers), an hour or two each week is enough. More time is needed upfront as the network administrator settles into the job and discovers the ins and outs of the network. After an initial settling-in period, though, network administration for a small office network doesn't take more than an hour or two per week. (Of course, larger networks take more time to manage.)

✔ Make sure that everyone knows who the network administrator is and that the network administrator has the authority to make decisions about the network, such as what access rights each user has, what files can and can't be stored on the server, how often backups are done, and so on.

✔ Pick someone who is assertive and willing to irritate people. A good network administrator should make sure that backups are working *before* a hard drive fails and make sure that antivirus protection is in place *before* a virus wipes out the entire network. This policing will irritate people, but it's for their own good.

✔ In most cases, the person who installs the network is also the network administrator. This is appropriate because no one understands the network better than the person who designs and installs it.

✔ The network administrator needs an understudy — someone who knows almost as much about the network, is eager to make a mark, and smiles when the worst network jobs are delegated.

✔ The network administrator has some sort of official title, such as Network Boss, Network Czar, Vice President in Charge of Network Operations, or Dr. Network. A badge, a personalized pocket protector, or a set of Spock ears helps, too.

The Three "Ups" of Network Management

Much of the network manager's job is routine stuff — the equivalent of vacuuming, dusting, and mopping, or changing your car's oil and rotating the tires.

Three of the most important routine tasks that a network administrator must do vigilantly are what I call the "Three Ups of Network Management." They are

✔ **Back up:** The network manager must ensure that the network is properly backed up. If something goes wrong and the network isn't backed up, guess who gets the blame? On the other hand, if disaster strikes yet you're able to recover everything from yesterday's backup with only a small amount of work lost, who gets the pat on the back, the fat bonus, and the vacation in the Bahamas? Chapter 20 describes the options for network backups. Read it *soon.*

✔ **Lock-up:** Another major task for a network administrator is sheltering the network from the evils of the outside world. These evils come in many forms, including hackers trying to break into your network and virus programs arriving through e-mail. Chapter 21 describes this task in more detail.

✔ **Clean-up:** Users think that the network server is like the attic: They want to throw files up there and leave them forever. No matter how much disk storage your network has, your users will fill it up sooner than you think, so the network manager gets the fun job of cleaning up the attic once in a while. The best advice I can offer is to continually complain about how messy it is up there and warn your users that spring cleaning is on the to-do list.

Managing Network Users

Managing network technology is the easiest part of network management. Computer technology can be confusing at first, but computers aren't as confusing as people. The real challenge of managing a network is managing the network's users.

The difference between managing technology and managing users is obvious: You can figure out computers, but who can ever really figure out people? The people who use the network are much less predictable than the network itself. Here are some tips for dealing with users:

✔ **Make user training a key part of the network manager's job.** Make sure that everyone who uses the network understands how it works and how to use it. If the network users don't understand how the network works, they may unintentionally do all kinds of weird things to it.

✔ **Treat network users respectfully.** If users don't understand how to use the network, it's not their fault. Explain it to them. Offer a class. Buy each one a copy of this book, and tell them to read it during the lunch hour. Hold their hands. Just don't treat them like idiots.

✔ **Create a network cheat sheet.** It should contain everything users need to know about using the network — on one page. Everyone needs a copy.

✔ **Be as responsive as possible.** If you don't quickly fix a network user's problem, he may try to fix it. You don't want that to happen.

The better you understand the psychology of network users, the more prepared you are for the strangeness they often serve up. Toward that end, I recommend that you read the *Diagnostic and Statistical Manual of Mental Disorders* (also known as *DSM-5*) from cover to cover.

Acquiring Software Tools for Network Administrators

Network managers need certain tools to get their jobs done. Managers of big, complicated, expensive networks need big, complicated, expensive tools. Managers of small networks need small tools.

Some tools that a manager needs are hardware tools, such as screwdrivers, cable crimpers, and hammers. The tools I'm talking about, however, are software tools. I mention a couple of them earlier in this chapter: Visio (to help you draw network diagrams) and a network-discovery tool to help you map your network. Here are a few others:

✔ **Built-in TCP/IP commands:** Many of the software tools that you need in order to manage a network come with the network itself. As the network manager, you should read through the manuals that come with your network software to see which management tools are available. For example, Windows includes a `net diag` command that you can use to make sure that all the computers on a network can communicate with each other. (You can run `net diag` from an MS-DOS prompt.) For TCP/IP networks, you can use the TCP/IP diagnostic commands that I summarize in Table 18-1.

Table 18-1	TCP/IP Diagnostic Commands
Command	*What It Displays*
`arp`	Address resolution information used by the Address Resolution Protocol (ARP)
`hostname`	Your computer's host name
`ipconfig`	Current TCP/IP settings
`nbtstat`	The status of NetBIOS over TCP/IP connections
`netstat`	Statistics for TCP/IP
`nslookup`	DNS information
`ping`	Verification that a specified computer can be reached
`route`	The PC's routing tables
`tracert`	The route from your computer to a specified host

✔ **System Information:** This program, which comes with Windows, is a useful utility for network managers.

✔ **Hotfix Checker:** This handy tool from Microsoft scans your computers to see which patches need to be applied. You can download the Hotfix Checker for free from the Microsoft website. Just go to www.microsoft.com and search for **hotfix**.

✔ **Baseline Security Analyzer:** If you prefer GUI-based tools, check out this program, which you can download for free from the Microsoft website. To find it, go to www.microsoft.com and search for **Microsoft Baseline Security Analyzer**.

✔ **Protocol analyzer:** A *protocol analyzer* (or *packet sniffer*) can monitor and log the individual packets that travel along your network. You can configure the protocol analyzer to filter specific types of packets, watch for specific types of problems, and provide statistical analysis of the captured packets.

Most network administrators agree that Sniffer, by NetScout Systems, Inc. (www.netscout.com) is the best protocol analyzer available. However, it's also one of the most expensive. If you prefer a free alternative, check out *Wireshark,* which you can download for free from www.wireshark.org.

✔ **Network Monitor:** All current versions of Windows include a program called Network Monitor, which provides basic protocol analysis and can often help solve pesky network problems.

Building a Library

Scotty delivered one of his best lines in the original *Star Trek* series when he refused to take shore leave so that he could get caught up on his technical journals. "Don't you ever relax?" asked Kirk. "I am relaxing!" Scotty replied.

To be a good network administrator, you need to read computer books — lots of them. And you need to enjoy doing it. If you're the type who takes computer books with you to the beach, you'll make a great network administrator.

Read books on a variety of topics. I don't recommend specific titles, but I do recommend that you get a good, comprehensive book on each of these topics:

✔ Network security and hacking

✔ Wireless networking

✔ Network cabling and hardware

- ✔ Ethernet

- ✔ Windows Server 2008 or 2012

- ✔ Windows 7 or 8

- ✔ Linux

- ✔ TCP/IP

- ✔ DNS

- ✔ Sendmail or Microsoft Exchange Server, depending on which e-mail server you use

In addition to books, you may also want to subscribe to some magazines to keep up with what's happening in the networking industry. Here are a few you should probably consider, along with their web addresses:

- ✔ *InformationWeek:* www.informationweek.com

- ✔ *InfoWorld:* www.infoworld.com

- ✔ *Network Computing:* www.networkcomputing.com

- ✔ *Network World:* www.networkworld.com

- ✔ *2600 The Hacker Quarterly* (a great magazine on computer hacking and security): www.2600.com

The Internet is one of the best sources of technical information for network administrators. You'll want to stock your browser's Favorites menu with plenty of websites that contain useful networking information. In addition, you may want to subscribe to one of the many online newsletters that deliver fresh information on a regular basis via e-mail.

Pursuing Certification

Remember the scene near the end of *The Wizard of Oz* when the Wizard grants the Scarecrow a diploma, the Cowardly Lion a medal, and the Tin Man a testimonial?

Network certifications are kind of like that. I can picture the scene now:

The Wizard: "And as for you, my network-burdened friend, any geek with thick glasses can administer a network. Back where I come from, there are people who do nothing but configure Cisco routers all day long. And they don't have any more brains than you do. But they do have one thing you don't have: certification. And so, by the authority vested in me by the

Universita Committeeatum E Pluribus Unum, I hereby confer upon you the coveted certification of CND."

You: "CND?"

The Wizard: "Yes, that's, uh, *Certified Network Dummy.*"

You: "The Seven Layers of the OSI Reference Model are equal to the Sum of the Layers on the Opposite Side. Oh, joy, rapture! I feel like a network administrator already!"

My point is that certification in and of itself doesn't guarantee that you really know how to administer a network. That ability comes from real-world experience — not exam crams.

Nevertheless, certification is becoming increasingly important in today's competitive job market. So you may want to pursue certification, not just to improve your skills, but also to improve your resume. Certification is an expensive proposition. Each test can cost several hundred dollars, and depending on your technical skills, you may need to buy books to study or enroll in training courses before you take the tests.

You can pursue two basic types of certification: vendor-specific certification and vendor-neutral certification. The major software vendors such as Microsoft and Cisco provide certification programs for their own equipment and software. CompTIA, a nonprofit industry trade association, provides the best-known vendor-neutral certification.

Helpful Bluffs and Excuses

As network administrator, you just won't be able to solve a problem sometimes, at least not immediately. You can do two things in this situation. The first is to explain that the problem is particularly difficult and that you'll have a solution as soon as possible. The second solution is to look the user in the eyes and, with a straight face, try one of these phony explanations:

- ✔ Blame it on the version of whatever software you're using. "Oh, they fixed that with version 39."
- ✔ Blame it on cheap, imported memory chips.
- ✔ Blame it on Democrats. Or Republicans. Doesn't matter.
- ✔ Blame it on oil company executives.
- ✔ Blame it on global warming.

✔ Hope that the problem wasn't caused by stray static electricity. Those types of problems are very difficult to track down. Tell your users that not properly discharging themselves before using their computers can cause all kinds of problems.

✔ You need more memory.

✔ You need a bigger hard drive.

✔ You need a faster processor.

✔ Blame it on Jar-Jar Binks.

✔ You can't do that in Windows 8.

✔ You can only do that in Windows 8.

✔ Could be a virus.

✔ Or sunspots.

✔ No beer and no TV make Homer something something something.

Chapter 19

Solving Network Problems

- -

In This Chapter

▶ Checking the obvious things

▶ Fixing computers that have expired

▶ Pinpointing the cause of trouble

▶ Restarting client and server computers

▶ Reviewing network event logs

▶ Keeping a record of network woes

- -

*F*ace it: Networks are prone to breaking.

They have too many parts. Cables. Connectors. Cards. Switches. Routers. All these parts must be held together in a delicate balance, and the network equilibrium is all too easy to disturb. Even the best-designed computer networks sometimes act as if they're held together with baling wire, chewing gum, and duct tape.

To make matters worse, networks breed suspicion. After your computer is attached to a network, users begin to blame the network every time something goes wrong, regardless of whether the problem has anything to do with the network. You can't get columns to line up in a Word document? Must be the network. Your spreadsheet doesn't add up? The @@#$% network's acting up again. The stock market's down? Arghhh!!!!!!

The worst thing about network failures is that sometimes they can shut down an entire company. It's not so bad if just one user can't access a particular shared folder on a file server. If a critical server goes down, however, your network users may be locked out of their files, applications, e-mail, and everything else they need to conduct business as usual. When that happens, they'll be beating down your doors and won't stop until you get the network back up and running.

In this chapter, I review some of the most likely causes of network trouble and suggest some basic troubleshooting techniques that you can employ when your network goes on the fritz.

When Bad Things Happen to Good Computers

Here are some basic troubleshooting steps explaining what you should examine at the first sign of network trouble. In many (if not most) of the cases, one of the following steps can get your network back up and running:

1. **Make sure that your computer and everything attached to it is plugged in.**

   Computer geeks love it when a user calls for help, and they get to tell the user that the computer isn't plugged in or that its power strip is turned off. They write it down in their geek logs so that they can tell their geek friends about it later. They may even want to take your picture so that they can show it to their geek friends. (Most "accidents" involving computer geeks are a direct result of this kind of behavior. So try to be tactful when you ask a user whether he or she is sure the computer is actually turned on.)

2. **Make sure that your computer is properly connected to the network.**

3. **Note any error messages that appear on-screen.**

4. **Try restarting the computer.**

   An amazing number of computer problems are cleared up by a simple restart of the computer. Of course, in many cases, the problem recurs, so you'll have to eventually isolate the cause and fix the problem. Some problems are only intermittent, and a simple reboot is all that's needed.

5. **Try the built-in Windows network troubleshooter.**

   For more information, see the section, "Using the Windows Networking Troubleshooter," later in this chapter.

6. **Check the free disk space on your computer and on the server.**

   When a computer runs out of disk space or comes close to it, strange things can happen. Sometimes you get a clear error message indicating such a situation, but not always. Sometimes the computer just grinds to a halt; operations that used to take a few seconds now take a few minutes.

7. **Do a little experimenting to find out whether the problem is indeed a network problem or just a problem with the computer itself.**

   See the section, "Time to Experiment," later in this chapter, for some simple things that you can do to isolate a network problem.

8. **Try restarting the network server.**

   See the section, "Restarting a Network Server," later in this chapter.

Fixing Dead Computers

If a computer seems totally dead, here are some things to check:

- ✔ **Make sure that the computer is plugged in.**

- ✔ **If the computer is plugged into a surge protector or a power strip, make sure that the surge protector or power strip is plugged in and turned on.** If the surge protector or power strip has a light, it should be glowing. Also, the surge protector may have a reset button that needs to be pressed.

- ✔ **Make sure that the computer's On/Off switch is turned on.** This advice sounds too basic to even include here, but many computers have two power switches: an on/off switch on the back of the computer and a push-button on the front that actually starts the computer. If you push the front button and nothing happens, check the switch on the back to make sure it's in the ON position.

To complicate matters, newer computers have a Sleep feature, in which they appear to be turned off but really they're just sleeping. All you have to do to wake such a computer is jiggle the mouse a little. (I used to have an uncle like that.) It's easy to assume that the computer is turned off, press the power button, wonder why nothing happened, and then press the power button and hold it down, hoping it will take. If you hold down the power button long enough, the computer will actually turn itself off. Then, when you turn the computer back on, you get a message saying the computer wasn't shut down properly. Arghhh! The moral of the story is to jiggle the mouse if the computer seems to have nodded off.

- ✔ **If you think the computer isn't plugged in but it looks like it is, listen for the fan.** If the fan is running, the computer is getting power, and the problem is more serious than an unplugged power cord. (If the fan isn't running but the computer is plugged in and the power is on, the fan may be out to lunch.)

- ✔ **If the computer is plugged in and turned on but still not running, plug a lamp into the outlet to make sure that power is getting to the outlet.** You may need to reset a tripped circuit breaker or replace a bad surge protector. Or you may need to call the power company. (If you live in California, don't bother calling the power company. It probably won't do any good.)

- ✔ **Check the surge protector.** Surge protectors have a limited life span. After a few years of use, many surge protectors continue to provide electrical power for your computer, but the components that protect your computer from power surges no longer work. If you're using a surge protector that is more than two or three years old, replace the old surge protector with a new one.

✔ **Make sure that the monitor is plugged in and turned on.** The monitor has a separate power cord and switch. (The monitor actually has two cables that must be plugged in. One runs from the back of the monitor to the back of the computer; the other is a power cord that comes from the back of the monitor and must be plugged into an electrical outlet.)

✔ **Make sure that all cables are plugged in securely.** Your keyboard, monitor, mouse, and printer are all connected to the back of your computer by cables.

Make sure that the other ends of the monitor and printer cables are plugged in properly, too.

✔ **If the computer is running but the display is dark, try adjusting the monitor's contrast and brightness.** Some monitors have knobs that you can use to adjust the contrast and brightness of the monitor's display. They may have been turned down all the way.

Ways to Check a Network Connection

The cables that connect client computers to the rest of the network are finicky beasts. They can break at a moment's notice, and by "break," I don't necessarily mean "to physically break in two." Although some broken cables look like someone got to the cable with pruning shears, most cable problems aren't visible to the naked eye.

✔ **Twisted-pair cable:** If your network uses twisted-pair cable, you can quickly tell whether the cable connection to the network is good by looking at the back of your computer. Look for a small light located near where the cable plugs in; if this light is glowing steadily, the cable is good. If the light is dark or it's flashing intermittently, you have a cable problem (or a problem with the network card or the hub or switch that the other end of the cable is plugged in to).

If the light isn't glowing steadily, try removing the cable from your computer and reinserting it. This action may cure the weak connection.

✔ **Patch cable:** Hopefully, your network is wired so that each computer is connected to the network with a short (six feet or so) patch cable. One end of the patch cable plugs into the computer, and the other end plugs into a cable connector mounted on the wall. Try quickly disconnecting and reconnecting the patch cable. If that doesn't do the trick, try to find a spare patch cable that you can use.

✔ **Switches:** Switches are prone to having cable problems, too — especially switches that are wired in a "professional manner," involving a rat's nest of patch cables. Be careful whenever you enter the lair of the rat's nest. If you need to replace a patch cable, be very careful when you disconnect the suspected bad cable and reconnect the good cable in its place.

A Bunch of Error Messages Just Flew By!

Error messages that display when your computer boots can provide invaluable clues to determine the source of the problem.

If you see error messages when you start up the computer, keep the following points in mind:

✔ **Don't panic if you see a lot of error messages.** Sometimes, a simple problem that's easy to correct can cause a plethora of error messages when you start your computer. The messages may look as if your computer is falling to pieces, but the fix may be very simple.

✔ **If the messages fly by so fast that you can't see them, press your computer's Pause key.** Your computer comes to a screeching halt, giving you a chance to catch up on your error-message reading. After you've read enough, press the Pause key again to get things moving. (On keyboards that don't have a Pause key, pressing Ctrl+Num Lock or Ctrl+S does the same thing.)

✔ **If you miss the error messages the first time, restart the computer and watch them again.**

✔ **Better yet, press F8 when you see the Starting Windows message.** This displays a menu that allows you to select from several startup options.

Double-Checking Your Network Settings

I swear that there are little green men who sneak into offices at night, turn on computers, and mess up TCP/IP configuration settings just for kicks. These little green men are affectionately known as *networchons*.

Remarkably, network configuration settings sometimes get inadvertently changed so that a computer, which enjoyed the network for months or even years, one day finds itself unable to access the network. So one of the first things you do, after making sure that the computers are actually on and that the cables aren't broken, is a basic review of the computer's network settings. Check the following:

✔ **At a command prompt, run ipconfig to make sure that TCP/IP is up and running on the computer and that the IP addresses, subnet masks, and default gateway settings look right.**

✔ **Call up the network connection's Properties dialog box and make sure that the necessary protocols are installed correctly.**

✔ **Open the System Properties dialog box (double-click System in Control Panel) and check the Computer Name tab.**

Make sure that the computer name is unique and also that the domain or workgroup name is spelled properly.

✔ **Double-check the user account to make sure that the user really has permission to access the resources he needs.**

Using the Windows Networking Troubleshooter

Windows comes with a built-in troubleshooter that can often help you to pin down the cause of a network problem. Figure 19-1 shows the Windows 8 version. Answer the questions asked by the troubleshooter and click Next to move from screen to screen. The Networking Troubleshooter can't solve all networking problems, but it does point out the causes of the most common problems.

Figure 19-1: The Windows 8 Networking Trouble-shooter.

The procedure for starting Networking Troubleshooter depends on which version of Windows you're using:

- **Windows 8 and Windows 7:** Open Control Panel, click View Network Status and Tasks, and then click Troubleshoot Problems. Then select the troubleshooter that seems most directly related to the problem you're experiencing. You'll find troubleshooters for wireless network problems, home networks, and local area network (LAN) and Internet connections.

- **Windows Vista:** Choose Start⇨Help and Support, click Troubleshooting, and then click the link for the network troubleshooter that seems most directly related to the problem you're experiencing. You'll find trouble-shooters for wireless network problems, home networks, and LAN and Internet connections.

- **Windows XP:** Choose Start⇨Help and Support⇨Networking and the Web⇨Fixing Network or Web Problems. Then click Home and Small Office Networking Troubleshooter.

Time to Experiment

If you can't find some obvious explanation for your troubles — say, the computer is unplugged — you need to do some experimenting to narrow down the possibilities. Design your experiments to answer one basic question: Is it a network problem or a local computer problem?

Here are some ways you can narrow down the cause of the problem:

- **Try performing the same operation on someone else's computer.** If no one on the network can access a network drive or printer, something is probably wrong with the network. On the other hand, if the error occurs on only one computer, the problem is likely with that computer. The wayward computer may not be reliably communicating with the network or configured properly for the network, or the problem may have nothing to do with the network at all.

- **If you can perform the operation on another computer without problems, try logging on to the network with another computer using your own username.** Then see whether you can perform the operation without error. If you can, the problem is probably on your computer. If you can't, the problem may be with the way your user account is configured.

- **If you can't log on at another computer, try waiting for a bit.** Your account may be temporarily locked out. This can happen for a variety of reasons — the most common of which is trying to log on with the wrong password several times in a row. If you're still locked out an hour later, call the network administrator and offer a doughnut.

Who's on First?

When troubleshooting a networking problem, find out who is actually logged on to a network server. For example, if a user can't access a file on the server, you can check whether the user is logged on. If so, you know that the user's account is valid. Even so, the user may not have permission to access the particular file or folder that he's attempting to access. On the other hand, if the user isn't logged on, the problem may lie with the account itself or how the user is attempting to connect to the server.

I also recommend finding out who's logged on in case you need to restart the server. For more information about restarting a server, see the section, "Restarting a Network Server," later in this chapter.

To find out who is currently logged on to a Windows server, right-click the Computer icon on the desktop and choose Manage from the menu that appears. This brings up the Computer Management window. Open System Tools in the tree list and then open Shared Folders and select Sessions. A list of users who are logged on appears.

You can immediately disconnect all users by right-clicking Sessions in the Computer Management window and choosing All Tasks➪Disconnect All. Be warned, however, that this can cause users to lose data.

Restarting a Client Computer

Sometimes, trouble gets a computer so tied up in knots that the only thing you can do is reboot. In some cases, the computer just starts acting weird. Strange characters appear on the screen, or Windows goes haywire and doesn't let you exit a program. Sometimes, the computer gets so confused that it can't even move. It just sits there, like a deer staring at oncoming headlights. It won't move, no matter how hard you press Esc or Enter. You can move the mouse all over your desktop, or you can even throw it across the room, but the mouse pointer on the screen stays perfectly still.

When a computer starts acting strange, you need to reboot. If you must reboot, you should do so as cleanly as possible. I know this procedure may seem elementary, but the technique for safely restarting a client computer is worth repeating, even if it is basic:

1. **Save your work if you can.**

   Use the File⇨Save command to save any documents or files that you were editing when things started to go haywire. If you can't use the menus, try clicking the Save button on the toolbar. If that doesn't work, try pressing Ctrl+S (the standard keyboard shortcut for the Save command).

2. **Close any running programs if you can.**

   Use the File⇨Exit command or click the Close button in the upper-right corner of the program window. Or press Alt+F4.

   If a program refuses to close, you can usually shut it down by using Windows Task Manager. Right-click the Windows task bar and choose Start Task Manager. Then select the program you want to close and click the End Task button.

3. **Restart the computer.**

   - *Windows XP:* Choose Start⇨Turn Off Computer to summon the Shut Down Windows dialog box. Select the Restart option and then click OK.

   - *Windows 7 and Vista:* Click the Start button, click the right arrow that appears at the bottom-right corner of the Start menu, and then click Restart.

   - *Windows 8:* Oddly enough, shutting down Windows 8 is a bit challenging. You can stare at the Windows 8 desktop all day and not find an intuitive way to shut down your computer. The secret lies in the Charms Bar, which you can find by hovering the mouse over the lower-right corner of the screen. Next, click the Settings icon, and then click the Shut Down icon.

If restarting your computer doesn't seem to fix the problem, you may need to turn off your computer and then turn it on again. To do so, follow the previous procedure but choose Shut Down instead of Restart.

Here are a few things to try if you have trouble restarting your computer:

1. **If your computer refuses to respond to the Start⇨Shut Down command, try pressing Ctrl+Alt+Delete.**

   This is called the "three-finger salute." It's appropriate to say, "Queueue" while you do it.

   When you press Ctrl+Alt+Delete, Windows displays a dialog box that enables you to close any running programs or shut down your computer entirely.

2. **If pressing Ctrl+Alt+Delete doesn't do anything, you've reached the last resort. The only thing left to do is turn off the computer by pressing the power On/Off button and holding it down for a few seconds.**

Turning off your computer by pressing the power button is a drastic action that you should take only after your computer becomes completely unresponsive. Any work you haven't yet saved to disk is lost. (Sniff.) (If your computer doesn't have a Reset button, turn off the computer, wait a few moments, and then turn the computer back on again.)

If at all possible, save your work before restarting your computer. Any work you haven't saved is lost. Unfortunately, if your computer is totally tied up in knots, you probably can't save your work. In that case, you have no choice but to push your computer off the digital cliff.

Booting in Safe Mode

Windows provides a special start-up mode called *Safe Mode* that's designed to help fix misbehaving computers. When you start your computer in Safe Mode, Windows loads only the most essential parts of itself into memory — the bare minimum required for Windows to work. Safe Mode is especially useful when your computer has developed a problem that prevents you from using the computer at all.

To boot your computer in Safe Mode, first restart the computer. Then, as soon as the computer begins to restart, start pressing the F8 key — just tap away at it until a menu titled Advanced Boot Options appears. One of the options on this menu is Safe Mode; use the up- or down-arrow keys to select that option, and then press Enter to boot in Safe Mode.

Using System Restore

System Restore is a Windows feature that periodically saves important Windows configuration information and allows you to later return your system to a previously saved configuration. This can often fix problems by reverting your computer to a time when it was working.

By default, Windows saves *restore points* whenever you install new software on your computer or apply a system update. Restore points are also saved automatically every seven days.

Although System Restore is turned on by default, you should verify that System Restore is active and running to make sure that System Restore points are being created. To do that, right-click Computer from the Start menu, choose Properties, and then click the System Protection tab. The dialog box shown in Figure 19-2 is displayed. Verify that the Protection status for your computer's C: drive is On. If it isn't, select the C: drive and click the Configure button to configure System Restore for the drive.

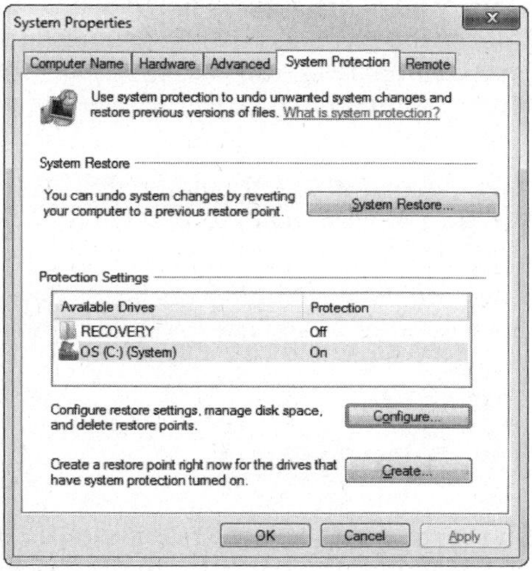

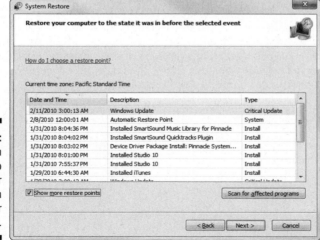

Figure 19-2:
The System Protection tab of the System Properties dialog box.

If your computer develops a problem, you can restore it to a previously saved restore point by clicking the System Protection tab. This brings up the System Restore Wizard, as shown in Figure 19-3. This wizard allows you to select the restore point you want to use.

Figure 19-3:
Use System Restore to restore your system to an earlier configuration.

Here are a few additional thoughts to remember about System Restore:

- System Restore *does not* delete data files from your system. Thus, files in your Documents folder won't be lost.

- System Restore *does* remove any applications or system updates you've installed since the restore point was made. Thus, you need to reinstall those applications or system updates — unless, of course, you determine that an application or system update was the cause of your problem in the first place.

- System Restore automatically restarts your computer. The restart may be slow because some of the changes made by System Restore happen after the restart.

- Do *not* turn off or cut power to your computer during System Restore. Doing so may leave your computer in an unrecoverable state.

Restarting Network Services

Once in a while, the operating system (OS) service that supports the task that's causing you trouble inexplicably stops or gets stuck. If users can't access a server, it may be because one of the key network services has stopped or is stuck.

You can review the status of services by using the Services tool, as shown in Figure 19-4. To display it, right-click Computer from the Start menu and choose Manage; then, expand the Services and Applications node and click Services. Review this list to make sure that all key services are running. If an important service is paused or stopped, restart it.

Which services qualify as "important" depends on what roles you define for the server. Table 19-1 lists a few important services that are common to most Windows network operating systems (NOSes). However, many servers require additional services besides these. In fact, a typical server will have many dozens of services running simultaneously.

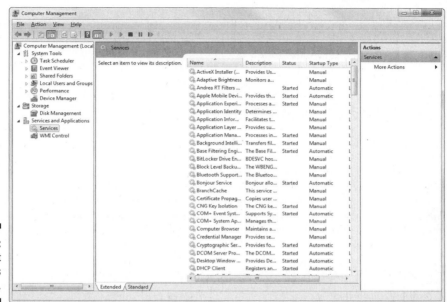

Figure 19-4:
Looking at services (Windows 8).

Table 19-1	Key Windows Services
Service	**Description**
Computer Browser	Maintains a list of computers on the network that can be accessed. If this service is disabled, the computer won't be able to use browsing services, such as My Network Places.
DHCP Client	Enables the computer to obtain its IP address from a Dynamic Host Configuration Protocol (DHCP) server. If this service is disabled, the computer's IP address won't be configured properly.
DNS Client	Enables the computer to access a Domain Name Server (DNS) server to resolve DNS names. If this service is disabled, the computer won't be able to handle DNS names, including Internet addresses and Active Directory (AD) names.
Server	Provides basic file- and printer-sharing services for the server. If this service is stopped, clients won't be able to connect to the server to access files or printers.
Workstation	Enables the computer to establish client connections with other servers. If this service is disabled, the computer won't be able to connect to other servers.

Key services usually stop for a reason, so simply restarting a stopped service probably won't solve your network's problem — at least, not for long. You should review the System log to look for any error messages that may explain why the service stopped in the first place.

Restarting a Network Server

Sometimes, the only way to flush out a network problem is to restart the network server that's experiencing trouble.

Restarting a network server is something you should do only as a last resort. Windows Server is designed to run for months or even years at a time without rebooting. Restarting a server invariably results in a temporary shutdown of the network. If you must restart a server, try to do it during off hours if possible.

Before you restart a server, check whether a specific service that's required has been paused or stopped. You may be able to just restart the individual service rather than the entire server. For more information, see the section, "Restarting Network Services," earlier in this chapter.

Here's the basic procedure for restarting a network server:

1. **Make sure that everyone is logged off the server.**

   The easiest way to do that is to restart the server after normal business hours, when everyone has gone home for the day. Then, you can just shut down the server and let the shutdown process forcibly log off any remaining users.

   To find out who's logged on, refer to the earlier section, "Who's on First?"

2. **After you're sure the users have logged off, shut down the network server.**

   You want to do this step behaving like a good citizen if possible — decently, and in order. Use the Start⇨Shut Down command to shut down the server. This summons a dialog box that requires you to indicate the reason for the shutdown. The information you supply here is entered into the server's System log, which you can review by using Event Viewer. See the next section for more on Event Viewer.

3. **Reboot the server computer or turn it off and then on again.**

   Watch the server start up to make sure that no error messages appear.

4. **Tell everyone to log back on and make sure that everyone can now access the network.**

Heed the following when you consider restarting the network server:

✔ **Restarting the network server is more drastic than restarting a client computer.** Make sure that everyone saves his or her work and logs off the network before you do it! You can cause major problems if you blindly turn off the server computer while users are logged on.

✔ **Obviously, restarting a network server is a major inconvenience to every network user.** Better offer treats.

Looking at Event Logs

One of the most useful troubleshooting techniques for diagnosing network problems is to review the network operating system's built-in event logs. These logs contain information about interesting and potentially troublesome events that occur during the daily operation of your network. Ordinarily, these logs run in the background, quietly gathering information about network events. When something goes wrong, you can check the logs to see whether the problem generated a noteworthy event. In many cases, the event logs contain an entry that pinpoints the exact cause of the problem and suggests a solution.

To display the event logs in a Windows server, use Event Viewer, which is available from the Administrative Tools menu. For example, Figure 19-5 shows an Event Viewer from a Windows Server 2012 system. The tree listing on the left side of Event Viewer lists five categories of events that are tracked: Application, Security, Setup, System, and Forwarded Events. Select one of these options to see the log that you want to view. For details about a particular event, double-click the event to display a dialog box with detailed information about the event.

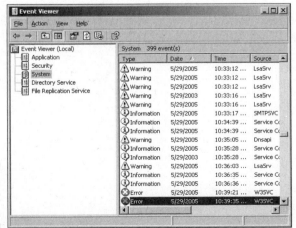

Figure 19-5:
View event logs here.

Documenting Your Trials and Tribulations

For a large network, you probably want to invest in problem-management software that tracks each problem through the entire process of troubleshooting, from initial report to final resolution. For small- and medium-sized networks, it's probably sufficient to put together a three-ring binder with pre-printed forms. Or record your log in a Word document or an Excel spreadsheet.

Regardless of how you track your network problems, the tracking log should include the following information:

- ✔ **The real name and the network username of the person reporting the problem**

- ✔ **The date the problem was first reported**

- ✔ **An indication of the severity of the problem**

   Is it merely an inconvenience, or is a user unable to complete his or her work because of the problem? Does a workaround exist?

- ✔ **The name of the person assigned to resolve the problem**

- ✔ **A description of the problem**

- ✔ **A list of the software involved, including versions**

- ✔ **A description of the steps taken to solve the problem**

- ✔ **A description of any intermediate steps that were taken to try to solve the problem, along with an indication of whether those steps were "undone" when they didn't help solve the problem**

- ✔ **The date the problem was finally resolved**

Chapter 20

Backing Up Your Data

- -

In This Chapter

▶ Understanding the need for backups

▶ Working with tape drives and other backup media

▶ Understanding the different types of backups

▶ Mastering tape rotation and other details

- -

*I*f you're the hapless network manager, the safety of the data on your network is your responsibility. In fact, it's your primary responsibility. You get paid to lie awake at night worrying about your data. Will it be there tomorrow? If it's not, can you get it back? And — most important — if you can't get it back, will you have a job tomorrow?

This chapter covers the ins and outs of being a good, responsible, trustworthy network manager. No one gives out merit badges for this stuff, but someone should.

Backing Up Your Data

Having data backed up is the cornerstone of any disaster recovery plan. Without backups, a simple hard drive failure can set your company back days or even weeks while it tries to reconstruct lost data. In fact, without backups, your company's very existence is in jeopardy.

The fundamental goal of backing up is simple: Keep a spare copy of your network's critical data so that no matter what happens, you never lose more than one day's work. The stock market may crash, Earth may be hit by a giant asteroid, or the Cleveland Browns might win the Super Bowl. But as long as you're on top of your backups, you'll survive.

The way to meet the primary goal of backups is, naturally, to make sure that data is reliably backed up every day. For many networks, you can back up all the network hard drives every night. And even if full nightly backups aren't possible, you can still use techniques that can ensure that every file on the network has a backup copy that's no more than one day old.

Choosing Where to Back Up Your Data

If you plan on backing up the data on your network server's hard drives, you obviously need some type of media on which to back up the data. You could copy the data onto CDs, but a 500GB hard drive would need more than 750 CDs for a full backup. That's a few more discs than most people want to keep in the closet. You could use DVDs, but you'll still need about a dozen of them, as well as an hour or so to fill each one. Sigh. That means devoting every Saturday to creating your backups.

Because of the limitations of CDs and DVDs, most network administrators back up network data to some other type of storage device. The three most common options are

- ✓ **Tape:** Magnetic tape, the oldest storage medium for backups, is still one of the most widely used types. One of the biggest advantages of tape backups is that tape cartridges are small and can thus be easily transported to an offsite location.

- ✓ **Network Attached Storage (NAS):** A *Network Attached Storage* device connects directly to your network. NAS devices are often used as backup devices because they are inexpensive. In addition, they are relatively small and easy to remove, so like tape, they can be transported offsite.

- ✓ **Cloud backup:** An increasingly popular option is to use a third-party service to back up your data to a remote location via the Internet. Cloud backup has the advantage of already being offsite.

Backing Up to Tape

Another benefit of using a tape backup is that you can run it unattended. In fact, you can schedule a tape backup to run automatically during off hours when no one is using the network. For unattended backups to work, though, you must ensure that you have enough tape capacity to back up your entire network server's hard drive without having to manually switch tapes. If your network server has only 100GB of data, you can easily back it up onto a single tape. If you have 1,000GB of data, however, invest in a tape drive that features a magazine changer that can hold several tapes and automatically cycle them in and out of the drive. That way, you can run your backups unattended.

You have several distinct types of tape backup systems to choose from:

✔ **Travan drives:** A popular style of tape backup for small servers is a Travan drive, which comes in a variety of models with tape capacities ranging from 20GB to 40GB. You can purchase a 20GB drive for less than $200.

✔ **DAT, DLT, and LTO units:** For larger networks, you can get tape backup units that offer higher capacity and faster backup speed than Travan drives — for more money, of course. Digital audio tape (DAT) units can back up as much as 80GB on a single tape, and DLT (digital linear tape) drives can store up to 800GB on one tape. Linear tape open (LTO) drives can store 1.5TB on a single tape. DAT, DLT, and LTO drives can cost $1,000 or more, depending on the capacity.

✔ **Robotic units:** If you're really up the backup creek, with hundreds of gigabytes to back up, you can get robotic tape backup units that automatically fetch and load tape cartridges from a library. That way, you can do complete backups without having to load tapes manually. As you can likely guess, these units aren't inexpensive: Small ones, which have a library of about eight tapes and a total backup capacity of more than 5,000GB, start at about $4,000.

Understanding Backup Software

All versions of Windows come with a built-in backup program. In addition, most tape drives come with backup programs that are often faster or more flexible than the standard Windows backup.

You can also purchase sophisticated backup programs that are specially designed for networks that have multiple servers with data that must be backed up. For a basic Windows file server, you can use the backup program that comes with Windows Server. Server versions of Windows come with a decent backup program that can run scheduled, unattended tape backups.

Backup programs do more than just copy data from your hard drive to tape. Backup programs use special compression techniques to squeeze your data so that you can cram more data onto fewer tapes. Compression factors of 2:1 are common, so you can usually squeeze 100GB of data onto a tape that would hold only 50GB of data without compression. (Tape drive manufacturers tend to state the capacity of their drives by using compressed data, assuming a

2:1 compression ratio. Thus, a 200GB tape has an uncompressed capacity of 100GB.)

Whether you achieve a compression factor of 2:1 depends on the nature of the data you're backing up:

- **Documents:** If your network is used primarily for Microsoft Office applications and is filled with Word and Excel documents, you'll probably get better than 2:1 compression.

- **Graphics:** If your network data consists primarily of graphic image files, you probably won't get much compression. Most graphic image file formats are already compressed, so they can't be compressed much more by the backup software's compression methods.

Backup programs also help you keep track of which data has been backed up and which hasn't. They also offer options, such as incremental or differential backups that can streamline the backup process, as I describe in the next section.

If your network has more than one server, invest in good backup software. The most popular is Yosemite Backup, made by BarracudaWare (`www.barracuda ware.com`). Besides being able to handle multiple servers, one of the main advantages of backup software (such as Yosemite Backup) is that it can properly back up Microsoft Exchange server data.

Comparing Types of Backups

You can perform five different types of backups. Many backup schemes rely on full daily backups, but for some networks, using a scheme that relies on two or more of these backup types is more practical.

The differences among the five types of backups involve a little technical detail known as the "archive bit," which indicates whether a file has been modified since it was backed up. The archive bit is a little flag stored along with the filename, creation date, and other directory information. Any time a program modifies a file, the archive bit is set to the On position. That way, backup programs know that the file has been modified and needs to be backed up.

The differences among the various types of backups center on whether they use the archive bit to determine which files to back up, as well as whether they flip the archive bit to the Off position after they back up a file. Table 20-1 summarizes these differences, which I explain in the following sections.

Backup programs allow you to select any combination of drives and folders to back up. As a result, you can customize the file selection for a backup operation to suit your needs. For example, you can set up one backup plan that backs up all a server's shared folders and drives, plus its mail server stores, but then leaves out folders that rarely change, such as the operating system folders or installed program folders. You can then back up those folders on a less-regular basis. The drives and folders that you select for a backup operation are collectively called the *backup selection*.

Table 20-1	How Backup Types Use the Archive Bit	
Backup Type	*Selects Files Based on Archive Bit?*	*Resets Archive Bits After Backing Up?*
Normal	No	Yes
Copy	No	No
Daily	No*	No
Incremental	Yes	Yes
Differential	Yes	No

Selects files based on the Last Modified date.

The archive bit would have made a good Abbott and Costello routine. ("All right, I wanna know who modified the archive bit." "What." "Who?" "No, What." "Wait a minute . . . just tell me what's the name of the guy who modified the archive bit!" "Right.")

Normal backups

A *normal backup* — also called a *full backup* — is the basic type of backup. In a normal backup, all files in the backup selection are backed up regardless of whether the archive bit has been set. In other words, the files are backed up even if they haven't been modified since the last time they were backed up. When each file is backed up, its archive bit is reset, so backups that select files based on the archive bit setting won't back up the files.

When a normal backup finishes, none of the files in the backup selection has its archive bit set. As a result, if you immediately follow a normal backup with an incremental backup or a differential backup, files won't be selected for backup by the incremental or differential backup because no file will have its archive bit set.

The easiest backup scheme is to simply schedule a normal backup every night. That way, all your data is backed up on a daily basis. Then, if the need arises, you can restore files from a single tape or set of tapes. Restoring files is more complicated when other types of backups are involved.

Do normal backups nightly if you have the tape capacity to do them unattended — that is, without having to swap tapes. If you can't do an unattended normal backup because the amount of data to be backed up is greater than the capacity of your tape drive(s), you have to use other types of backups in combination with normal backups.

If you can't get a normal backup on a single tape, and you can't afford a second tape drive or a tape changer, take a hard look at the data that's being included in the backup selection. I recently worked on a network that was difficult to back up onto a single tape. When I examined the data that was being backed up, I discovered a large amount of static data that was essentially an online archive of old projects. This data was necessary because network users needed it for research purposes, but the data was read-only. Even though the data never changed, it was being backed up to tape every night, and the backups required two tapes. After I removed this data from the cycle of nightly backups, the backups were able to squeeze onto a single tape again.

If you remove static data from the nightly backup, make sure that you have a secure backup of the static data on tape, CD-RW, or some other media.

Copy backups

A *copy backup* is similar to a normal backup except that the archive bit isn't reset when each file is copied. As a result, copy backups don't disrupt the cycle of normal and incremental or differential backups.

Copy backups usually aren't incorporated into regular, scheduled backups. Instead, you use a copy backup when you want to do an occasional one-shot backup. If you're about to perform an operating system upgrade, for example, you should back up the server before proceeding. If you do a full backup, the archive bits are reset, and your regular backups are disrupted. If you do a copy backup, however, the archive bits of any modified files remain unchanged. As a result, your regular normal and incremental or differential backups are unaffected.

If you don't incorporate incremental or differential backups into your backup routine, the difference between a copy backup and a normal backup is moot.

Daily backups

A *daily backup* backs up just those files that changed the same day when the backup was performed. A daily backup examines the modification date stored with each file's directory entry to determine whether a file should be backed up. Daily backups don't reset the archive bit.

I'm not a big fan of this option because of the small possibility that some files may slip through the cracks. Someone may be working late one night and modify a file after the evening's backups have completed — but before midnight — meaning that those files won't be included in the following night's backups. Incremental or differential backups, which rely on the archive bit rather than the modification date, are more reliable.

Incremental backups

An *incremental backup* backs up only those files that were modified since the last time you did a backup. Incremental backups are a lot faster than full backups because your network users probably modify only a small portion of the files on the server on any given day. As a result, if a full backup takes three tapes, you can probably fit an entire week's worth of incremental backups on a single tape.

When an incremental backup copies each file, it resets the file's archive bit. That way, the file will be backed up again before your next normal backup only when a user modifies the file again.

Here are some thoughts about using incremental backups:

✔ **The easiest way to use incremental backups is the following:**

- A *normal* backup every Monday

  If your full backup takes more than 12 hours, you may want to do it on Friday so that it can run over the weekend.

- An *incremental* backup on each remaining normal business day (for example, Tuesday, Wednesday, Thursday, and Friday)

✔ **When you use incremental backups, the complete backup consists of the full backup tapes and all the incremental backup tapes that you've made since you did the full backup.**

If the hard drive crashes, and you have to restore the data onto a new drive, you first restore Monday's normal backup and then restore each of the subsequent incremental backups.

✓ **Incremental backups complicate restoring individual files because the most recent copy of the file may be on the full backup tape or on any of the incremental backups.**

  Backup programs keep track of the location of the most recent version of each file to simplify the process.

  ✓ **When you use incremental backups, you can choose whether you want to**

  • Store each incremental backup on its own tape.

  • Append each backup to the end of an existing tape.

  Often, you can use a single tape for a week of incremental backups.

Differential backups

A *differential backup* is similar to an incremental backup except that it doesn't reset the archive bit when files are backed up. As a result, each differential backup represents the difference between the last normal backup and the current state of the hard drive.

To do a full restore from a differential backup, you first restore the last normal backup and then restore the most recent differential backup.

Suppose that you do a normal backup on Monday and differential backups on Tuesday, Wednesday, and Thursday, and your hard drive crashes Friday morning. On Friday afternoon, you install a new hard drive. To restore the data, you first restore the normal backup from Monday. Then you restore the differential backup from Thursday. The Tuesday and Wednesday differential backups aren't needed.

The main difference between incremental and differential backups is that

  ✓ *Incremental* backups result in smaller and faster backups.

  ✓ *Differential* backups are easier to restore.

  If your users often ask you to restore individual files, consider using differential backups.

Choosing between Local and Network Backups

When you back up network data, you have two basic approaches to running the backup software:

✔ You can perform a *local backup,* in which the backup software runs on the file server itself and backs up data to a tape drive that's installed in the server.

✔ Or you can perform a *network backup,* in which you use one network computer to back up data from another network computer. In a network backup, the data has to travel over the network to get to the computer that's running the backup.

If you run the backups from the file server, you'll tie up the server while the backup is running, and users will complain that their server access has slowed to a snail's pace. On the other hand, if you run the backup over the network from a client computer or a dedicated backup server, you'll flood the network with gigabytes of data being backed up. Then your users will complain that the entire network has slowed to a snail's pace.

Network performance is one of the main reasons why you should try to run your backups during off hours, when other users aren't accessing the network. Another reason to run backups during off hours is so that you can perform a more thorough backup. If you run your backup while other users are accessing files, the backup program is likely to skip any files that are being accessed by users at the time the backup runs. As a result, your backup won't include those files. Ironically, the files most likely to get left out of the backup are often the files that need backing up the most, because they're the files that are being used and modified.

Here are some extra thoughts on client and server backups:

✔ **Backing up directly from the server isn't necessarily more efficient than backing up from a client because data doesn't have to travel over the network.** The network may well be faster than the tape drive. The network probably won't slow down backups unless you back up during the busiest time of the day, when hordes of network users are storming the network gates.

✔ **To improve network backup speed and to minimize the effect that network backups have on the rest of the network, consider using a 1,000 Mbps switch instead of a normal 100 Mbps switch to connect the servers and the backup client.** That way, network traffic between the server and the backup client won't bog down the rest of the network.

✔ **Any files that are open while the backups are running won't get backed up.** That's usually not a problem, because backups are run at off hours when people have gone home. If someone leaves his computer on with a Word document open, however, that Word document won't be backed up. One way to solve this problem is to set up the server so that it automatically logs everyone off the network before the backups begin.

✔ **Some backup programs have special features that enable them to back up open files.** The backup programs that come with Windows Server (versions 2003 and later) do this by creating a snapshot of the volume when it begins, thus making temporary copies of any files that are modified during the backup. The backup backs up the temporary copies rather than the versions being modified. When the backup finishes, the temporary copies are deleted.

Deciding How Many Sets of Backups to Keep

Don't try to cut costs by purchasing one backup tape and reusing it every day. What happens if you accidentally delete an important file on Tuesday and don't discover your mistake until Thursday? Because the file didn't exist on Wednesday, it won't be on Wednesday's backup tape. If you have only one tape that's reused every day, you're outta luck.

The safest scheme is to use a new backup tape every day and keep all your old tapes in a vault. Pretty soon, though, your tape vault can start looking like the warehouse where they stored the Ark of the Covenant at the end of *Raiders of the Lost Ark.*

As a compromise between these two extremes, most users purchase several tapes and rotate them. That way, you always have several backup tapes to fall back on, just in case the file you need isn't on the most recent backup tape. This technique is *tape rotation,* and several variations are commonly used:

✔ **The simplest approach is to purchase three tapes and label them A, B, and C.** You use the tapes on a daily basis in sequence: A the first day, B the second day, and C the third day; then A the fourth day, B the fifth day, C the sixth day, and so on. On any given day, you have three generations of backups: today's, yesterday's, and the day-before-yesterday's. Computer geeks like to call these the *grandfather, father,* and *son* tapes.

✔ **Another simple approach is to purchase five tapes and use one each day of the workweek.**

✔ **A variation of the preceding bullet is to buy eight tapes.** Take four of them, and write *Tuesday* on one label, *Wednesday* on the second, *Thursday* on the third, and *Friday* on the fourth label. On the other four tapes, write *Monday 1, Monday 2, Monday 3,* and *Monday 4.* Now tack up a calendar on the wall near the computer, and number all the Mondays in the year: 1, 2, 3, 4, 1, 2, 3, 4, and so on.

On Tuesday through Friday, you use the appropriate daily backup tape. When you run a full backup on Monday, consult the calendar to decide which Monday tape to use. With this scheme, you always have four weeks' worth of Monday backup tapes, plus individual backup tapes for the rest of the week.

✔ **If bookkeeping data lives on the network, make a backup copy of all your files (or at least all your accounting files) immediately before closing the books each month; then retain those backups for each month of the year.** This doesn't necessarily mean that you should purchase 12 additional tapes. If you back up just your accounting files, you can probably fit all 12 months on a single tape. Just make sure that you back up with the Append to Tape option rather than the Erase Tape option so that the previous contents of the tape aren't destroyed. Also, treat this accounting backup as completely separate from your normal daily backup routine.

Keep at least one recent full backup at another location. That way, if your office should fall victim to an errant Scud missile or a rogue asteroid, you can re-create your data from the backup copy that you stored offsite. Make sure that the person entrusted with the task of taking the backups to this offsite location is trustworthy.

Verifying Tape Reliability

From experience, I've found that although tape drives are very reliable, they do run amok once in a while. The problem is that they don't always tell you when they're not working. A tape drive (especially one of the less-expensive Travan drives; refer to "Backing Up to Tape," earlier in this chapter) can spin along for hours, pretending to back up your data — but in reality, your data isn't being written reliably to the tape. In other words, a tape drive can trick you into thinking that your backups are working just fine. Then, when disaster strikes and you need your backup tapes, you may just discover that the tapes are worthless.

Don't panic! Here's a simple way to assure yourself that your tape drive is working. Just activate the "compare after backup" feature of your backup software. As soon as your backup program finishes backing up your data, it rewinds the tape, reads each backed-up file, and compares it with the original version on the hard drive. If all files compare, you know that your backups are trustworthy.

Here are some additional thoughts about the reliability of tapes:

- The compare-after-backup feature doubles the time required to do a backup, but that doesn't matter if your entire backup fits on one tape. You can just run the backup after hours. Whether the backup and repair operation takes one hour or ten doesn't matter, as long as it's finished by the time the network users arrive at work the next morning.

- If your backups require more than one tape, you may not want to run the compare-after-backup feature every day. Be sure to run it periodically, however, to check that your tape drive is working.

- If your backup program reports errors, throw away the tape, and use a new tape.

- Actually, you should ignore that last comment about waiting for your backup program to report errors. You should discard tapes *before* your backup program reports errors. Most experts recommend that you should use a tape only about 20 times before discarding it. If you use the same tape every day, replace it monthly. If you have tapes for each day of the week, replace them twice yearly. If you have more tapes than that, figure out a cycle that replaces tapes after about 20 uses.

Keeping Backup Equipment Clean and Reliable

An important aspect of backup reliability is proper maintenance of your tape drives. Every time you back up to tape, little bits and specks of the tape rub off onto the read and write heads inside the tape drive. Eventually, the heads become too dirty to read or write data reliably.

To counteract this problem, clean the tape heads regularly. The easiest way to clean them is to use a cleaning cartridge for the tape drive. The drive automatically recognizes when you insert a cleaning cartridge and then performs a routine that wipes the cleaning tape back and forth over the heads to clean them. When the cleaning routine is done, the tape is ejected. The whole process takes only about 30 seconds.

Because the maintenance requirements of drives differ, check each drive's user's manual to find out how and how often to clean the drive. As a general rule, clean drives once weekly.

The most annoying aspect of tape drive cleaning is that the cleaning cartridges have a limited life span, and unfortunately, if you insert a used-up cleaning cartridge, the drive accepts it and pretends to clean the drive. For this reason, keep track of how many times you use a cleaning cartridge and replace it as recommended by the manufacturer.

Setting Backup Security

Backups create an often-overlooked security exposure for your network: No matter how carefully you set up user accounts and enforce password policies, if any user (including a guest) can perform a backup of the system, that user may make an unauthorized backup. In addition, your backup tapes themselves are vulnerable to theft. As a result, make sure that your backup policies and procedures are secure by taking the following measures:

✔ **Set up a user account for the user who does backups.** Because this user account has backup permission for the entire server, guard its password carefully. Anyone who knows the username and password of the backup account can log on and bypass any security restrictions that you place on that user's normal user ID.

✔ **Counter potential security problems by restricting the backup user ID to a certain client and a certain time of the day.** If you're really clever (and paranoid), you can probably set up the backup user's account so that the only program it can run is the backup program.

✔ **Use encryption to protect the contents of your backup tapes.**

✔ **Secure the backup tapes in a safe location, such as . . . um, a safe.**

Chapter 21

Securing Your Network

*B*efore you had a network, computer security was easy. You simply locked your door when you left work for the day. You could rest easy, secure in the knowledge that the bad guys would have to break down the door to get to your computer.

The network changes all that. Now, anyone with access to any computer on the network can break into the network and steal *your* files. Not only do you have to lock your door, but you have to make sure that other people lock their doors, too.

Fortunately, network operating systems (NOSes) have built-in provisions for network security, deterring someone from stealing your files even if he does break down the door. All modern NOSES have security features that are more than adequate for all but the most paranoid users.

When I say *more* than adequate, I mean it. Most networks have security features that would make even Maxwell Smart happy. Using all these security features is kind of like Smart insisting that the Chief lower the "Cone of Silence" (which worked so well that Max and the Chief couldn't hear each other!). Don't make your system so secure that even the good guys can't get their work done.

If any computer on your network is connected to the Internet, you must harden your network against intrusion via the Internet. For more information, see Chapter 23. Also, if your network supports wireless devices, you have wireless security issues. For information about security for wireless networks, see Chapter 9.

Do You Need Security?

Most small networks are in small businesses or departments where everyone knows and trusts everyone else. Folks don't lock up their desks when they take a coffee break, and although everyone knows where the petty cash box is, money never disappears.

Network security isn't necessary in an idyllic setting like this one, is it? You bet it is. Here's why any network should be set up with at least some concern for security:

- ✔ Even in the friendliest office environment, some information is and should be confidential. If this information is stored on the network, you want to store it in a directory that's available only to authorized users.

- ✔ Not all security breaches are malicious. A network user may be routinely scanning through files and come across a filename that isn't familiar. The user may then call up the file, only to discover that it contains confidential personnel information, juicy office gossip, or your résumé. Curiosity, rather than malice, is often the source of security breaches.

- ✔ Sure, everyone at the office is trustworthy now. However, what if someone becomes disgruntled, a screw pops loose, and he decides to trash the network files before jumping out the window? What if someone decides to print a few $1,000 checks before packing off to Tahiti?

- ✔ Sometimes the mere opportunity for fraud or theft can be too much for some people to resist. Give people free access to the payroll files, and they may decide to vote themselves a raise when no one is looking.

- ✔ If you think that your network doesn't contain any data worth stealing, think again. For example, your personnel records probably contain more than enough information for an identity thief: names, addresses, phone numbers, Social Security numbers, and so on. Also, your customer files may contain your customers' credit card numbers.

- ✔ Hackers who break into your network may be looking to plant a Trojan horse program on your server, enabling them to use your server for their own purposes. For example, someone may use your server to send thousands of unsolicited spam e-mail messages. The spam won't be traced back to the hackers; it'll be traced back to *you.*

- ✔ Not everyone on the network knows enough about how Windows and the network work to be trusted with full access to your network's data and systems. A careless mouse click can wipe out a directory of network files. One of the best reasons for activating your network's security features is to protect the network from mistakes made by users who don't know what they're doing.

Two Approaches to Security

When you're planning how to implement security on your network, first consider which of two basic approaches to security you'll take:

- ✔ **Open door:** You grant everyone access to everything by default and then place restrictions just on those resources to which you want to limit access.

- ✔ **Closed door:** You begin by denying access to everything and then grant specific users access to the specific resources that they need.

In most cases, an open door policy is easier to implement. Typically, only a small portion of the data on a network really needs security, such as confidential employee records, or secrets, such as the Coke recipe. The rest of the information on a network can be safely made available to everyone who can access the network.

If you choose a closed door approach, you set up each user so that he has access to nothing. Then, you grant each user access only to those specific files or folders that he needs.

A closed door approach results in tighter security but can lead to the Cone of Silence Syndrome: Like how Max and the Chief can't hear each other but still talk while they're under the Cone of Silence, your network users will constantly complain that they can't access the information that they need. As a result, you'll find yourself often adjusting users' access rights. Choose a closed door approach only if your network contains a lot of sensitive information, and only if you're willing to invest time administrating your network's security policy.

You can think of an open door approach as an *entitlement model,* in which the basic assumption is that users are entitled to network access. In contrast, the closed-door policy is a *permissions model,* in which the basic assumption is that users aren't entitled to anything but must get permissions for every network resource that they access.

If you've never heard of the Cone of Silence, go to YouTube (www.youtube.com) and search for *Cone of Silence.* You'll find several clips from the original *Get Smart* series.

Physical Security: Locking Your Doors

The first level of security in any computer network is *physical security.* I'm amazed when I walk into the reception area of an accounting firm and see an unattended computer sitting on the receptionist's desk. Often, the reception-ist has logged on to the system and then walked away from the desk, leaving the computer unattended.

Physical security is important for workstations but vital for servers. Any good hacker can quickly defeat all but the most paranoid security measures if they can gain physical access to a server. To protect the server, follow these guidelines:

- ✔ Lock the computer room.
- ✔ Give the key only to people you trust.
- ✔ Keep track of who has the keys.
- ✔ Mount the servers on cases or racks that have locks.
- ✔ Disable the floppy drive on the server.

  A common hacking technique is to boot the server from a floppy, thus bypassing the security features of the NOS.

- ✔ Keep a trained guard dog in the computer room and feed it only enough to keep it hungry and mad. (Just kidding.)

There's a big difference between a door with a lock and a locked door. And locks are quite worthless if you don't use them.

Client computers should be physically secure:

- ✔ Instruct users to not leave their computers unattended while they're logged on.
- ✔ In high-traffic areas (such as the receptionist's desk), users should secure their computers with the keylock, if the computer has one.
- ✔ Users should lock their office doors when they leave.

Here are some other threats to physical security that you may not have considered:

- ✔ The nightly cleaning crew probably has complete access to your facility. How do you know that the person who vacuums your office every night doesn't really work for your chief competitor or doesn't consider com-puter hacking to be a sideline hobby? You don't, so consider the clean-ing crew to be a threat.
- ✔ What about your trash? Paper shredders aren't just for Enron accountants. Your trash can contain all sorts of useful information: sales reports, security logs, printed copies of the company's security policy, even hand-written passwords. For the best security, every piece of paper that leaves your building via the trash bin should first go through a shredder.

✔ Where do you store your backup tapes? Don't just stack them up next to the server. Not only does that make them easy to steal, it also defeats one of the main purposes of backing up your data in the first place: securing your server from physical threats, such as fires. If a fire burns down your computer room and the backup tapes are sitting unprotected next to the server, your company may go out of business and you'll certainly be out of a job. Store the backup tapes securely in a fireproof safe and keep a copy off-site, too.

✔ I've seen some networks in which the servers are in a locked computer room, but the hubs or switches are in an unsecured closet. Remember that every unused port on a hub or a switch represents an open door to your network. The hubs and switches should be secured just like the servers.

Securing User Accounts

Next to physical security, the careful use of user accounts is the most important type of security for your network. Properly configured user accounts can prevent unauthorized users from accessing the network, even if they gain physical access to the network. The following sections describe some of the steps that you can take to strengthen your network's use of user accounts.

Obfuscating your usernames

Huh? When it comes to security, *obfuscation* simply means picking obscure usernames. For example, most network administrators assign usernames based on some combination of the user's first and last name, such as `BarnyM` or `baMiller`. However, a hacker can easily guess such a user ID if he or she knows the name of at least one employee. After the hacker knows a username, he or she can focus on breaking the password.

You can slow down a hacker by using names that are more obscure. Here are some suggestions on how to do that:

✔ Add a random three-digit number to the end of the name. For example: BarnyM320 or baMiller977.

✔ Throw a number or two into the middle of the name. For example: Bar6nyM or ba9Miller2.

✔ Make sure that usernames are different from e-mail addresses. For example, if a user's e-mail address is `baMiller@Mydomain.com`, do *not* use baMiller as the user's account name. Use a more obscure name.

Do *not* rely on obfuscation to keep people out of your network! Security by obfuscation doesn't work. A resourceful hacker can discover the most obscure names. Obfuscation can *slow* intruders, not stop them. If you slow intruders down, you're more likely to discover them before they crack your network.

Using passwords wisely

One of the most important aspects of network security is the use of passwords.

Usernames aren't usually considered *secret*. Even if you use obscure names, even casual hackers will eventually figure them out.

Passwords, on the other hand, are top secret. Your network password is the one thing that keeps an impostor from logging on to the network by using your username and therefore receiving the same access rights that you ordinarily have. *Guard your password with your life.*

Here are some tips for creating good passwords:

- ✔ Don't use obvious passwords, such as your last name, your kid's name, or your dog's name.

- ✔ Don't pick passwords based on your hobbies. A friend of mine is a boater, and his password is the name of his boat. Anyone who knows him can quickly guess his password. Five lashes for naming your password after your boat.

- ✔ Store your password in your head — not on paper.

    Especially bad: Writing your password down on a sticky note and sticking it on your computer's monitor.

- ✔ Most network operating systems enable you to set an expiration time for passwords. For example, you can specify that passwords expire after 30 days. When a user's password expires, the user must change it. Your users may consider this process a hassle, but it helps to limit the risk of someone swiping a password and then trying to break into your computer system later.

- ✔ You can configure user accounts so that when they change passwords, they can't reuse a *recent* password. For example, you can specify that the new password can't be identical to any of the user's past three passwords.

- ✔ You can also configure security policies so that passwords must include a mixture of uppercase letters, lowercase letters, numerals, and special symbols. Thus, passwords like DIMWIT or DUFUS are out. Passwords like 87dIM@wit or duF39&US are in.

✔ Some administrators of small networks opt against passwords altogether because they feel that security isn't an issue on their network. Or short of that, they choose obvious passwords, assign every user the same password, or print the passwords on giant posters and hang them throughout the building. Ignoring basic password security is rarely a good idea, even in small networks. You should consider not using passwords only if your network is very small (say, two or three computers), if you don't keep sensitive data on a file server, or if the main reason for the network is to share access to a printer rather than sharing files. (Even if you don't use passwords, imposing basic security precautions, like limiting access that certain users have to certain network directories, is still possible. Just remember that if passwords aren't used, nothing prevents a user from signing on by using someone else's username.)

Generating passwords For Dummies

How do you come up with passwords that no one can guess but that you can remember? Most security experts say that the best passwords don't correspond to any words in the English language but consist of a random sequence of letters, numbers, and special characters. Yet, how in the heck are you supposed to memorize a password like Dks4%DJ2? Especially when you have to change it three weeks later to something like 3pQ&X(d8.

Here's a compromise solution that enables you to create passwords that consist of two four-letter words back to back. Take your favorite book (if it's this one, you need to get a life) and turn to any page at random. Find the first four- or five-letter word on the page. Suppose that word is *When.* Then repeat the process to find another four- or five-letter word; say you pick the word *Most* the second time. Now combine the words to make your password: WhenMost. I think you'll agree that WhenMost is easier to remember than 3PQ&X(D8 and is probably just about as hard to guess. I probably wouldn't want the folks at the Los Alamos Nuclear Laboratory using this scheme, but it's good enough for most of us.

Here are additional thoughts on concocting passwords from your favorite book:

✔ If the words end up being the same, pick another word. And pick different words if the combination seems too commonplace, such as WestWind or FootBall.

✔ For an interesting variation, insert a couple of numerals or special characters between the words. You end up with passwords like into#cat, ball3%and, or tree47wing. If you want, use the page number of the second word as a separator. For example, if the words are *know* and *click* and the second word comes from page 435, use know435click.

✔ To further confuse your friends and enemies, use medieval passwords by picking words from Chaucer's *Canterbury Tales.* Chaucer is a great source for passwords because he lived before the days of word processors with spell-checkers. He wrote *seyd* instead of *said, gret* instead of *great, welk* instead of *walked, litel* instead of *little.* And he used lots of seven-letter and eight-letter words suitable for passwords, such as *glotenye* (gluttony), *benygne* (benign), and *opynyoun* (opinion). And he got A's in English.

✔ If you use any of these password schemes and someone breaks into your network, don't blame me. You're the one who's too lazy to memorize D#Sc$h4@bb3xaz5.

✔ If you do decide to go with passwords, such as KdI22UR3xdkL, you can find random password generators on the Internet. Just go to a search engine, such as Google, and search for Password Generator. You'll find Web pages that generate random passwords based on criteria that you specify, such as how long the password should be, whether it should include letters, numbers, punctuation, uppercase and lowercase letters, and so on.

Secure the Administrator account

It stands to reason that at least one network user must have the authority to use the network without any of the restrictions imposed on other users. This user is the *administrator.* The administrator is responsible for setting up the network's security system. To do that, the administrator must be exempt from all security restrictions.

Many networks automatically create an administrator user account when you install the network software. The username and password for this initial administrator are published in the network's documentation and are the same for all networks that use the same network operating system. One of the first things that you must do after getting your network up and running is to change the password for this standard administrator account. Otherwise, your elaborate security precautions are a complete waste of time. Anyone who knows the default administrator username and password can access your system with full administrator rights and privileges, thus bypassing the security restrictions that you so carefully set up.

Don't forget the password for the administrator account! If a network user forgets his or her password, you can log on as the supervisor and change that user's password. If you forget the administrator's password, though, you're stuck.

Managing User Security

User accounts are the backbone of network security administration. Through the use of user accounts, you can determine who can access your network as well as what network resources each user can and can't access. You can restrict access to the network to just specific computers or to certain hours of the day. In addition, you can lock out users who no longer need to access your network. The following sections describe the basics of setting up user security for your network.

User accounts

Every user who accesses a network must have a *user account*. User accounts allow the network administrator to determine who can access the network and what network resources each user can access. In addition, the user account can be customized to provide many convenient features for users, such as a personalized Start menu or a display of recently used documents.

Every user account is associated with a *username* (sometimes called a *user ID*), which the user must enter when logging on to the network. Each account also has other information associated with it. In particular:

✔ **The user's password:** This also includes the password policy, such as how often the user has to change his or her password, how complicated the password must be, and so on.

✔ **The user's contact information:** This includes full name, phone number, e-mail address, mailing address, and other related information.

✔ **Account restrictions:** This includes restrictions that allow the user to log on only during certain times of the day. This feature can restrict your users to normal working hours so that they can't sneak in at 2 a.m. to do unauthorized work. This feature also discourages your users from working overtime because they can't access the network after hours, so use it judiciously. You can also specify that the user can log on only at certain computers.

✔ **Account status:** You can temporarily disable a user account so the user can't log on.

✔ **Home directory:** This specifies a shared network folder where the user can store documents.

✔ **Dial-in permissions:** These authorize the user to access the network remotely via a dialup connection.

✔ **Group memberships:** These grant the user certain rights based on groups to which she belongs.

For more information, see the section, "Group therapy," later in this chapter.

Built-in accounts

Most network operating systems come preconfigured with two built-in accounts, Administrator and Guest. In addition, some server services, such as web or database servers, create their own user accounts under which to run. The following sections describe the characteristics of these accounts.

✔ **The Administrator account:** The Administrator account is the King of the Network. This user account isn't subject to any of the account restrictions to which mere mortal accounts must succumb. If you log on as the administrator, you can do anything. For this reason, avoid using the Administrator account for routine tasks. Log in as the Administrator only when you really need to.

Because the Administrator account has unlimited access to your network, it's imperative that you secure it immediately after you install the server. When the NOS Setup program asks for a password for the Administrator account, start with a good random mix of uppercase and lowercase letters, numbers, and symbols. Don't pick some easy-to-remember password to get started, thinking you'll change it to something more cryptic later. You'll forget, and in the meantime, someone will break in and reformat the server's C: drive or steal your customer's credit card numbers.

✔ **The Guest account:** Another commonly created default account is the *Guest account.* This account is set up with a blank password and — if any — access rights. The Guest account is designed to allow anyone to step up to a computer and log on, but after they do, it then prevents them from doing anything. Sounds like a waste of time to me. I suggest you disable the Guest account.

✔ **Service accounts:** Some network users aren't actual people. I don't mean that some of your users are subhuman. Rather, some users are actually software processes that require access to secure resources, and therefore, require user accounts. These user accounts are usually created automatically for you when you install or configure server software.

For example, when you install Microsoft's web server (IIS), an Internet user account called IUSR is created. The complete name for this account is IUSR_<servername>. So if the server is named WEB1, the account is named IUSR_WEB1. IIS uses this account to allow anonymous Internet users to access the files of your website.

Don't mess with these accounts unless you know what you're doing. For example, if you delete or rename the IUSR account, you must reconfigure IIS to use the changed account. If you don't, IIS will deny access to anyone trying to reach your site. (Assuming that you *do* know what you're doing, renaming these accounts can increase your network's security. However, don't start playing with these accounts until you've researched the ramifications.)

Network rights we want to see

The network rights allowed by most NOSes are pretty boring. Here are a few rights I wish would be allowed:

✔ **Cheat:** Provides a special option that enables you to see what cards the other players are holding when you're playing Hearts.

✔ **Spy:** Eavesdrops on other users' Internet sessions so you can find out what websites they're viewing.

✔ **Grumble:** Automatically sends e-mail messages to other users that explain how busy, tired, or upset you are.

✔ **Set pay:** Grants you special access to the payroll system so that you can give yourself a pay raise.

✔ **Sue:** In America, everyone has the right to sue. So this right should be granted automatically to all users.

✔ **Fire:** Wouldn't it be great if the network could grant you the right to play Donald Trump and fire your annoying co-workers?

User rights

User accounts and passwords are the front line of defense in the game of network security. After a user accesses the network by typing a valid user ID and password, the second line of security defense — *rights* — comes into play.

In the harsh realities of network life, all users are created equal, but some users are more equal than others. The Preamble to the Declaration of Network Independence contains the statement "We hold these truths to be self-evident, that *some* users are endowed by the network administrator with certain inalienable rights. . . ."

The rights that you can assign to network users depend on which network operating system you use. These are some of the possible user rights for Windows servers:

✔ **Log on locally:** The user can log on to the server computer directly from the server's keyboard.

✔ **Change system time:** The user can change the time and date registered by the server.

✔ **Shut down the system:** The user can perform an orderly shutdown of the server.

✔ **Back up files and directories:** The user can perform a backup of files and directories on the server.

✔ **Restore files and directories:** The user can restore backed-up files.

✔ **Take ownership of files and other objects:** The user can take over files and other network resources that belong to other users.

NetWare has a similar set of user rights.

Permissions (who gets what)

User rights control what a user can do on a network-wide basis. *Permissions* enable you to fine-tune your network security by controlling access to specific network resources, such as files or printers, for individual users or groups. For example, you can set up permissions to allow users into the accounting department to access files in the server's \ACCTG directory. Permissions can also enable some users to read certain files but not modify or delete them.

Each network operating system manages permissions in a different way. Whatever the details, the effect is that you can give permission to each user to access certain files, folders, or drives in certain ways. For example, you might grant a user full access to some files but grant read-only access to other files.

Any permissions you specify for a folder apply automatically to any of that folder's subfolders, unless you explicitly specify different permissions for the subfolder.

You can use Windows permissions only for files or folders that are created on drives formatted as NTFS or ReFS volumes. If you insist on using FAT or FAT32 for your Windows shared drives, you can't protect individual files or folders on the drives. This is one of the main reasons for using NTFS for your Windows servers.

Group therapy

A *group account* is an account that doesn't represent an individual user. Instead, it represents a group of users who use the network in a similar way. Instead of granting access rights to each of these users individually, you can grant the rights to the group and then assign individual users to the group. When you assign a user to a group, that user inherits the rights specified for the group.

For example, suppose that you create a group named Accounting for the accounting staff and then allow members of the Accounting group access to the network's accounting files and applications. Then, instead of granting each accounting user access to those files and applications, you simply make each accounting user a member of the Accounting group.

Here are a few additional details about groups:

✔ Groups are one of the keys to network management nirvana. As much as possible, avoid managing network users individually. Instead, clump them into groups and manage the groups. When all 50 users in the accounting department need access to a new file share, would you rather update 50 user accounts or just 1 group account?

✔ A user can belong to more than one group. Then, the user inherits the rights of each group. For example, you can have groups set up for Accounting, Sales, Marketing, and Finance. A user who needs to access both Accounting and Finance information can be made a member of both groups. Likewise, a user who needs access to both Sales and Marketing information can be made a member of both the Sales and Marketing groups.

✔ You can grant or revoke specific rights to individual users to override the group settings. For example, you may grant a few extra permissions for the manager of the accounting department. You may also impose a few extra restrictions on certain users.

User profiles

User profiles are a Windows feature that keeps track of an individual user's preferences for his or her Windows configuration. For a non-networked computer, profiles enable two or more users to use the same computer, each with his or her own desktop settings, such as wallpaper, colors, Start menu options, and so on.

The real benefit of user profiles becomes apparent when profiles are used on a network. A user's profile can be stored on a server computer and accessed whenever that user logs on to the network from any Windows computer on the network.

The following are some of the elements of Windows that are governed by settings in the user profile:

✔ Desktop settings from the Display Properties dialog box, including wallpaper, screen savers, and color schemes

✔ Start menu programs and Windows toolbar options

✔ Favorites, which provide easy access to the files and folders that the user accesses often

✔ Network settings, including drive mappings, network printers, and recently visited network locations

✔ Application settings, such as option settings for Microsoft Word

✔ The My Documents folder

Logon scripts

A *logon script* is a batch file that runs automatically whenever a user logs on. Logon scripts can perform several important logon tasks for you, such as mapping network drives, starting applications, synchronizing the client computer's time-of-day clock, and so on. Logon scripts reside on the server. Each user account can specify whether to use a logon script and which script to use.

This sample logon script maps a few network drives and synchronizes the time:

```
net use m: \\MYSERVER\Acct
net use n: \\MYSERVER\Admin
net use o: \\MYSERVER\Dev
net time \\MYSERVER /set /yes
```

Logon scripts are a little out of vogue because most of what a logon script does can be done via user profiles. Still, many administrators prefer the simplicity of logon scripts, so they're still used even on Windows 2012 Server systems.

Securing Your Users

Security techniques, such as physical security, user account security, server security, and locking down your servers are child's play compared with the most difficult job of network security: securing your network's users. All the best-laid security plans will go for naught if your users write their passwords on sticky notes and post them on their computers.

The key to securing your network users is to create a written network security policy and to stick to it. Have a meeting with everyone to go over the security policy to make sure that everyone understands the rules. Also, make sure to have consequences when violations occur.

Here are some suggestions for some basic security rules that can be incorporated into your security policy:

✔ Never write down your password or give it to someone else.

✔ Accounts shouldn't be shared. Never use someone else's account to access a resource that you can't access under your own account. If you need access to some network resource that isn't available to you, formally request access under your own account.

✔ Likewise, never give your account information to a co-worker so that he or she can access a needed resource. Your co-worker should instead formally request access under his or her own account.

✔ Don't install any software or hardware on your computer without first obtaining permission. This especially includes wireless access devices or modems.

✔ Don't enable file and printer sharing on workstations without first getting permission.

✔ Never attempt to disable or bypass the network's security features.

Chapter 22

Hardening Your Network

· ·

· ·

*1*f your network is connected to the Internet, a whole host of security issues bubble to the surface. You probably connected your network to the Internet so that your network's users could get out to the Internet. Unfortunately, however, your Internet connection is a two-way street. Not only does it enable your network's users to step outside the bounds of your network to access the Internet, but it also enables others to step in and access your network.

And step in they will. The world is filled with hackers who are looking for networks like yours to break into. They may do it just for the fun of it, or they may do it to steal your customer's credit card numbers or to coerce your mail server into sending thousands of spam messages on their behalf. Whatever their motive, rest assured that your network will be broken into if you leave it unprotected.

This chapter presents an overview of three basic techniques for securing your network's Internet connection: controlling access via a firewall, detecting viruses with antivirus software, and fixing security flaws with software patches.

Firewalls

A *firewall* is a security-conscious router that sits between the Internet and your network with a single-minded task: preventing *them* from getting to *us*. The firewall acts as a security guard between the Internet and your local area network (LAN). All network traffic into and out of the LAN must pass through the firewall, which prevents unauthorized access to the network.

Some type of firewall is a must-have if your network has a connection to the Internet, whether that connection is broadband (cable modem or DSL), T1, or some other high-speed connection. Without it, sooner or later a hacker will discover your unprotected network and tell his friends about it. Within a few hours your network will be toast.

You can set up a firewall using two basic ways. The easiest way is to purchase a *firewall appliance,* which is basically a self-contained router with built-in firewall features. Most firewall appliances include a web-based interface that enables you to connect to the firewall from any computer on your network using a browser. You can then customize the firewall settings to suit your needs.

Alternatively, you can set up a server computer to function as a firewall computer. The server can run just about any network operating system, but most dedicated firewall systems run Linux.

Whether you use a firewall appliance or a firewall computer, the firewall must be located between your network and the Internet, as shown in Figure 22-1. Here, one end of the firewall is connected to a network hub, which is, in turn, connected to the other computers on the network. The other end of the firewall is connected to the Internet. As a result, all traffic from the LAN to the Internet and vice versa must travel through the firewall.

Figure 22-1:
A firewall
router
creates a
secure link
between a
network and
the Internet.

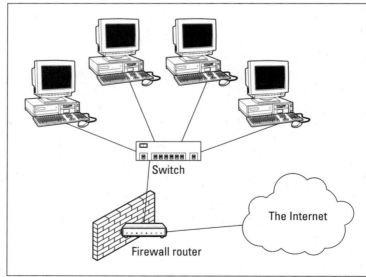

The term *perimeter* is sometimes used to describe the location of a firewall on your network. In short, a firewall is like a perimeter fence that completely surrounds your property and forces all visitors to enter through the front gate.

In large networks — especially campus-wide or even metropolitan networks — it's sometimes hard to figure out exactly where the perimeter is located. If your network has two or more wide area network (WAN) connections, make sure that every one of those connections connects to a firewall and not directly to the network. You can do this by providing a separate firewall for each WAN connection or by using a firewall with more than one WAN port.

The Many Types of Firewalls

Firewalls employ four basic techniques to keep unwelcome visitors out of your network. The following sections describe these basic firewall techniques.

Packet filtering

A *packet-filtering* firewall examines each packet that crosses the firewall and tests the packet according to a set of rules that you set up. If the packet passes the test, it's allowed to pass. If the packet doesn't pass, it's rejected.

Packet filters are the least expensive type of firewall. As a result, packet-filtering firewalls are very common. However, packet filtering has a number of flaws that knowledgeable hackers can exploit. As a result, packet filtering by itself doesn't make for a fully effective firewall.

Packet filters work by inspecting the source and destination IP and port addresses contained in each TCP/IP packet. *TCP/IP ports* are numbers that are assigned to specific services that help to identify for which service each packet is intended. For example, the port number for the HTTP protocol is 80. As a result, any incoming packets headed for an HTTP server will specify port 80 as the destination port.

Port numbers are often specified with a colon following an IP address. For example, the HTTP service on a server whose IP address is 192.168.10.133 would be 192.168.10.133:80.

Literally thousands of established ports are in use. Table 22-1 lists a few of the most popular ports.

Table 22-1	Some Well-Known TCP/IP Ports
Port	*Description*
20	File Transfer Protocol (FTP)
21	File Transfer Protocol (FTP)
22	Secure Shell Protocol (SSH)
23	Telnet
25	Simple Mail Transfer Protocol (SMTP)
53	Domain Name Server (DNS)
80	World Wide Web (HTTP)
110	Post Office Protocol (POP3)
119	Network News Transfer Protocol (NNTP)
137	NetBIOS Name Service
138	NetBIOS Datagram Service
139	NetBIOS Session Service
143	Internet Message Access Protocol (IMAP)
161	Simple Network Management Protocol (SNMP)
194	Internet Relay Chat (IRC)
389	Lightweight Directory Access Protocol (LDAP)
396	NetWare over IP
443	HTTP over TLS/SSL (HTTPS)

The rules that you set up for the packet filter either permit or deny packets that specify certain IP addresses or ports. For example, you may permit packets that are intended for your mail server or your web server and deny all other packets. Or, you may set up a rule that specifically denies packets that are heading for the ports used by NetBIOS. This rule keeps Internet hackers from trying to access NetBIOS server resources, such as files or printers.

One of the biggest weaknesses of packet filtering is that it pretty much trusts that the packets themselves are telling the truth when they say who they're from and who they're going to. Hackers exploit this weakness by using a hacking technique called *IP spoofing,* in which they insert fake IP addresses in packets that they send to your network.

Another weakness of packet filtering is that it examines each packet in isolation, without considering what packets have gone through the firewall before and what packets may follow. In other words, packet filtering is *stateless.* Rest assured that hackers have figured out how to exploit the stateless nature of packet filtering to get through firewalls.

In spite of these weaknesses, packet filter firewalls have several advantages that explain why they're commonly used:

- ✔ **Packet filters are very efficient.** They hold up each inbound and outbound packet for only a few milliseconds while they look inside the packet to determine the destination and source ports and addresses. After these addresses and ports have been determined, the packet filter quickly applies its rules and either sends the packet along or rejects it. In contrast, other firewall techniques have a more noticeable performance overhead.

- ✔ **Packet filters are almost completely transparent to users.** The only time a user will be aware that a packet filter firewall is being used is when the firewall rejects packets. Other firewall techniques require that clients and/or servers be specially configured to work with the firewall.

- ✔ **Packet filters are inexpensive.** Most routers include built-in packet filtering.

Stateful packet inspection (SPI)

Stateful packet inspection (SPI), is a step up in intelligence from simple packet filtering. A firewall with SPI looks at packets in groups rather than individually. It keeps track of which packets have passed through the firewall and can detect patterns that indicate unauthorized access. In some cases, the firewall may hold on to packets as they arrive until the firewall has gathered enough information to make a decision about whether the packets should be authorized or rejected.

Stateful packet inspection was once found only on expensive, enterprise-level routers. Now, however, SPI firewalls are affordable enough for small- or medium-sized networks to use.

Circuit-level gateway

A *circuit-level gateway* manages connections between clients and servers based on TCP/IP addresses and port numbers. After the connection is established, the gateway doesn't interfere with packets flowing between the systems.

For example, you could use a Telnet circuit-level gateway to allow Telnet connections (port 23) to a particular server and prohibit other types of connections to that server. After the connection is established, the circuit-level gateway allows packets to flow freely over the connection. As a result, the circuit-level gateway can't prevent a Telnet user from running specific programs or using specific commands.

Application gateway

An *application gateway* is a firewall system that's more intelligent than a packet-filtering, stateful packet inspection, or circuit-level gateway firewall. Packet filters treat all TCP/IP packets the same. In contrast, application gateways know the details about the applications that generate the packets that pass through the firewall. For example, a Web application gateway is aware of the details of HTTP packets. As a result, it can examine more than just the source and destination addresses and ports to determine whether the packets should be allowed to pass through the firewall.

In addition, application gateways work as proxy servers. Simply put, a *proxy server* is a server that sits between a client computer and a real server. The proxy server intercepts packets that are intended for the real server and processes them. The proxy server can examine the packet and decide to pass it on to the real server, or it can reject the packet. Or the proxy server may be able to respond to the packet itself, without involving the real server at all.

For example, web proxies often store copies of commonly used web pages in a local cache. When a user requests a web page from a remote web server, the proxy server intercepts the request and checks to see whether it already has a copy of the page in its cache. If so, the web proxy returns the page directly to the user. If not, the proxy passes the request on to the real server.

Application gateways are aware of the details of how various types of TCP/IP servers handle sequences of TCP/IP packets, so they can make more intelligent decisions about whether an incoming packet is legitimate or is part of an attack. As a result, application gateways are more secure than simple packet-filtering firewalls, which can deal with only one packet at a time.

The improved security of application gateways, however, comes at a price. Application gateways are more expensive than packet filters, both in terms of their purchase price and in the cost of configuring and maintaining them. In addition, application gateways slow down the network performance because they do more detailed checking of packets before allowing them to pass.

The Built-In Windows Firewall

All versions of Windows since Windows XP come with a built-in packet-filtering firewall. If you don't have a separate firewall router, you can use this built-in firewall to provide a basic level of protection. See Chapter 8 for the steps to follow to configure the Windows Firewall.

Do *not* enable the Windows Firewall if you're using a separate firewall router to protect your network. Because the other computers on the network are connected directly to the router and not to your computer, the firewall won't protect the rest of the network. Additionally, as an unwanted side effect, the rest of the network will lose the ability to access your computer.

Virus Protection

Viruses are one of the most misunderstood computer phenomena around these days. What is a virus? How does it work? How does it spread from computer to computer? I'm glad you asked.

What is a virus?

Make no mistake — viruses are real. Now that most people are connected to the Internet, viruses have really taken off. Every computer user is susceptible to attacks by computer viruses, and using a network increases your vulnerability because it exposes all network users to the risk of being infected by a virus that lands on any one network user's computer.

Viruses don't just spontaneously appear out of nowhere. *Viruses* are computer programs that are created by malicious programmers who've lost a few screws and should be locked up.

What makes a virus a virus is its capability to make copies of itself that can be spread to other computers. These copies, in turn, make still more copies that spread to still more computers, and so on, ad nauseam.

Then, the virus waits patiently until something triggers it — perhaps when you type a particular command or press a certain key, when a certain date arrives, or when the virus creator sends the virus a message. What the virus does when it strikes also depends on what the virus creator wants the virus to do. Some viruses harmlessly display a "gotcha" message. Some send e-mail to everyone it finds in your address book. Some wipe out all the data on your hard drive. Ouch.

A few years back, viruses moved from one computer to another by latching themselves onto floppy disks. Whenever you borrowed a floppy disk from a buddy, you ran the risk of infecting your own computer with a virus that may have stowed away on the disk.

Nowadays, virus programmers have discovered that e-mail is a much more efficient method to spread their viruses. Typically, a virus masquerades as a useful or interesting e-mail attachment, such as instructions on how to make $1,000,000 in your spare time, pictures of naked celebrities, or a Valentine's Day greeting from your long-lost sweetheart. When a curious but unsuspecting user double-clicks the attachment, the virus springs to life, copying itself onto the user's computer and, in some cases, sending copies of itself to all the names in the user's address book.

After the virus has worked its way onto a networked computer, the virus can then figure out how to spread itself to other computers on the network.

Here are some more tidbits about protecting your network from virus attacks:

- The term *virus* is often used to refer not only to true virus programs (which can replicate themselves) but also to any other type of program that's designed to harm your computer. These programs include so-called *Trojan horse* programs that usually look like games but are, in reality, hard drive formatters.

- A *worm* is similar to a virus, but it doesn't actually infect other files. Instead, it just copies itself onto other computers on a network. After a worm has copied itself onto your computer, there's no telling what it may do there. For example, a worm may scan your hard drive for interesting information, such as passwords or credit card numbers, and then e-mail them to the worm's author.

- Computer virus experts have identified several thousand "strains" of viruses. Many of them have colorful names, such as the I Love You virus, the Stoned virus, and the Michelangelo virus.

- Antivirus programs can recognize known viruses and remove them from your system, and they can spot the telltale signs of unknown viruses. Unfortunately, the idiots who write viruses aren't idiots (in the intellectual sense), so they're constantly developing new techniques to evade detection by antivirus programs. New viruses are frequently discovered, and antivirus programs are periodically updated to detect and remove them.

Antivirus programs

The best way to protect your network from virus infection is to use an antivirus program. These programs have a catalog of several thousand known viruses that they can detect and remove. In addition, they can spot the types of changes that viruses typically make to your computer's files, thus decreasing the likelihood that some previously unknown virus will go undetected.

Although Windows doesn't come with built-in antivirus software, you can download an excellent free antivirus solution from Microsoft called Microsoft Security Essentials. Popular alternatives to Microsoft's free product include Norton AntiVirus, Webroot SecureAnywhere Antivirus, and Kapersky Antivirus.

The people who make antivirus programs have their fingers on the pulse of the virus world and often release updates to their software to combat the latest viruses. Because virus writers are constantly developing new viruses, your antivirus software is next to worthless unless you keep it up-to-date by downloading the latest updates.

The following are several approaches to deploying antivirus protection on your network:

- ✔ You can install antivirus software on each network user's computer. This technique would be the most effective if you could count on all your users to keep their antivirus software up-to-date. Because that's an unlikely proposition, you may want to adopt a more reliable approach to virus protection.

- ✔ Managed antivirus services place antivirus client software on each client computer in your network. Then, an antivirus server automatically updates the clients on a regular basis to make sure that they're kept up to date.

- ✔ Server-based antivirus software protects your network servers from viruses. For example, you can install antivirus software on your mail server to scan all incoming mail for viruses and remove them before your network users ever see them.

- ✔ Some firewall appliances include antivirus enforcement checks that don't allow your users to access the Internet unless their antivirus software is up to date. This type of firewall provides the best antivirus protection available.

Safe computing

Besides using an antivirus program, you can take a few additional precautions to ensure virus-free computing. If you haven't talked to your kids about these safe-computing practices, you had better do so soon.

- ✓ Regularly back up your data. If a virus hits you and your antivirus software can't repair the damage, you may need the backup to recover your data. Make sure that you restore from a backup that was created before you were infected by the virus!

- ✓ If you buy software from a store and discover that the seal has been broken on the disk package, take the software back. Don't try to install it on your computer. You don't hear about tainted software as often as you hear about tainted beef, but if you buy software that's been opened, it may well be laced with a virus infection.

- ✓ Use your antivirus software to scan your disk for virus infection after your computer has been to a repair shop or worked on by a consultant. These guys don't intend harm, but they occasionally spread viruses accidentally, simply because they work on so many strange computers.

- ✓ Don't open e-mail attachments from people you don't know or attachments you weren't expecting.

- ✓ Use your antivirus software to scan any CD-ROM or flash drive that doesn't belong to you before you access any of its files.

Patching Things Up

One of the annoyances that every network manager faces is applying software patches to keep the operating system and other software up to date. A software *patch* is a minor update that fixes the small glitches that crop up from time to time, such as minor security or performance issues. These glitches aren't significant enough to merit a new version of the software, but they're important enough to require fixing. Most of the patches correct security flaws that computer hackers have uncovered in their relentless attempts to prove that they are smarter than the security programmers at Microsoft.

Periodically, all the recently released patches are combined into a *service pack.* Although the most diligent network administrators apply all patches when they're released, many administrators just wait for the service packs:

- ✔ For all versions of Windows, you can use the Windows Update website to apply patches to keep your operating system and other Microsoft software up to date. Windows Update scans your computer's software and creates a list of software patches and other components that you can download and install. To use Windows Update, open the Control Panel, click System and Security, and then click Windows Update.

- ✔ You can configure Windows Update to automatically notify you of updates so you don't have to remember to check for new patches.

- ✔ You can subscribe to a service that automatically sends you e-mail to let you know of new patches and updates.

Keeping a large network patched can be one of the major challenges of network administration. If you have more than a few dozen computers on your network, consider investing in server-based software that's designed to simplify the process. For example, Lumension (`www.lumension.com`) is a server-based program that collects software patches from a variety of manufacturers and lets you create distributions that are automatically pushed out to client computers. With software like Lumension, you don't have to rely on end users to download and install patches, and you don't have to visit each computer individually to install patches.

Chapter 23

Network Performance Anxiety

he term *network performance* refers to how efficiently the network responds to users' needs. Obviously, any access to resources that involves the network is slower than similar access that doesn't involve the network. For example, opening a Word document that resides on a network file server takes longer than opening a similar document that resides on the user's local hard drive. However, it shouldn't take *much* longer. If it does, you have a network performance problem.

This chapter is a general introduction to the practice of tuning your network so that it performs as well as possible. Keep in mind that many specific bits of network tuning advice are scattered throughout this book. In this chapter, you can find some specific techniques for analyzing your network's performance, taking corrective action when a performance problem develops, and charting your progress.

Why Administrators Hate Performance Problems

Network performance problems are among the most difficult network problems to track down and solve. If a user simply can't access the network, it usually doesn't take long to figure out why: The cable is unplugged, a network card is malfunctioning, or the user doesn't have permission to access the resource, for example. After you do a little investigating, the problem usually reveals itself, and you fix it and move on to the next problem.

Unfortunately, performance problems are messier. Here are just a few reasons that network administrators hate performance problems:

- **Performance problems are difficult to quantify.** Exactly how much slower is the network now than it was a week ago, a month ago, or even a year ago? Sometimes the network just *feels* slow, but you can't quite define exactly how slow it really is.

- **Performance problems usually develop gradually.** Sometimes a network slows down suddenly and drastically. More often, though, the network gradually gets slower, a little bit at a time, until one day its users notice that the network is slow.

- **Performance problems often go unreported.** Users gripe about the problem to each other around the water cooler, but they don't formally contact you to let you know that the network seems 10 percent slower than usual. As long as they can still access the network, they just assume that the problem is temporary or that they're imagining a problem.

- **Many performance problems are intermittent.** Sometimes a user calls you and complains that a certain network operation has become slower than molasses, and by the time you get to that person's desk, the operation performs in a snap. Sometimes you can find a pattern to the intermittent behavior, such as it's slower in the morning than in the afternoon or it's slow only while backups are running or while the printer is working. At other times, you can't find a pattern: Sometimes the operation is slow, and sometimes it isn't.

- **Performance tuning isn't an exact science.** Improving performance sometimes involves educated guesswork. Will upgrading all users from 100 Mbps to 1 Gbps improve performance? Probably. Will segmenting the network improve performance? Maybe. Will adding another 8GB of RAM to the server improve performance? Hopefully.

- **The solution to a performance problem is sometimes a hard sell.** If a user can't access the network because of a malfunctioning component, the purchase of a replacement is usually undeniably justified. However, if the network is slow and you think that you can fix it by upgrading the entire network to Gigabit Ethernet, you may have trouble selling management on the upgrade.

What Exactly Is a Bottleneck?

The term *bottleneck* doesn't refer in any way to the physique of the typical computer geek. Rather, computer geeks coined the phrase when they discovered that the tapered shape of a bottle of Jolt cola limited the rate at which they could consume the beverage. "Hey," a computer geek said one day, "the gently tapered narrowness of this bottle's neck imposes a distinct limiting effect upon the rate at which I can consume the tasty caffeine-laden beverage contained within. This observation draws to mind a hitherto undiscovered yet obvious analogy to the limiting effect that a single slow component of a computer system can have upon the performance of the system as a whole."

"Fascinating," replied all the other computer geeks, who were fortunate enough to be present at that historic moment.

The term stuck and is used to this day to draw attention to the simple fact that a computer system is only as fast as its slowest component. It's the computer equivalent of the old truism that a chain is only as strong as its weakest link.

For a simple demonstration of this concept, consider what happens when you print a word-processing document on a slow printer. Your word-processing program reads the data from disk and sends it to the printer. Then you sit and wait while the printer prints the document.

Would buying a faster CPU or adding more memory make the document print faster? No. The CPU is already much faster than the printer, and your computer already has more than enough memory to print the document. The printer itself is the bottleneck, so the only way to print the document faster is to replace the slow printer with a faster one.

Here are some other, random thoughts about bottlenecks:

- ✔ **A computer system always has a bottleneck.** Suppose that you decide that the bottleneck on your file server is a slow 10,000 RPM SCSI disk drive, so you replace it with a fast 15,000 RPM drive. Now the hard drive is no longer the bottleneck: The drive can process information faster than the controller card to which the disk is connected. You didn't really eliminate the bottleneck — you just moved it from the hard drive to the disk controller. No matter what you do, the computer will always have a component that limits the overall performance of the system.

- ✔ **One way to limit the effect of a bottleneck is to avoid waiting for the bottleneck.** For example, print spooling lets you avoid waiting for a slow printer. Although spooling doesn't speed up the printer, it frees you to do other work while the printer chugs along. Similarly, disk caching lets you avoid waiting for a slow hard drive.

The Five Most Common Network Bottlenecks

Direct from the home office in sunny Fresno, California, here are the top five most common network bottlenecks, in no particular order.

The hardware inside your servers

Your servers should be powerful computers capable of handling all the work your network will throw at them. Don't cut corners by using a bottom-of-the-line computer that you bought at a discount computer store.

The following list describes the four most important components of your server hardware:

- **Processor:** Your server should have a powerful processor. Any processor that's available in a $500 computer from a low-cost general appliance store is generally not a processor that you want to see in your file server. In other words, avoid processors designed for consumer-grade home computers.

- **Memory:** You can't have too much memory. Memory is cheap, so don't skimp. Don't even think about running a server with fewer than 4GB of RAM.

- **Disk:** Don't mess around with inexpensive IDE hard drives. To have a respectable system, you should have nothing but SCSI or SAS (Serially Attached SCSI) drives.

- **Network interface:** A $9.95 network card may be fine for your home network, but don't use one in a file server that supports 100 users and expect to be happy with the server's performance. Remember that the server computer uses the network more often than any clients do. Make sure your servers are equipped with good high-speed network interfaces.

The server's configuration options

All network operating systems (NOSes) have options that you can configure. Some of these options can make the difference between a pokey network and a zippy network. Unfortunately, no hard-and-fast rules exist for setting these options. Otherwise, you wouldn't have options.

The following important tuning options are available for most servers:

- **Virtual memory options:** *Virtual memory* refers to disk paging files that the server uses when it doesn't have enough real memory to do its work. Few servers ever have enough real memory, so virtual memory is always an important server feature. You can specify the size and location of the virtual memory paging files.

For the best performance, provide at least as much virtual memory as your computer has real memory. For example, if your server has 16GB of real memory, allocate at least 16GB of virtual memory. If necessary, you can increase this size later.

- **Disk striping:** Use the disk defragmenter to optimize the data storage on your server's disks.

  If the server has more than one hard drive, you can increase performance by creating *striped volumes,* which allow disk I/O operations to run concurrently on each of the drives in the stripe set.

- **Network protocols:** Make sure that your network protocols are configured correctly and remove any protocols that aren't necessary.

- **Free disk space on the server:** Servers like to have plenty of breathing room on their disks.

  If the amount of free disk space on your server drops precipitously low, the server chokes up and slows to a crawl. Make sure that your server has plenty of space — a few gigabytes of unused disk space provides a healthy buffer.

Servers that do too much

One common source of network performance problems is a server overloaded with too many duties. Just because a modern network operating system comes equipped with dozens of different types of services doesn't mean that you should enable and use them all on a single server. If a single server is bogged down because of too much work, add a second server to relieve the first server of some of its chores. Remember the old saying: "Many hands make light work."

For example, if your network needs more disk space, consider adding a second file server rather than adding another drive to the server that already has four nearly full drives. Better yet, purchase a file server appliance dedicated to the task of serving files.

As a side benefit, your network will be easier to administer and more reliable if you place separate functions on separate servers. For example, if a single server doubles as a file server and a mail server, you lose both services if you have to take down the server to perform an upgrade or repair a failed component. However, if you have separate file and mail server computers, only one of the services is interrupted if you have to take down one of the servers.

The network infrastructure

The infrastructure consists of the cables and any switches, hubs, routers, and other components that sit between your clients and your servers.

The following network infrastructure items can slow down your network:

- **Hubs:** If you have old network hubs rather than switches, replace them immediately. Do not pass go, do not collect $200.

- **Segment sizes:** Keep the number of computers and other devices on each network segment to a reasonable number. About 20 devices is usually the right number. (Note that if you replace your hubs with switches, you instantly cut the size of each segment because each port on a switch constitutes a separate segment.)

- **The network's speed:** If you have a really old network, you may discover that many — if not all — of your users are still working at 10 Mbps. Upgrading to 100 Mbps speeds up the network dramatically. Upgrading to 1 Gbps speeds it up even more.

- **The backbone speed:** If your network uses a backbone to connect segments, consider upgrading the backbone to 1 Gbps.

The hardest part about improving the performance of a network is determining where the bottlenecks are. With sophisticated test equipment and years of experience, network gurus can make good educated guesses. Without the equipment and experience, you can still make good uneducated guesses.

Malfunctioning components

Sometimes a malfunctioning network card or other component slows down the network. For example, a switch may malfunction intermittently, occasionally letting packets through but dropping enough of them to slow down the network. After you identify the faulty component, replacing it restores the network to its original speed.

Tune Your Network the Compulsive Way

You can tune your network in one of two ways. The first is to think about it a bit, take a guess at an approach that may improve performance, try that approach, and see whether the network seems to run faster. This strategy is the way most people go about tuning the network.

You can also try the compulsive way, which is suitable for people who organize their sock drawers by color and their food cupboards alphabetically by food group. The compulsive approach to tuning a network goes something like this:

1. Establish a method for objectively testing the performance of some aspect of the network.

   In this method, you create a *benchmark*. The result of your benchmark is a *baseline*.

2. Change one variable of your network configuration and rerun the test.

   For example, you may think that increasing the size of the disk cache can improve performance. Change the cache size, restart the server, and run the benchmark test. Note whether performance improves, stays the same, or becomes worse.

3. Repeat Step 2 for each variable that you want to test.

Here are some salient points to keep in mind if you decide to tune your network the compulsive way:

- ✔ **If possible, test each variable separately.** In other words, before proceeding, reverse the changes you made to other network variables.

- ✔ **Write down the results of each test so that you have an accurate record of the effect that each change makes on your network's performance.**

- ✔ **Be sure to change only one aspect of the network each time you run the benchmark.** If you make several changes, you don't know which one caused the change. One change may improve performance, but the other change may worsen performance so that the changes cancel each other out — kind of like offsetting penalties in a football game.

- ✔ **If possible, conduct the baseline test during normal working hours, when the network is undergoing its normal workload.**

- ✔ **To establish the network's baseline performance, run the benchmark test two or three times to make sure that the results are repeatable.**

Monitoring Network Performance

One way to monitor network performance is to use a stopwatch to see how long it actually takes to complete common network tasks, such as opening documents or printing reports. If you choose to monitor your network by using the stopwatch technique, you'll want to get a clipboard, baseball cap, and gray sweat suit to complete the ensemble.

A more high-tech approach to monitoring network performance is to use a monitor program that automatically gathers network statistics for you. After you set up the monitor, it plugs away, silently spying on your network and recording what it sees in performance logs. You can then review the performance logs to see how your network is doing.

For large networks, you can purchase sophisticated monitoring programs that run on their own dedicated servers. For small- and medium-sized networks, you can probably get by with the built-in monitoring facilities that come with the network operating system. For example, Figure 23-1 shows the Performance Monitor tool that comes with Windows Server 2012. Other operating systems come with similar tools.

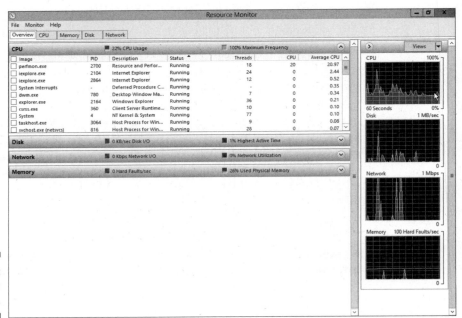

Figure 23-1:
Monitoring
performance.

Windows Performance Monitor lets you keep track of several different aspects of system performance at once. You track each performance aspect by setting up a counter. You can choose from dozens of different counters. Table 23-1 describes some of the most commonly used counters. Note that each counter refers to a server object, such as physical disk, memory, or the processor.

Table 23-1	Commonly Used Performance Counters	
Object	*Counter*	*Description*
Physical Disk	% Free Space	Percentage of free space on the server's physical disks. Should be at least 15%.
Physical Disk Length	Average Queue	Indicates how many disk operations are waiting while the disk is busy servicing other disk operations. Should be two or fewer.
Memory	Pages/second	Number of pages retrieved from the virtual memory page files per second (pps). A typical threshold is about 2,500 pps.
Processor	% Processor Time	Indicates the percentage of the processor's time that it's busy doing work rather than sitting idle. Should be 85% or less.

Here are a few more things to consider about performance monitoring:

- **Performance Monitor enables you to view real-time data or to view data that you can save in a log file.** Real-time data gives you an idea about what's happening with the network at a particular moment, but the more useful information comes from the logs.

- **You can schedule logging to occur at certain times of the day and for certain intervals.** For example, you may schedule the log to gather data every 15 seconds from 9:00 to 9:30 every morning and then again from 3:00 to 3:30 every afternoon.

- **Even if you don't have a performance problem now, you should set up performance logging and let it run for a few weeks to gather baseline data.** If you develop a problem, this baseline data will prove invaluable while you research the problem.

- **Don't leave performance logging turned on all the time.** Gathering performance data slows down your server. Use it only occasionally to gather baseline data or when you're experiencing a performance problem.

More Performance Tips

Here are a few last-minute performance tips that barely made it in:

- **You can often find the source of a slow network by staring at the network hubs or switches for a few minutes.** These devices have colorful arrays of green and red lights. The green lights flash whenever data is transmitted; the red lights flash when a collision occurs. An occasional red flash is normal, but if one or more of the red lights is flashing repeatedly, the network interface card (NIC) connected to that port may be faulty.

✔ **Check for scheduled tasks, such as backups, batched database updates, or report jobs.** If at all possible, schedule these tasks to run after normal business hours, such as at night when no one is in the office. These jobs tend to slow down the network by hogging the server's hard drives.

✔ **Sometimes, faulty application programs can degrade performance.** For example, some programs develop a *memory leak.* They use memory but then forget to release the memory after they finish. Programs with memory leaks can slowly eat up all the memory on a server, until the server runs out and grinds to a halt. If you think a program has a memory leak, contact the manufacturer of the program to see whether a fix is available.

✔ **Spyware can slow a system to a crawl.** A common source of performance problems on client computers is *spyware,* those annoying programs that you almost can't help but pick up when you surf the Internet. Fortunately, you can remove spyware with a variety of free or inexpensive spyware removal tools. For more information, use Google or another search engine to search for spyware removal.

Part VI
More Ways to Network

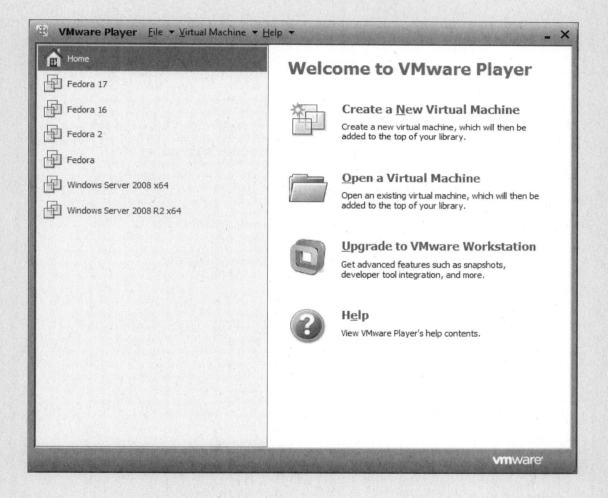

 Find out how to virtualize your desktop with products such as VMWare at www.dummies.com/extras/networking

In this part...

- ✔ Considering how the concept of virtualization can make your network more efficient and more cost effective

- ✔ Learning about Linux, a commonly used alternative to the Windows Server operating system for server computers

- ✔ Connecting to your network with an Apple Mac computer

Chapter 24

Going Virtual

*V*irtualization is one of the hottest trends in networking today. According to some industry pundits, virtualization is the best thing to happen to computers since the invention of the transistor. If you haven't already begun to virtualize your network, you're standing on the platform watching as the train is pulling out.

This chapter is a brief introduction to virtualization, with an emphasis on using it to leverage your network server hardware to provide more servers using less hardware. In addition to the general concepts of virtualization, you find out how to experiment with virtualization by using VMware's free virtualization product, VMware Player.

Mastering a virtualization environment calls for a book of its own. I recommend two titles: *Virtualization For Dummies,* by Bernard Golden, and *VMware Infrastructure 3 For Dummies,* by William Lowe (no relation, honest).

Understanding Virtualization

The basic idea behind virtualization is to use software to simulate the existence of hardware. This powerful idea enables you to run more than one independent computer system on a single physical computer system. Suppose that your organization requires a total of 12 servers to meet its needs. You could run each of these 12 servers on a separate computer, in which case you would have 12 computers in your server room, or you could use virtualization to run these 12 servers on just 2 computers. In effect, each of those computers would simulate six separate computer systems, each running one of your servers.

Each of the simulated computers is a virtual machine (VM). For all intents and purposes, each virtual machine appears to be a complete, self-contained computer system with its own processor (or, more likely, processors), memory, disk drives, CD-ROM/DVD drives, keyboard, mouse, monitor, network interfaces, USB ports, and so on.

Like a real computer, each virtual machine requires an operating system to do productive work. In a typical network server environment, each virtual machine runs its own copy of Windows Server 2012 (or an earlier version). The operating system has no idea that it's running on a virtual machine rather than on a real machine.

Here are a few terms you need to be familiar with if you expect to discuss virtualization intelligently:

- **Host:** The actual physical computer on which one or more virtual machines run.

- **Bare metal:** Another term for the host computer that runs one or more virtual machines.

- **Guest:** Another term for a virtual machine running on a host.

- **Guest operating system:** An operating system that runs within a virtual machine. By itself, a guest is just a machine; it requires an operating system to run. The guest operating system is what brings the guest to life.

    As far as licensing is concerned, Microsoft treats each virtual machine as a separate computer. Thus, if you run six guests on a single host, and each guest runs Windows Server 2012, you need six licenses of Windows Server 2012.

- **Hypervisor:** The virtualization operating system that creates and runs virtual machines.

    The two basic types of hypervisors are Type 1 and Type 2. A *Type 1 hypervisor* is a hypervisor that itself runs directly on the bare metal. A *Type 2 hypervisor* is a hypervisor that runs within an operating system, which in turn runs on the bare metal.

    For production use, you should always use Type 1 hypervisors because they're much more efficient than Type 2 hypervisors. Type 1 hypervisors are considerably more expensive than Type 2 hypervisors, however. As a result, many people use inexpensive or free Type 2 hypervisors to experiment with virtualization before making a commitment to purchase an expensive Type 1 hypervisor.

The long trek of virtualization

Kids these days think they invented everything, including virtualization.

Little do they know.

Virtualization was developed for PC-based computers in the early 1990s, around the time Captain Picard was flying the Enterprise around in *Star Trek: The Next Generation*.

But the idea is much older than that.

The first virtualized server computers predate Captain Picard by about 20 years. In 1972, IBM released an operating system called simply VM, which had nearly all the basic features found in today's virtualization products.

VM allowed the administrators of IBM's System/370 mainframe computers to create multiple independent virtual machines, each of which was called (you guessed it) a virtual machine, or VM. This terminology is still in use today.

Each VM could run one of the various guest operating systems that were compatible with the System/370 and appeared to this guest operating system to be a complete, independent System/370 computer with its own processor cores, virtual memory, disk partitions, and input/output devices.

The core of the VM system itself was called the *hypervisor* — another term that persists to this day.

The VM product that IBM released in 1972 was actually based on an experimental product that IBM released on a limited basis in 1967.

So whenever someone tells you about this new technology called *virtualization,* you can tell them that it was invented when *Star Trek* was TV. When they ask, "You mean the one with Picard?" you can say, "No, the one with Kirk."

Looking at the Benefits of Virtualization

You might suspect that virtualization is inefficient because a real computer is inherently faster than a simulated computer. Although it's true that real computers are faster than simulated computers, virtualization technology has become so advanced that the performance penalty for running on a virtualized machine rather than a real machine is only a few percent.

The small amount of overhead imposed by virtualization is usually more than made up for by the simple fact that even the most heavily used servers spend most of their time twiddling their digital thumbs, waiting for something to do. In fact, many servers spend nearly *all* their time doing nothing. As computers get faster and faster, they spend even more of their time with nothing to do.

Virtualization is a great way to put all this unused processing power to good use.

Besides this basic efficiency benefit, virtualization has several compelling benefits:

✔ **Hardware cost:** You typically can save a lot of money by reducing hardware costs when you use virtualization. Suppose that you replace ten servers that cost $4,000 each with one host server. Granted, you'll probably spend more than $4,000 on that server, because it needs to be maxed out with memory, processor cores, network interfaces, and so on. So you'll probably end up spending $15,000 or $20,000 for the host server. Also, you'll end up spending something like $5,000 for the hypervisor software. But that's still a lot less than the $40,000 you would have spent on ten separate computers at $4,000 each.

✔ **Energy costs:** Many organizations have found that going virtual has reduced their overall electricity consumption for server computers by 80 percent. This savings is a direct result of using less computer hardware to do more work. One host computer running ten virtual servers uses approximately one-tenth the energy that would be used if each of the ten servers ran on separate hardware.

✔ **Recoverability:** One of the biggest benefits of virtualization isn't the cost savings, but the ability to recover quickly from hardware failures. Suppose that your organization has ten servers, each running on separate hardware. If any one of those servers goes down due to a hardware failure — say, a bad motherboard — that server will remain down until you can fix the computer. On the other hand, if those ten servers are running as virtual machines on two different hosts, and one of the hosts fails, the virtual machines that were running on the failed host can be brought up on the other host in a matter of minutes.

Granted, the servers will run less efficiently on a single host than they would have on two hosts, but the point is that they'll all be running after only a short downtime.

In fact, with the most advanced hypervisors available, the transfer from a failing host to another host can be done automatically and instantaneously, so downtime is all but eliminated.

✔ **Disaster recovery:** Besides the benefit of recoverability when hardware failures occur, an even bigger benefit of virtualization comes into play in a true disaster-recovery situation. Suppose that your organization's server infrastructure consists of 20 separate servers. In the case of a devastating disaster, such as a fire in the server room that destroys all hardware, how long will it take you to get all 20 of those servers back up and running on new hardware? Quite possibly, the recovery time will be measured in weeks.

By contrast, virtual machines are actually nothing more than files that can be backed up onto tape. As a result, in a disaster-recovery situation, all you have to do is rebuild a single host computer and reinstall the hypervisor software. Then you can restore the virtual-machine backups from tape, restart the virtual machines, and get back up and running in a matter of days instead of weeks.

Getting Started with Virtualization

Virtualization is a complex subject, and mastering the ins and outs of working with a full-fledged virtualization system like VMware Infrastructure is a topic that's beyond the scope of this book. You can dip your toes into the shallow end of the virtualization pond, however, by downloading and experimenting with VMware's free virtualization product, called VMware Player. You can download it from www.vmware.com.

Figure 24-1 shows the VMware Player main screen. From this screen, you can create a new virtual machine or run one of the virtual machines you've already created. As you can see in the figure, I've created several virtual machines, including a few that run various versions of Fedora (a popular Linux distribution) as well as two that run Windows Server 2008.

Figure 24-1:
VMware Player lets you experiment with virtualization.

You can run an existing virtual machine by selecting the VM and clicking Play Virtual Machine. This launches the virtual machine, which opens in a new window, as shown in Figure 24-2. When you launch a virtual machine, the VM behaves exactly as a real computer would when you power it up: First, it initializes its virtual hardware devices; then it loads the guest OS that has been installed in the VM. In Figure 24-2, Windows Server 2008 has booted up and is waiting for you to press Ctrl+Alt+Del to log on.

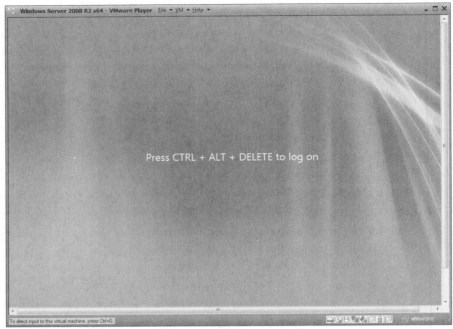

Press CTRL + ALT + DELETE to log on

To direct input to this virtual machine, press Ctrl+G.

Figure 24-2:
A virtual
machine
running
Windows
Server
2008 R2.

The prompt to press Ctrl+Alt+Del shown in Figure 24-2 illustrates one of the peculiar details of running a virtual machine within a host operating system (in this case, running Windows Server 2008 R2 within Windows 7 Ultimate). When you press Ctrl+Alt+Del, which OS — the host or the guest — responds? The answer is that the host OS responds to Ctrl+Alt+Del, so the guest OS never sees it.

To get around this limitation, VMware uses the special keyboard shortcut Ctrl+Alt+End to send a Ctrl+Alt+Del to the guest OS. Alternatively, you can use the VM pull-down menu that appears in the menu bar above the virtual-machine menu. This menu lists several actions that can be applied to the virtual machine, including Send Ctrl+Alt+Del.

Another detail you should know about when working with a VM is that when you click in the virtual machine's window, the VM captures your mouse and keyboard, so your input will be directed to the virtual machine rather than the host computer. If you want to break the bonds of the virtual machine and return to the host computer, press Ctrl and Alt simultaneously.

Creating a Virtual Machine

Creating a new virtual machine in VMware Player is relatively easy. In fact, the most challenging part is getting hold of the installation disc for the operating system you want to install on the VM. Remember that a virtual machine is useless without a guest operating system, so you need to have the installation disc available before you create the virtual machine.

If you just want to experiment with virtualization and don't have extra licenses of a Windows server operating system, you can always download an evaluation copy of Windows Server from Microsoft at `www.microsoft.com/en-us/server-cloud/windows-server`. The evaluation period is six months, so you'll have plenty of time to experiment.

The downloadable trial version of Windows Server comes in the form of an ISO file, which is an image of a DVD file that you can mount within your virtual machine as though it were a real disk.

When you have your ISO file or installation disc ready to go, you can create a new virtual machine by following these steps:

1. **Click Create a New Virtual Machine on the VMware Player home screen (refer to Figure 24-1).**

   This brings up the New Virtual Machine Wizard, as shown in Figure 24-3.

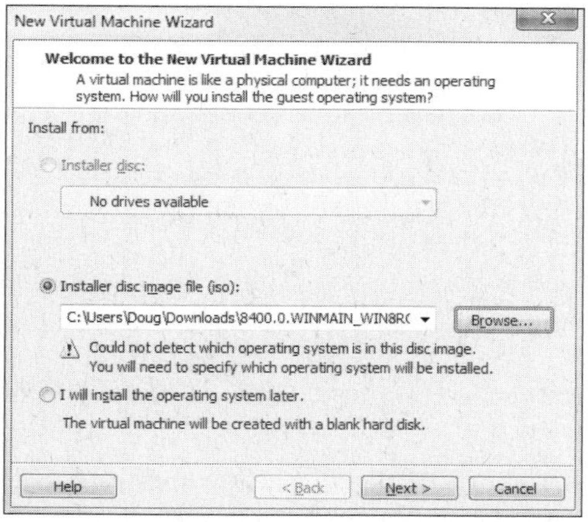

Figure 24-3:
The first page of the New Virtual Machine Wizard.

2. **Choose the installation option you want to use.**

   You have three choices:

   - *Installer Disc:* Select this option and then choose from the drop-down list the drive you'll install from if you want to install from an actual CD or DVD.

   - *Install Disc Image File (iso):* Select this option, click the Browse button, and browse to the ISO file that contains the installation image.

   - *I Will Install the Operating System Later:* Select this option if you want to create the virtual machine now but install the operating system later.

   Note that the remaining steps in this procedure assume that you select a Windows Server 2012 ISO file as the installation option.

3. **Click Next.**

   The screen shown in Figure 24-4 appears. You can enter the product key now or skip this step until later.

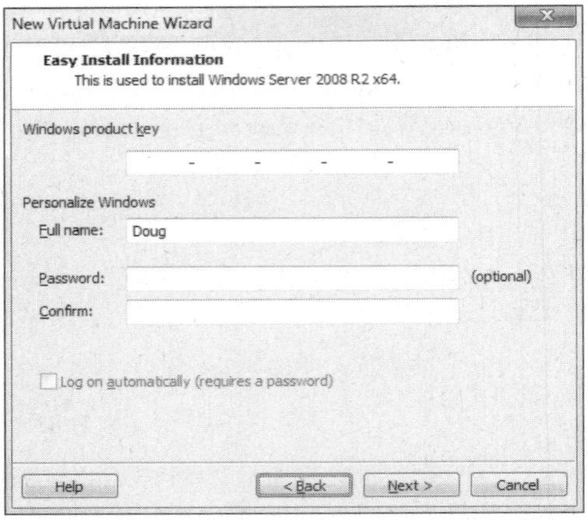

Figure 24-4:
The New Virtual Machine Wizard asks for your product key.

4. **If you have the Windows product key, enter it, and click Next; otherwise, just click Next.**

   You can always enter the product key later if you don't have it handy now. Either way, the screen shown in Figure 24-5 appears next.

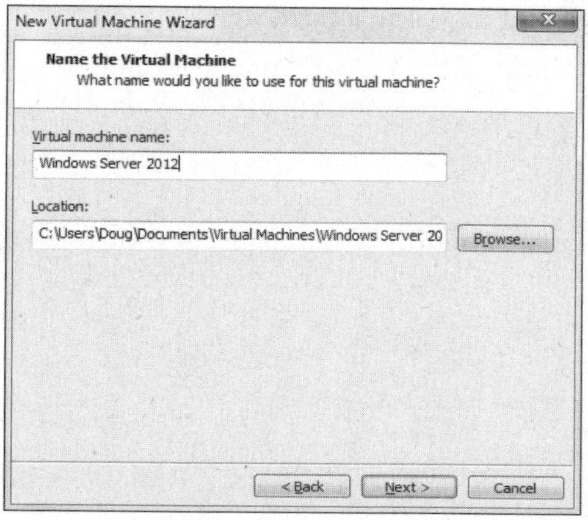

Figure 24-5:
Create a
name and
specify the
VM disk
location.

5. **Enter a name for the virtual machine.**

6. **Enter the location of the virtual machine's disk file.**

   If you want, you can click the Browse button and browse to the folder where you want to create the file.

7. **Click Next.**

   The wizard asks for the size of the disk to create for the virtual machine, as shown in Figure 24-6.

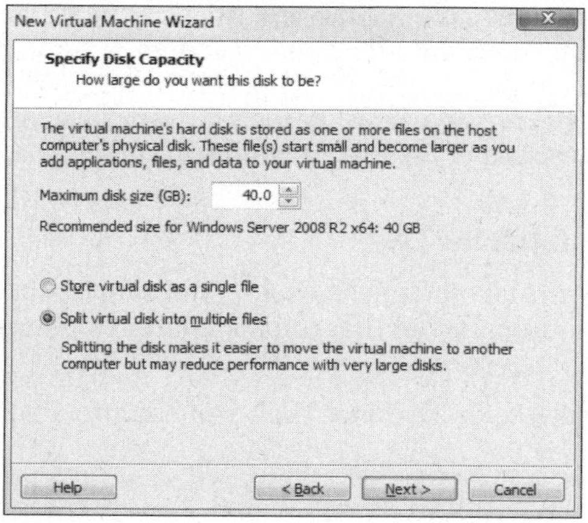

Figure 24-6:
Specify the
VM disk
size.

8. **Set the size of the virtual machine's hard drive.**

   The default setting is 40GB, but you can change it depending on your needs. Note that you must have sufficient space available on the host computer's disk drive.

9. **Click Next.**

   The wizard displays a final confirmation page, as shown in Figure 24-7.

Figure 24-7: VMware is ready to create the virtual machine.

10. **Click Finish.**

    The wizard creates the virtual machine and then starts it. Because the machine doesn't have an operating system installed, it boots from the CD/DVD installation image you specified back in Step 2. In this case, I booted with the Windows Server evaluation software disk image, so the new virtual machine displays the Install Windows screen, as shown in Figure 24-8.

11. **Follow the steps to install the OS.**

    Installing an OS in a virtual machine is exactly the same as installing it on a physical computer, except that the installation screens appear within a virtual-machine window.

    When the OS is installed, you're done! Then you can proceed to use the virtual machine.

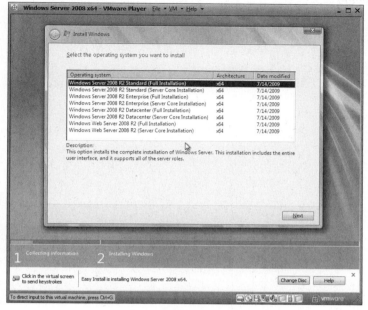

Figure 24-8:
Installing
Windows
Server in
a virtual
machine.

You can adjust the hardware configuration of a virtual machine by choosing
VM⇨Settings while the virtual machine is running. This command brings up the
Virtual Machine Settings dialog box, as shown in Figure 24-9. From this dialog
box, you can adjust the virtual machine's hardware configuration, including the
amount of RAM available to the VM and the number of processor cores. You
can also adjust the disk drive size; add CD, DVD, or floppy drives; and configure
network adapters, USB connections, and sound and display settings.

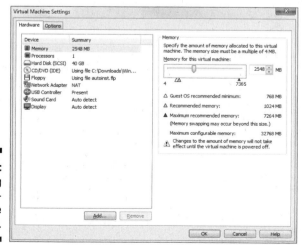

Figure 24-9:
Configuring
virtual-
machine
settings.

Chapter 25

Networking with Linux

. . . .

. . . .

L inux, the free operating system (OS) based on Unix, is a popular alternative to Windows Server, especially for specific applications such as web servers or e-mail servers. Linux can also be used as a firewall or as a file server and print server on your local area network (LAN).

Linux has many advantages over Windows, not the least of which is that it is free. But price isn't the only advantage. Many network administrators have found that Linux is more stable than Windows, crashing less often and requiring less downtime for maintenance. In addition, Linux has a solid reputation for efficiency and security.

Linux was created in 1991 by Linus Torvalds, who was then an undergraduate student at the University of Helsinki in Finland. Linus thought it'd be fun to create his own OS based on Unix for his brand-new PC. In the nearly two decades since Linux was first conceived, Linux has become a full-featured operating system that is fast and reliable.

This chapter shows the basics of setting up a Linux server on your network and using it as a file server, as a web server for the Internet or an intranet, as an e-mail server, and as a router and firewall to help connect your network to the Internet.

Linux is a complicated OS. Understanding how to use it can be a daunting task, especially if your only prior computer experience is with Windows. John Wiley & Sons, Inc., has *For Dummies* books that make Linux less painful. You'll find more comprehensive information about Linux in my book, *Networking All-in-One For Dummies,* 5th Edition; and you may also want to check out *Linux For Dummies,* 9th Edition, by Richard Blum.

Comparing Linux with Windows

If your only computer experience is with Windows, you're in for a steep learning curve when you first get into Linux. There are many fundamental differences between the Linux operating system and Windows. Here are some of the more important differences:

- **Linux is a multiuser operating system.** More than one user can log on and use a Linux computer at the same time:

  - Two or more users can log on to a Linux computer from the same keyboard and monitor by using virtual consoles, which let you switch from one user session to another with a special key combination.

  - Users can log on to the Linux computer from a terminal window running on another computer on the network.

  Most versions of Windows are single-user systems. Only one user at a time can log on to a Windows computer and run commands. (Windows Server can be configured as a multiuser system with terminal services.)

- **Linux doesn't have a built-in graphical user interface (GUI) as Windows does.** The GUI in Linux is provided by an optional component called *X Window System*. You can run Linux without X Window, in which case you interact with Linux by typing commands. If you prefer to use a GUI, you must install and run X Window.

  X Window is split into two parts:

  - *A server component* — X Server — manages multiple windows and provides graphics services for application programs.

  - *A UI component* — a window manager — provides user interface (UI) features, such as menus, buttons, toolbars, and a taskbar.

  Several window managers are available, each with a different look and feel. With Windows, you're stuck with the UI that Microsoft designed. With Linux, you can use the UI of your choosing.

- **Linux can't run Windows programs.** Nope, you can't run Microsoft Office on a Linux system; instead, you must find a similar program that's written specifically for Linux. Many Linux distributions come with the OpenOffice suite, which provides word processing, spreadsheet, presentation, graphics, database, e-mail, calendar, and scheduling software. Thousands of other programs are available for Linux.

  Windows emulator programs — the best-known is Wine — can run *some* Windows programs on Linux. However, the emulators run only some Windows programs, and they run them slower than they would run on a Windows system.

- **Linux doesn't do Plug and Play the way Windows does.** Major Linux distributions come with configuration programs that can automatically detect and configure the most common hardware components, but Linux doesn't have built-in support for Plug-and-Play hardware devices. You're more likely to run into a hardware-configuration problem with Linux than with Windows.

✔ **Linux uses a different system for accessing disk drives and files than Windows does.** For an explanation of how the Linux file system works, see the "I can't see my C drive!" sidebar that's coming up in this chapter.

✔ **Linux runs better on older hardware than the current incarnations of Windows do.** Linux is an ideal OS for an older Pentium computer with at least 32MB of RAM and 2GB of hard drive space.

If you're fond of antiques, Linux can run well on even a 486 computer with as little as 4MB of RAM and a few hundred MB of disk space.

I can't see my C drive!

Well, no, but that's normal. Linux and Windows have completely different ways of referring to your computer's disk drives and partitions. The differences can take some getting used to for experienced Windows users.

Windows uses a separate letter for each drive and partition on your system. For example, if you have a single drive formatted into three partitions, Windows identifies the partitions as drives C, D, and E. Each of these drives has its own `root` directory, which can in turn contain additional directories used to organize your files. As far as Windows is concerned, drives C, D, and E are completely separate drives even though the drives are actually just partitions on a single drive.

Linux doesn't use drive letters. Instead, Linux combines all the drives and partitions into a single directory hierarchy. In Linux, one of the partitions is designated as the `root` partition. The `root` is roughly analogous to the C drive on a Windows system. Then, the other partitions can be mounted on the `root` partition and treated as if they were directories on the `root` partition. For example, you might designate the first partition as the `root` partition and then mount the second partition as `/user` and the third partition as `/var`. Then any files

stored in the `/user` directory would actually be stored in the second partition, and files stored in the `/var` directory would be stored in the third partition.

The directory where a drive mounts is the drive's _mount point._

Notice that Linux uses regular forward-slash characters (`/`) to separate directory names rather than the backward-slash characters (`\`) used by Windows. Typing backslashes instead of regular slashes is one of the most common mistakes made by new Linux users.

While I'm on the subject, Linux uses a different convention for naming files, too. In Windows, filenames end in a three-letter (sometimes more letters than that) extension separated from the rest of the filename by a period. The extension is used to indicate the file type. For example, files that end in `.exe` are program files, but files that end in `.doc` are word-processing documents.

Linux doesn't use filename extensions, but periods are often used in Linux filenames to separate different parts of the name — and the last part often indicates the file type. For example, `ldap.conf` and `pine.conf` are both configuration files.

Choosing a Linux Distribution

Because the *kernel* (the core operating functions) of the Linux OS is free, several companies have created their own distributions of Linux, which include the Linux OS along with a bundle of packages, such as administration tools, web servers, and other useful utilities as well as printed documentation.

The following are some of the more popular Linux distributions:

- **Fedora:** One of the popular Linux distributions. You can download Fedora free from `http://fedoraproject.org`. You can also obtain it by purchasing any of several books on Fedora that include the Fedora distribution on DVD or CD-ROM.

  All the examples in this chapter are based on Fedora 17.

- **Mandriva Linux:** Another popular Linux distribution, one that is often recommended as the easiest for first-time Linux users to install. This distribution was formerly known as *Mandrake Linux*. Go to `www.mandriva.com` for more information.

- **Ubuntu:** A Linux distribution that has gained popularity in recent years. It focuses on ease of use. For more information, go to `www.ubuntu.com`.

- **SUSE:** Pronounced *SOO-zuh,* like the name of the famous composer of marches; a popular Linux distribution sponsored by Novell. You can find more information at `www.suse.com`.

- **Slackware:** One of the oldest Linux distributions and still popular, especially among Linux old-timers. A full installation of Slackware gives you all the tools that you need to set up a network or Internet server. See `www.slackware.com` for more information.

All distributions of Linux include the same core components: the Linux kernel, an X Server, popular windows managers (such as GNOME and KDE), compilers, Internet programs such as Apache, Sendmail, and so on. However, not all Linux distributions are created equal. In particular, the manufacturer of each distribution creates its own installation and configuration programs to install and configure Linux.

The installation program is what makes or breaks a Linux distribution. All the distributions I list in this section have easy-to-use installation programs that automatically detect the hardware that's present on your computer and configure Linux to work with that hardware, thus eliminating most — if not all — manual configuration chores. The installation programs also let you select the Linux packages that you want to install and let you set up one or more user accounts besides the root account.

Installing Linux

All the Linux distributions I describe in the earlier section, "Choosing a Linux Distribution," include an installation program that simplifies installing Linux on your computer. The installation program asks you a series of questions about your hardware, what components of Linux you want to install, and how you want to configure certain features. Then it copies the appropriate files to your hard drive and configures your Linux system.

If the thought of installing Linux gives you hives, you can buy computers with Linux preinstalled, just as you can buy computers with Windows already installed.

An excellent way to dip your feet into the Linux waters is to install it on a virtual machine, using a free virtual platform such as VMware Player or Oracle's VirtualBox.

Before you begin to install Linux, I recommend several planning steps:

✔ **Hardware:** Make a list of all the hardware components on your computer and how they're configured.

✔ **Partitioning:** Decide how you want to partition your hard drive for Linux.

Although Windows is usually installed into a single disk partition, Linux installations typically require at least three hard-drive partitions:

- *A boot partition:* This should be small; 16MB is recommended. The boot partition contains the OS kernel and is required to start Linux properly on some computers.

- *A swap partition:* This should be about twice the size of your computer's RAM. For example, if the computer has 2GB of RAM, allocate a 4GB swap partition. Linux uses this partition as an extension of your computer's RAM.

- *A* root *partition:* This, in most cases, uses up the remaining free space on the disk. The root partition contains all the files and data used by your Linux system.

You can also create additional partitions if you wish. The installation program includes a disk-partitioning feature that lets you set up your disk partitions and indicate the mount point for each partition. (For more information about disk partitions, see the sidebar, "I can't see my C drive!," earlier in this chapter.)

✔ **Packages:** Decide which optional Linux packages to install along with the Linux kernel:

- *All:* If you have enough drive space, install all the packages that come with your distribution. That way, if you decide you need to use a package, you won't have to figure out how to install the package outside of the installation program.

- *Pick and choose:* If you're tight on space, make sure that you at least install the basic network and Internet server packages, including Apache, Sendmail, FTP, and Samba.

✔ **Password:** Set the password for the `root` account.

✔ **User accounts:** In most distributions, you choose whether to create at least one user account.

Create at least one user account during installation so you can log on to Linux as a user (not with the `root` account). As a user, you can experiment with Linux commands without accidentally deleting or corrupting a needed system file.

On Again, Off Again

Any user who accesses a Linux system, whether locally or over a network, must be authenticated by a valid user account on the system. The following sections lay out the whys, hows, and wherefores of logging on and logging off a Linux system — and how to shut down the system.

Logging on

When Linux boots up, it displays a series of startup messages while it starts the various services that make up a working Linux system. Assuming that you selected X Server when you installed Linux, you're eventually greeted by the screen, as shown in Figure 25-1. To log on to Linux, click your user ID if is displayed. If your user ID isn't displayed, click Not Listed and then enter your user ID. Then, when prompted, type your password and press Enter.

As a part of the installation process, the Setup Agent creates a user account for you. Use this user account rather than the `root` user account whenever possible. Use the `root` account only when you're making major changes to the system's configuration. When you're doing routine work, log on as an ordinary user to avoid accidentally corrupting your system.

When you log on, Linux grinds its gears for a moment and then displays the GNOME desktop, which I describe later in this chapter.

Figure 25-1:
Logging on
to Linux.

Logging off

After you log on, you probably want to know how to log off. To do so, hover the mouse over your name in the top right corner of the screen, then choose Log Out.

Shutting down

Like with any OS, you shouldn't turn off the power to a Linux server without shutting down the system. The two ways to shut down Linux are

- ✔ Press Ctrl+Alt+Delete.
- ✔ Click your user name in the upper right of the screen and then click Shutdown.

Using GNOME

Figure 25-2 shows a typical GNOME desktop. Although the GNOME desktop looks a lot different from the Windows desktop, many of the basic skills used for working with Microsoft Windows — moving or resizing windows, minimizing or maximizing windows, and using drag-and-drop to move items between windows — are almost exactly the same in GNOME.

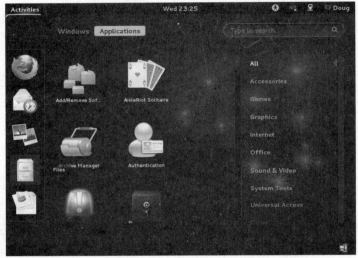

Figure 25-2:
A typical
GNOME
desktop.

Here are some key features of the GNOME desktop:

- ✔ **Activities:** The Activities Overview provides a single access point for all GNOME applications. It provides fast access to common functions, such as Internet browsing, e-mail, or file management, as well as desktop access to other applications. You can access Activities Overview by pressing the Windows key on the keyboard or clicking Activities in the top-left corner. (The screen in Figure 25-2 shows the Activities Overview open.)

- ✔ **Search box:** The search box in the top-right corner is the easiest way to find things in GNOME. For example, if you want to run the gedit program to edit a text file, search for "gedit." Or if you want to fiddle with network settings, search for "Network."

- ✔ **Settings:** To manage your system or user settings, click your name at the top right of the screen. This reveals a menu with options for various settings.

Getting to a Command Shell

A command shell is a text-based window in which you can enter Linux commands directly, bypassing the graphical user interface. You can get to a command shell in one of two basic ways when you need to run Linux commands directly.

The first is to press Ctrl+Alt+F*x* to switch to one of the virtual consoles, where F*x* is one of the function keys, from F1 through F12. (A *virtual console* is simply a text-mode command prompt.) Then, you can log on and run commands to your heart's content. When you're done, press Ctrl+Alt+F7 to return to GNOME.

Alternatively, you can open a command shell directly in GNOME by opening the Activities Overview, clicking Applications, and then clicking the Terminal icon. This opens a command shell in a window right on the GNOME desktop, as shown in Figure 25-3. Because this shell runs within the user account that GNOME is logged on as, you don't have to log on. You can just start typing commands. When you're done, type **Exit** to close the window.

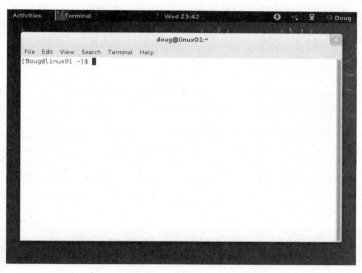

Figure 25-3:
Using a
Terminal
window to
run Linux
commands.

Managing User Accounts

One of the most common network administration tasks is adding a user account. The Setup Agent prompts you to create a user account the first time you start Linux after installing it. However, you'll probably need to create additional accounts.

Each Linux user account has the following information associated with it:

- ✔ **Username:** The name the user types to log on to the Linux system.
- ✔ **Full name:** The user's full name.

✔ **Home directory:** The directory where the user is placed when he logs on. In Fedora, the default home directory is `/home/username`. For example, if the username is `blowe`, the home directory will be `/home/blowe`.

✔ **Shell:** The program used to process Linux commands. Several shell programs are available. In most distributions, the default shell is `/bin/bash`.

✔ **Group:** You can create group accounts, which makes it easy to apply identical access rights to groups of users. Group accounts are option, but useful if you have more than just a few users.

✔ **User ID:** The internal identifier for the user.

You can add a new user by using the `useradd` command. For example, to create a user account named `slowe`, using default values for the other account information, open a Terminal window or switch to a virtual console and type this command:

```
# useradd slowe
```

The `useradd` command has many optional parameters that you can use to set account information, such as the user's home directory and shell.

Fortunately, most Linux distributions come with special programs that simplify routine system management tasks. For example, Fedora comes with the user Manager program, as shown in Figure 25-4. To start this program, click Activities, click Applications, and then double-click Users and Groups (scroll down to find it).

Figure 25-4:
Managing
users and
groups.

To create a user with User Manager, click the Add User button. This brings up a dialog box that asks for the user's name, password, and other information. Fill out this dialog box and then click OK.

The User Manager also lets you create groups. You can simplify the task of administering users by applying access rights to groups rather than individual users. Then, when a user needs access to a resource, you can add the user to the group that has the needed access.

To create a group, click the Add Group button. A dialog box appears, asking for the name of the new group. Type the name you want and then click OK.

To add a user to a group, click the Groups tab in the User Manager. Then, double-click the group to which you want to add users. This brings up the Group Properties dialog box. Click the Group Users tab and then select the users that you want to belong to the group.

Network Configuration

In many cases, configuring a Linux server for networking is a snap. When you install Linux, the Installation program automatically detects your network adapters and installs the appropriate drivers. Then you're prompted for basic network-configuration information, such as the computer's IP address, hostname, and so on.

You may need to manually change your network settings after installation or configure advanced networking features that aren't configured during installation. In the following sections, you get a look at the basic procedures for configuring Linux networking services.

Using the Network Configuration program

Before you can use a network interface to access a network, you have to configure the interface's basic TCP/IP options, such as its IP address, host name, Domain Name System (DNS) servers, and so on. This configuration is automatically set up when you install Linux, but you may need to change it later on. In this section, I show you how to do that by using Fedora's Network settings program. You can access this program by clicking your name in the top-right corner of the screen, choosing Settings, and then choosing Network.

Most other Linux distributions have similar programs.

The Network Configuration program lets you configure the basic TCP/IP settings for a network interface by pointing and clicking your way through tabbed windows. Figure 25-5 shows the Network Configuration program in action.

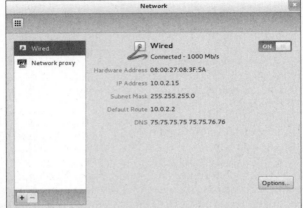

Figure 25-5:
The
Network
Configuration
program.

Notice that the main window of the Network Configuration lists all the network interfaces installed in your computer. You can double-click any of the interfaces to bring up a window similar to the one shown in Figure 25-6. This window lets you set the configuration options for the network interface, such as its IP address and other TCP/IP–configuration information.

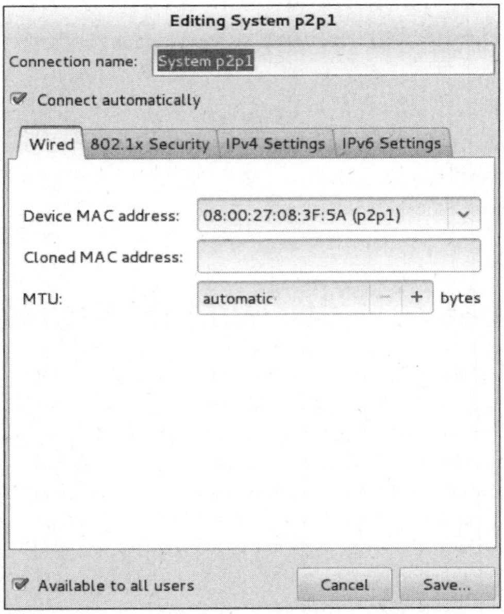

Figure 25-6:
Configure
basic TCP/
IP settings
here.

Restarting your network

Whenever you make a configuration change to your network, you must restart Linux networking services for the change to take effect. If you find that annoying, just be thankful that you don't have to restart the entire computer. Simply restarting the network services is sufficient.

Open a console by pressing Ctrl+Alt+*n*, where *n* is a number from 2–7. Log in using the root account and then enter the following command:

```
service network restart
```

To confirm that the service was properly restarted, you'll see a message similar to this:

```
Restarting network (via systemctl):                    [  OK  ]
```

Doing the Samba Dance

Until now, you probably thought of Samba as an intricate Brazilian dance with fun rhythms. But in the Linux world, *Samba* refers to a file- and printer-sharing program that allows Linux to mimic a Windows file-and-print server so Windows computers can use shared Linux directories and printers. If you want to use Linux as a file or print server in a Windows network, you have to know how to dance the Samba.

Understanding Samba

Because Linux and Windows have such different file systems, you can't create a Linux file server simply by granting Windows users access to Linux directories. Windows client computers wouldn't be able to access files in the Linux directories. Too many differences exist between the file systems. For example:

- ✔ **Case sensitivity:** Linux filenames are case sensitive, whereas Windows filenames are not. For example, in Windows, `File1.txt` and `file1.txt` are the same file. In Linux, they're different files.

- ✔ **File extensions:** In Linux, periods aren't used to denote file extensions.

  Linux filenames don't use extensions.

- ✔ **File attributes:** Windows has file attributes like *read-only* and *archive*. Linux doesn't have these.

More fundamentally, Windows networking uses the Server Message Block (SMB) protocol to manage the exchange of file data among file servers and clients. Linux doesn't have SMB support built in. And that's why Samba is required. Samba is a program that mimics the behavior of a Windows-based file server by implementing the SMB protocol. So when you run Samba on a Linux server, the Windows computers on your network see the Linux server as if it were a Windows server.

Like a Windows server, Samba works by designating certain directories as shares. A *share* is simply a directory that's made available to other users via the network. Each share has the following elements:

- ✔ **Name:** The name by which the share is known over the network

  Share names should be eight characters whenever possible.

- ✔ **Path:** The path to the directory on the Linux computer that's being shared, such as `\Users\Doug`

- ✔ **Description:** A one-line description of the share

- ✔ **Access:** A list of users or groups who have been granted access to the share

Samba also includes a client program that lets a Linux computer access Windows file servers.

Why did Samba's developers choose to call their program Samba? Simply because the protocol that Windows file and print servers use to communicate with each other is SMB. Add a couple of vowels to *SMB*, and you get *Samba*.

Installing Samba

If you didn't install Samba when you installed Linux, you'll have to install it now. Here are the steps:

1. **Click Activities, Applications, and then Add/Remove Software.**

   This summons the Add/Remove Software program.

2. **Type** Samba **in the search text box and click Find.**

   A list of Samba packages appears in the window's main list box.

3. **Select the package labeled Server and Client Software to Interoperate with Windows Machines.**

   This is the basic Samba package.

4. **Scroll down a bit and also choose the Samba Server Configuration Tool package.**

   This package provides a user-friendly interface for configuring Samba.

5. **Click Apply.**

   The Add/Remove Software program grinds and whirs for a moment and then installs the package you selected.

6. **Close the Add/Remove Software program.**

   Samba is now installed.

One sure way to render a Samba installation useless is to enable the default Linux firewall settings on the computer that runs Samba. The Linux firewall is designed to prevent users from accessing network services, such as Samba. It's designed to be used between the Internet and your local network — not between Samba and your local network. Although you can configure the firewall to allow access to Samba only to your internal network, a much better option is to run the firewall on a separate computer. That way, the firewall computer can concentrate on being a firewall, and the file server computer can concentrate on being a file server.

Starting and stopping Samba

Before you can use Samba, you must start its two daemons, smbd and nmbd. (*Daemon* is the Linux term for *service,* which is a program that runs as a background task.) Both daemons can be started at once by starting the SMB service. From a command shell, use this command:

```
service smb start
```

Whenever you make a configuration change, such as adding a new share or creating a new Samba user, you should stop and restart the service with this command:

```
service smb restart
```

If you prefer, you can stop and start the service with separate commands:

```
service smb stop
service smb start
```

If you're not sure whether Samba is running, enter this command:

```
service smb status
```

You get a message indicating whether the smbd and nmbd daemons are running.

To configure Samba to start automatically when you start Linux, use this command:

```
chkconfig -level 35 smb on
```

To make sure that the `chkconfig` command worked right, enter this command:

```
chkconfig –list smb
```

You should see output similar to the following:

```
Smb        0:off   1:off   2:off   3:on    4:off   5:on    6:off
```

You can independently configure services to start automatically for each of the six boot levels of Linux. Boot level 3 is normal operation without a GUI; level 5 is normal operation with a GUI. So setting SMB to start for levels 3 and 5 makes SMB available, regardless of whether you're using a GUI.

Using the Samba Server Configuration tool

Fedora includes a handy GNOME-based configuration tool that simplifies the task of configuring Samba. To start it, click Activities, click Applications, and then click Samba. When you do so, the Samba Server Configuration tool appears, as shown in Figure 25-7. This tool lets you configure basic server settings and manage shares.

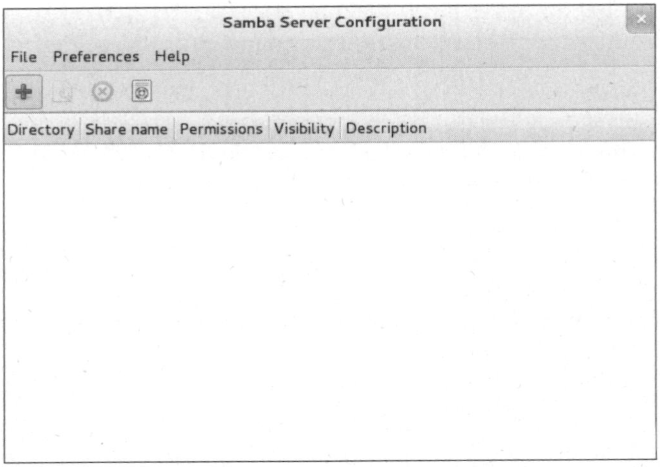

Figure 25-7: Using the Samba Server Configuration tool.

To make your Samba server visible on the network, choose Preferences⇨Server Settings. This brings up a dialog box that lets you set the workgroup name (which must match the workgroup or domain name you want the Samba server to belong to) and a description for the server, as well as some basic security settings that control how users can access the Samba server.

You can set four basic types of security for your Samba server:

- ✔ **Domain:** Configures the Samba server to use a Windows domain controller to verify the user. If you specify this option, you must

    - • Provide the domain controller's name in the Authentication Server field.

    - • Set Encrypted Passwords to Yes (if you use Domain mode).

- ✔ **Server:** Configures Samba to use another Samba server to authenticate users.

    If you have more than one Samba server, this feature lets you set up user accounts on just one of the servers. Then, in the Authentication Server field, specify the name of the Samba server that should perform the authentication.

- ✔ **Share:** Authorizes users separately for each share they attempt to access.

- ✔ **User:** Requires that users provide a valid username and password when they first connect to a Samba server. That authentication then grants them access to all shares on the server, subject to the restrictions of the account they're authorized under.

    User mode is the default.

For each network user who needs to access the Samba server, you must

1. Create a Linux user account for each user.

2. Create a separate Samba user account.

   To create a Samba user account, choose Preferences⇨Samba Users from the Samba Server Configuration window. This brings up the Samba Users dialog box, as shown in Figure 25-8. You can use this dialog box to add, edit, or delete users.

   The Samba user account maps to an existing Linux user account, so you must create the Linux user account first.

Figure 25-8:
The Samba Users dialog box lists your Samba users.

To be useful, a file server should offer one or more *shares* — directories that have been designated as publicly accessible via the network. Again, you use the Samba Server Configuration program to manage your shares. To add a share, click the Add button on the Samba Server Configuration program's toolbar. This brings up the Create Samba Share dialog box, as shown in Figure 25-9. You can then

✔ Enter the path for the directory you want to share.

✔ Enter a description for the share.

✔ Select whether to allow either read-only or read-write access.

✔ Click the Access tab if you want to set limits on access (for example, to specific users).

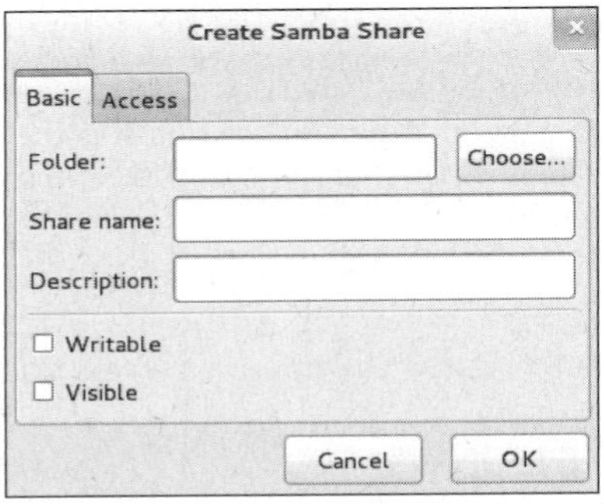

Figure 25-9:
The Create
Samba
Share
dialog box.

Create Samba Share ✕

| Basic | Access |

Folder: [   ] [Choose...]

Share name: [   ]

Description: [   ]

☐ Writable
☐ Visible

[Cancel] [OK]

When you create a new share using the Samba Configuration program, the share should be immediately visible to network users. If not, try restarting the Samba server, as I describe in the section, "Starting and stopping Samba," in this chapter.

Chapter 26

Macintosh Networking

· ·

· ·

This book dwells on mostly networking Windows-based computers, as though Microsoft were the only game in town. I'm sure plenty of people in Redmond, WA (where Microsoft is headquartered) wished that it were so. But alas, there is an entirely different breed of computer: the Apple Macintosh, more commonly referred to simply as *Mac*.

Every Macintosh ever built, even an original 1984 model, includes networking support. Newer Macintosh computers have better built-in networking features than older Macintosh computers, of course. The newest Macs include built-in Gigabit Ethernet connections or 802.11n wireless connections, or both. Support for these network connections is pretty much automatic, so all you have to do is plug your Mac into a network or connect to a wireless network, and you're ready to go.

This chapter presents what you need to know to network Mac computers running OS X, Apple's operating system for Mac computers. You'll see how to control basic Mac network options, such as TCP/IP and file sharing. I also show you how to join a Mac to a Windows domain network.

Basic Mac Network Settings

Most network settings on OS X are automatic. If you wish, you can look at and change the default network settings by following these steps:

1. **Choose System Preferences➪ Networking.**

   The Network preferences page appears, as shown in Figure 26-1.

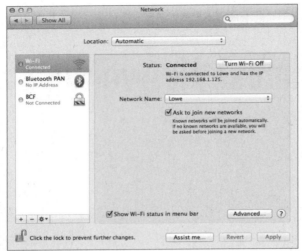

Figure 26-1:
Network
preferences.

2. Click Advanced.

The advanced network settings are displayed, as shown in Figure 26-2.

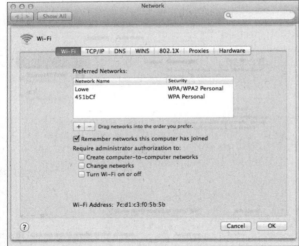

Figure 26-2:
Advanced
network
settings.

3. Click the TCP/IP tab to view or change the TCP/IP settings.

This brings up the TCP/IP settings, as shown in Figure 26-3. From this page, you can view the currently assigned IP address for the computer. And, if you wish, you can assign a static IP address by changing the Configure IPv4 drop-down from Using DHCP to Manually. Then, you can enter your own IP address, subnet mask, and router address. (For more information about IP addresses, refer to Chapter 5.)

4. Click the DNS tab to view or change the DNS settings.

This brings up the DNS settings shown in Figure 26-4. Here, you can see the DNS servers being used, and you can add additional DNS servers if you wish.

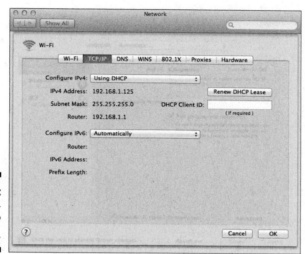

Figure 26-3:
Mac net-
work TCP/IP
settings.

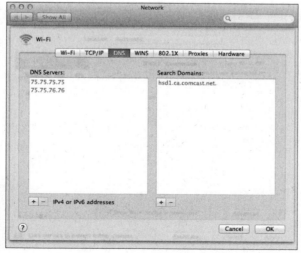

Figure 26-4:
DNS
settings.

5. **Click the Hardware tab to view hardware information.**

This brings up the settings page shown in Figure 26-5. The most useful bit of information on this tab is the MAC address, which is sometimes needed to set up wireless security. (For more information, refer to Chapter 9.)

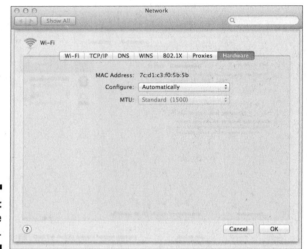

Figure 26-5:
Hardware settings.

What about OS X Server?

At one time, Apple offered the Mac OS X Server dedicated network operating system (NOS). In 2011, Apple merged Mac OS X Server with its desktop OS and made the server components of the OS available as an inexpensive add-on you can purchase from the App Store. For the latest version of OS X (10.8, released in July of 2012), the Server App enhancement can be purchased for about $20.

The Server App download adds a variety of network server features to OS X, including

- ✔ **Apache web server,** which also runs on Windows and Linux systems

- ✔ **MySQL,** which is also available in Windows and Linux versions

- ✔ **Wiki Server,** which lets you set up web-based wiki, blog, and calendaring sites

- ✔ **NetBoot,** a feature that simplifies the task of managing network client computers

- ✔ **Spotlight Server,** which lets you search for content on remote file servers

- ✔ **Podcast Producer,** which lets the create and distribute multimedia programs

Joining a Domain

If you're using a Mac in a Windows domain environment, you can join the Mac to the domain by following these steps:

1. **Choose Settings⇨Users & Groups.**

   This brings up the Users & Groups page, as shown in Figure 26-6.

Figure 26-6:
Users and
Groups.

2. **Select the user account you want to join to the domain and then click Login Options.**

   The Login Options page appears, as shown in Figure 26-7.

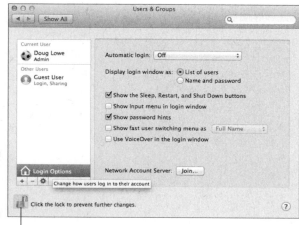

Figure 26-7:
Login
Options.

The lock icon

3. **If the lock icon at the bottom left of the page is locked, click it and enter your password when prompted.**

   By default, the user login options are locked to prevent unauthorized changes. This step unlocks the settings so that you can join the domain.

4. **Click the Join button.**

   You're prompted to enter the name of the domain you want to join, as shown in Figure 26-8.

Figure 26-8: Joining a domain.

5. **Enter the name of the domain you want to join.**

   When you enter the domain name, the dialog box expands to allow you to enter domain credentials to allow you to join the domain, as shown in Figure 26-9.

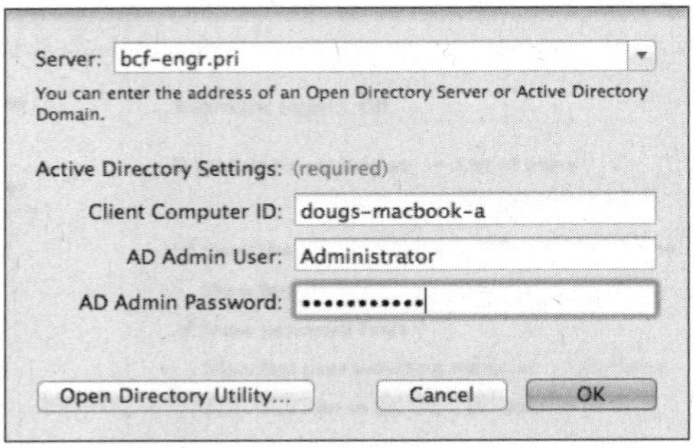

Figure 26-9: Authenticating with the domain.

6. **Enter the name and password of a domain administrator account; then click OK.**

   You return to the Login Options page, which shows that you have successfully joined the domain; see Figure 26-10.

7. **Close the Users & Groups window.**

Connecting to a Share

After you join a domain, you can access its network shares via the Finder. Just follow these steps:

1. **Click Finder.**

2. **Choose Go⇨Connect to Server.**

   The Connect to Server dialog box appears.

3. **Type the path that leads to the server share you want to connect to.**

   To type a network path, follow this syntax:

   ```
   smb://server-name/share-name
   ```

   Replace the *server-name* with the name of the server that contains the share and *share-name* with the name of the share. For example, to connect to a share named `files` on a server named `lowe01`, type `smb://lowe01/files`.

4. **Click Connect.**

   You'll be prompted for login credentials.

5. **Enter a domain username and password and then click OK.**

   Precede the user name with the domain name, separated by a backslash. For example, if the domain name is `lowewriter.pri` and the user name is `Doug`, enter `lowewriter.pri\Doug` as the username.

   After connection is complete, the files in the share display in the Finder window. You can then open files directly from the share (provided you have the right software, such as Microsoft Office, to read the files). You can also drag and drop files between the Mac and the file shares.

Part VII
The Part of Tens

Enjoy an additional Networking Part of Tens list online at www.dummies.com/extras/networking

In this part...

✔ Learn the unwritten rules of networking, which I call the Ten Networking Commandments

✔ Find out the common networking mistakes you should avoid

✔ Review my list of ten handy networking things you should keep in your closet

Chapter 27

Ten Networking Commandments

"Blessed is the network manager who walks not in the council of the ignorant, nor stands in the way of the oblivious, nor sits in the seat of the greenhorn, but delights in the Law of the Network and meditates on this Law day and night."

— Networks 1:1

And so it came to pass that these Ten Networking Commandments were handed down from generation to generation, to be worn as frontlets between the computer geeks' eyes (taped on the bridges of their broken glasses) and written upon their doorposts with Sharpie markers. Obey these commandments, and it shall go well with you, with your users, and with your users' users.

I. Thou Shalt Back Up Thy Hard Drive Religiously

Prayer is a good thing, and I heartily recommend it. But when it comes to protecting the data on your network, nothing beats a well-thought-out schedule of backups followed religiously. (If this were an actual network Bible, a footnote here would refer you to related verses in Chapter 21.)

II. Thou Shalt Protect Thy Network from Infidels

One of my favorite classic TV series is *M*A*S*H*. One of the recurring characters on that show was Colonel Flagg, who hid in trash cans looking for Communists. I don't recommend that you actually become him, but on the other hand, you don't want to ignore the possibility of getting zapped by a virus, your network being invaded by hackers, or your data being compromised by an unscrupulous user. Make sure that your Internet connection is properly secured with a firewall and don't allow any Internet access that circumvents your security.

To counter virus threats, use network-aware antivirus software to ensure that every user on your network has up-to-date virus protection. And teach your users so they know how to avoid those virus threats that manage to sneak past your virus protection.

III. Thou Shalt Keepeth Thy Network Drive Pure and Cleanse It of Old Files

Don't wait until your 2TB network drive is down to just 1GB of free space before you think about cleaning it up. Set up a routine schedule for disk housekeeping, where you wade through the files and directories on the network disk to remove old junk.

IV. Thou Shalt Not Tinker with Thine Network Configuration Unless Thou Knowest What Thou Art Doing

Networks are finicky things. After yours is up and running, don't mess with it unless you know what you're doing. You may be tempted to log on to your firewall router to see whether you can tweak some of its settings to squeeze another ounce of performance out of it. But unless you know what you're doing, be careful! (Be especially careful if you *think* you know what you're doing. It's the people who think they know what they're doing who get themselves into trouble!)

V. Thou Shalt Not Covet Thy Neighbor's Network

Network envy is a common malady among network managers. If your network users are humming along fine at 100 Mbps, don't covet your neighbor's Gigabit network. If your network users are happy with Windows 7, resist the urge to upgrade to Windows 8 unless you have a really good reason. And if you run Windows Server 2008, fantasizing about Windows Server 2012 is a venial sin.

You're especially susceptible to network envy if you're a gadget freak. There's always a better switch to be had or some fancy network-protocol gizmo to lust after. Don't give in to these base urges! Resist the devil, and he will flee!

VI. Thou Shalt Schedule Downtime before Working upon Thy Network

As a courtesy, try to give your users plenty of advance notice before you take down the network to work on it. Obviously, you can't predict when random problems strike. But if you know you're going to patch the server on Thursday morning, you earn points if you tell everyone about the inconvenience two days before rather than two minutes before. (You'll earn even more points if you patch the server Saturday morning. Tell your boss you'll take next Thursday morning off to make it up.)

VII. Thou Shalt Keep an Adequate Supply of Spare Parts

There's no reason that your network should be down for two days just because a cable breaks. Always make sure that you have at least a minimal supply of network spare parts on hand. (As luck would have it, Chapter 30 suggests ten things you should keep in your closet.)

VIII. Thou Shalt Not Steal Thy Neighbor's Program without a License

How would you like it if Inspector Clouseau (from the *Pink Panther* movies) barged into your office, looked over your shoulder as you ran Excel from a network server, and asked, "Do you have a *liesaunce*?"

"A *liesaunce*?" you reply, puzzled.

"Yes. of course, a *liesaunce* — that is what I said! The law specifically prohibits the playing of a computer program on a network without a proper *liesaunce*."

You don't want to get in trouble with Inspector Clouseau, do you? Then make sure you have the correct licenses for the applications you run on your network.

IX. Thou Shalt Train Thy Users in the Ways of the Network

Don't blame the users if they don't know how to use the network. It's not their fault. If you're the network administrator, your job is to provide training so the network users know how to use the network.

X. Thou Shalt Write Down Thy Network Configuration upon Tablets of Stone

Network documentation should be written down. If you cross the River Jordan, who else will know diddly-squat about the network if you don't write it down somewhere? Write down everything, put it in an official binder labeled *Network Bible,* and protect the binder as if it were sacred.

Your hope should be that 2,000 years from now, when archeologists are exploring caves in your area, they find your network documentation hidden in a jar and marvel at how meticulously the people of our time recorded their network configurations.

They'll probably draw ridiculous conclusions, such as we offered sacrifices of burnt data packets to a deity named TCP/IP and confessed our transgressions in a ritual known as "logging," but that makes it all the more fun.

Chapter 28

Ten Big Network Mistakes

*J*ust about the time you figure out how to avoid the most embarrassing computer mistakes (such as using your CD drive's tray as a cup holder), the network lands on your computer. Now you have a whole new list of dumb things you can do, mistakes that can give your average computer geek a belly laugh because they seem so basic to him. Well, that's because he's a computer geek. Nobody had to tell *him* not to fold the floppy disk — he was born with an extra gene that gave him an instinctive knowledge of such things.

Here's a list of some of the most common mistakes made by network novices. Avoid these mistakes and you deprive your local computer geek of the pleasure of a good laugh at your expense.

Skimping on Cable

If your network consists of more than a few computers or has computers located in different rooms, invest in a professional-quality cable installation, complete with wall-mounted jacks, patch panels, and high-quality network switches. It's tempting to cut costs by using cheap switches and by stringing inexpensive cable directly from the switches to each computer on the network. In the long run, though, the Scrooge approach may actually prove to be more expensive than investing in a good cable installation in the first place.

Here are just a few of the reasons it pays to do the cabling right in the first place:

✔ A good cable installation lasts much longer than the computers it services. A good cable installation can last 10 or 15 years, long after the computers on your network have been placed on display in a computer history museum.

✔ Installing cable is hard work. No one enjoys going up in the attic, poking his head up through ceiling panels and wiping fiberglass insulation out of his or her hair, or fishing cables through walls. If you're going to do it, do it right so you don't have to do it again in just a few years. Build your cable installation to last.

✔ Your network users may be satisfied with 100 Mbps networking now, but it won't be long before they demand gigahertz speed. And who knows how fast the next wave of networking will be? If you cut costs by using

> plain Cat5 cable instead of more expensive Cat6 cable, you'll have to replace it later.
>
> ✔ You might be tempted to skip the modular wall jacks and patch cables and instead just run the cable down the wall, out through a hole, and then directly to the computer or hub. That's a bad idea because the connectors are the point at which cables are most likely to fail. If a connector fails, you have to replace the entire cable — all the way up the wall, through the ceiling, and back to the switch. By wiring in a wall-jack and using a patch cable, you have to replace only the patch cable when a connector fails.

For more information about professional touches for installing cable, see Chapter 5.

Turning Off or Restarting a Server Computer While Users Are Logged On

The fastest way to blow your network users' accounts to kingdom come is to turn off a server computer while users are logged on. Restarting it by pressing its reset button can have the same disastrous effect.

If your network is set up with a dedicated file server, you probably won't be tempted to turn it off or restart it. But if your network is set up as a true peer-to-peer network, where each of the workstation computers — including your own — also doubles as a server computer, be careful about the impulsive urge to turn off or restart your computer. Someone may be accessing a file or printer on your computer at that very moment.

So, before you turn off or restart a server computer, find out whether anyone is logged on. If so, politely ask her to log off.

Many server problems don't require a server reboot. Instead, you can often correct the problem just by restarting the particular service that's affected.

Deleting Important Files on the Server

Without a network, you can do anything you want to your computer, and the only person you can hurt is yourself. (Kind of like the old "victimless crime" debate.) Put your computer on a network, though, and you take on a certain amount of responsibility. You must find out how to live like a responsible member of the network society.

Therefore, you can't capriciously delete files from a network server just because you don't need them. They may not be yours. You wouldn't want someone deleting your files, would you?

Be especially careful about files that are required to keep the network running. For example, some versions of Windows use a folder named wgpo0000 to hold e-mail. If you delete this folder, your e-mail is history. Look before you delete.

The first time you accidentally delete an important file from a network share, you may be unpleasantly surprised to discover that the Recycle Bin does not work for network files. The Recycle Bin saves copies of files you've deleted from your computer's local hard disk, but it does *not* save copies of files you delete from network shares. As a result, you can't undelete a file you've accidentally deleted from the network.

Copying a File from the Server, Changing It, and Then Copying It Back

Sometimes working on a network file is easier if you first copy the file to your local hard drive. Then you can access it from your application program more efficiently because you don't have to use the network. This is especially true for large database files that have to be sorted to print reports.

You're asking for trouble, though, if you copy the file to your PC's local hard drive, make changes to the file, and then copy the updated version of the file back to the server. Why? Because somebody else may be trying the same thing at the same time. If that happens, the updates made by one of you — whoever copies the file back to the server first — are lost.

Copying a file to a local drive is rarely a good idea.

Sending Something to the Printer Again Just Because It Didn't Print the First Time

What do you do if you send something to the printer and nothing happens?

- ✔ **Right answer:** Find out why nothing happened and *fix it.*
- ✔ **Wrong answer:** Send it again and see whether it works this time.

Some users keep sending it over and over again, hoping that one of these days, it'll take. The result is rather embarrassing when someone finally clears the paper jam and then watches 30 copies of the same letter print. Or when 30 copies of your document print on a different printer because you had the wrong printer selected.

Assuming That the Server Is Safely Backed Up

Some users make the unfortunate assumption that the network somehow represents an efficient and organized bureaucracy worthy of their trust. This is far from the truth. Never assume that the network jocks are doing their jobs backing up the network data every day, even if they are. Check up on them. Conduct a surprise inspection one day: Burst into the computer room wearing white gloves and demand to see the backup tapes. Check the tape rotation to make sure that more than one day's worth of backups is available.

If you're not impressed with your network's backup procedures, take it upon yourself to make sure that you never lose any of your data. Back up your most valued files to a flash drive.

Connecting to the Internet without Considering Security Issues

If you connect a non-networked computer to the Internet and then pick up a virus or get yourself hacked into, only that one computer is affected. But if you connect a networked computer to the Internet, the entire network becomes vulnerable.

Beware: Never connect a networked computer to the Internet without first considering the security issues:

- ✔ How will you protect yourself and the network from viruses?
- ✔ How will you ensure that the sensitive files located on your file server don't suddenly become accessible to the entire world?
- ✔ How can you prevent evil hackers from sneaking into your network, stealing your customer file, and selling your customer's credit card data on the black market?

For answers to these and other Internet-security questions, see Chapter 23.

Plugging In a Wireless Access Point without Asking

For that matter, plugging any device into your network without first getting permission from the network administrator is a big no-no. But wireless access points (WAPs) are particularly insidious. Many users fall for the marketing line that wireless networking is as easy as plugging in one of these devices to the network. Then, your wireless notebook PC or handheld device can instantly join the network.

The trouble is, so can anyone else within about one-quarter mile of the WAP. Therefore, you must employ extra security measures to make sure hackers can't get into your network via a wireless computer located in the parking lot or across the street.

If you think that's unlikely, think again. Several underground Web sites on the Internet actually display maps of unsecured wireless networks in major cities. For more information about securing a wireless network, see Chapter 9.

Thinking You Can't Work Just Because the Network Is Down

A few years back, I realized that I can't do my job without electricity. Should a power failure occur and I find myself without electricity, I can't even light a candle and work with pencil and paper because the only pencil sharpener I have is electric.

Some people have the same attitude about the network: They figure that if the network goes down, they may as well go home. That's not always the case. Just because your computer is attached to a network doesn't mean that it won't work when the network is down. True — if the wind flies out of the network sails, you can't access any network devices. You can't get files from network drives, and you can't print on network printers. But you can still use your computer for local work — accessing files and programs on your local hard drive and printing on your local printer (if you're lucky enough to have one).

Running Out of Space on a Server

One of the most disastrous mistakes to make on a network server is to let it run out of disk space. When you buy a new server with hundreds of gigabytes of disk space, you might think you'll never run out of space. It's amazing how quickly an entire network full of users can run through a few hundred gigabytes of disk space, though.

Unfortunately, bad things begin to happen when you get down to a few gigabytes of free space on a server. Windows begins to perform poorly and may even slow to a crawl. Errors start popping up. And, when you finally run out of space completely, users line up at your door demanding an immediate fix:

✔ The best way to avoid this unhappy situation is to monitor the free disk space on your servers on a daily basis. It's also a good idea to keep track of free disk space on a weekly basis so you can look for project trends. For example, if your file server has 100GB of free space and your users chew up about 5GB of space per week, you know you'll most likely run out of disk space in 20 weeks. With that knowledge in hand, you can formulate a plan.

✔ Adding additional disk storage to your servers isn't always the best solution to the problem of running out of disk space. Before you buy more disks, you should

- Look for old and unnecessary files that can be removed.

- Consider using disk quotas to limit the amount of network disk space your users can consume.

Always Blaming the Network

Some people treat the network kind of like the village idiot who can be blamed whenever anything goes wrong. Networks cause problems of their own, but they aren't the root of all evil:

✔ If your monitor displays only capital letters, it's probably because you pressed the Caps Lock key.

Don't blame the network.

✔ If you spill coffee on the keyboard, well, that's your fault.

Don't blame the network.

✔ If your toddler sticks Play-Doh in the floppy drive, kids will be kids.

Don't blame the network.

Get the point?

Chapter 29

Ten Things You Should Keep in Your Closet

When you first network your office computers, you need to find a closet where you can stash some network goodies. If you can't find a whole closet, shoot for a shelf, a drawer, or at least a sturdy cardboard box.

Here's a list of what stuff to keep on hand.

Duct Tape

Duct tape helped get the crew of Apollo 13 back from their near-disastrous moon voyage. You won't actually use it much to maintain your network, but it serves the symbolic purpose of demonstrating that you realize things sometimes go wrong and you're willing to improvise to get your network up and running.

If you don't like duct tape, a little baling wire and some chewing gum serve the same symbolic purpose.

Tools

Make sure that you have at least a basic computer toolkit, the kind you can pick up for $15 from just about any office supply store. At the minimum, you'll need a good set of screwdrivers, plus wire cutters, wire strippers, and cable crimpers for assembling RJ-45 connectors.

Patch Cables

Keep a good supply of patch cables on hand. You'll use them often: when you move users around from one office to another, when you add computers to your network, or when you need to rearrange things at the patch panels (assuming you wired your network using patch panels).

When you buy patch cables, buy them in a variety of lengths and colors. One good way to quickly make a mess of your patch panels is to use 15' cables when 3' cables will do the job. And having a variety of colors can help you sort out a mass of cables.

 The last place you should buy patch cables is from one of those big-box office supply or consumer electronics stores. Instead, get them online. Cables that sell for $15 or $20 each at chain stores can be purchased online for $3 or $4 each.

Cable Ties

Cable ties — those little plastic zip things that you wrap around a group of cables and pull to tighten — can go a long way toward helping keep your network cables neat and organized. You can buy them in bags of 1,000 at big-box home-improvement stores.

Twinkies

If left sealed in their little individually wrapped packages, Twinkies keep for years. In fact, they'll probably outlast the network itself. You can bequeath them to future network geeks, ensuring continued network support for generations to come.

In November of 2012, computer geeks throughout the world faced a crisis far more menacing than the end of the Mayan calendar: the possible end of Hostess and Twinkies. Fortunately, the gods intervened, and Twinkies were saved, thus ensuring the continued operation of computer networks throughout the globe.

Extra Network Cards

Ideally, nearly all your computers will have network interfaces built directly into the motherboard. However, you will occasionally find that the motherboard's network interface goes bad. Rather than replace the entire motherboard, you can often fix the problem by adding a cheap (less than $20) network card to use instead of the on-board network interface.

Cheap Network Switches

Keep a couple of inexpensive (about $20) four- or eight-port network switches on hand. You don't want to use them for your main network infrastructure, but they sure come in handy when you need to add a computer or printer somewhere, and you don't have an available network jack. For example, suppose one of your users has a short-term need for a second computer, but there's only one network jack in the user's office. Rather than pulling a new cable to the user's office, just plug a cheap switch into the existing jack and then plug both of the computers into the switch.

The Complete Documentation of the Network on Tablets of Stone

I mention several times in this book the importance of documenting your network. Don't spend hours documenting your network and then hide the documentation under a pile of old magazines behind your desk. Put the binder in the closet with the other network supplies so that you and everyone else always know where to find it. And keep backup copies of the Word, Excel, Visio, or other documents that make up the network binder in a fireproof safe or at another site.

Don't you dare chisel passwords into the network documentation, though. Shame on you for even thinking about it!

If you decide to chisel the network documentation onto actual stone tablets, consider using *sandstone*. It's attractive, inexpensive, and easy to update (just rub out the old info and chisel in the new). Keep in mind, however, that sandstone is subject to erosion from spilled Diet Coke. Oh, and make sure that you store it on a reinforced shelf.

The Network Manuals and Disks

In the Land of Oz, a common lament of the Network Scarecrow is, "If I only had the manual." True, the manual probably isn't a Pulitzer Prize candidate, but that doesn't mean you should toss it in a landfill, either.

Put the manuals and disks for all the software you use on your network where they belong — in the closet with all the other network tools and artifacts.

Ten Copies of This Book

Obviously, you want to keep an adequate supply of this book on hand to distribute to all your network users. The more they know, the more they stay off your back.

Sheesh, 10 copies may not be enough — 20 may be closer to what you need.

Index

• E •

● ●

● ●